the

Hitched
Chick's
to
Modern
Marriage

Essential Advice for Staying

Single-minded and

Happily Married

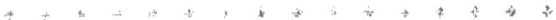

www.stmartins.com

BOOK DESIGN BY AMANDA DEWEY

Library of Congress Cataloging-in-Publication Data

Norwood, Mandi.
    The hitched chick's guide to modern marriage : essential advice for staying single-minded and happily married / Mandi Norwood.—[Rev. ed.]
        p. cm.
    Rev. ed. of: Sex & the married girl. C2003.
    ISBN 0-312-31214-8
    EAN 978-0312-31214-5
    1. Sex in marriage. 2. Married women—Sexual behavior. 3. Sex instruction for women. I. Norwood, Mandi. Sex & the married girl. 2004. II. Title.

HQ31.N875 2004
646.7'8—dc22   2004040676

First published in the United States by St. Martin's Press under the title *Sex & the Married Girl*

First St. Martin's Griffin Edition: May 2004

Mandi Norwood

ST. MARTIN'S GRIFFIN   NEW YORK

The Complete Truth About Twenty-first Century Marriage Revealed!

"This marriage primer is a perfect gift for the newly married girl or bride-to-be."

—*Publishers Weekly*

"Whether you want the best sex ever, or simply to secure your finances should the fairy tale falter, *The Hitched Chick's Guide to Modern Marriage* tells you precisely how. Norwood puts women on top, and just that makes you want to cheer."

—Anna Maxted, author of *Running in Heels*

"Chock-full of story and anecdote, it's as full of gory details as a night in with the gals."

—*Image*

"Couples have had a tough time of it these past six years. Ever since Helen Fielding coined the term 'smug marrieds,' getting hitched has been wildly unfashionable. *The Hitched Chick's Guide to Modern Marriage* is all about being young, happily married, and still getting it on. Hurrah!"

—*The Evening Standard*

"It's a scandal . . . laced with common sense."

—Lauren Stover, author of *The Bombshell Manual of Style*

"Norwood proudly presents a lineup of women who have cheerfully jettisoned docility and domesticity for married lives that focus on themselves."

—*The Times of London*

Contents

the Hitched Chick's

Chick's

to Modern

Marriage

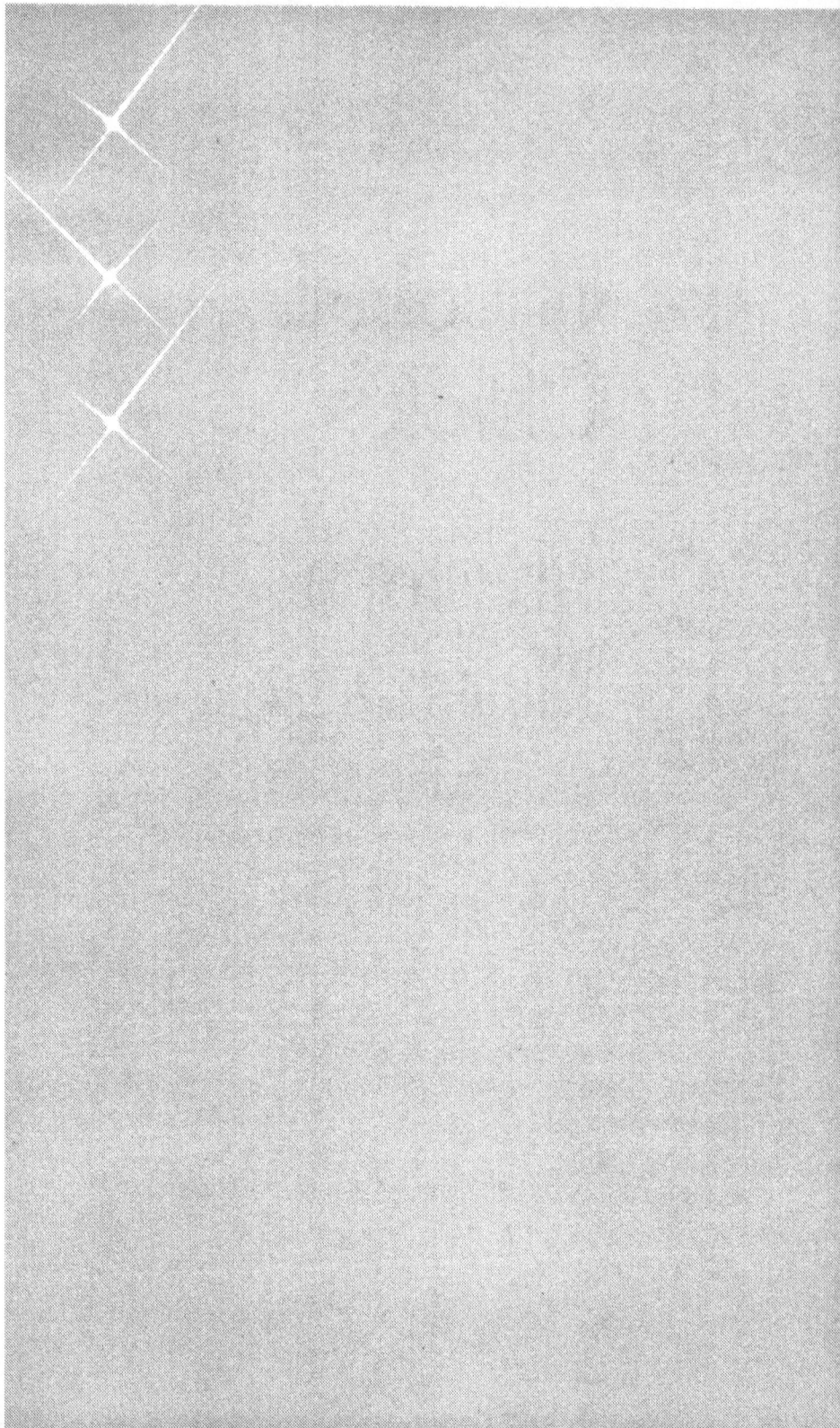

Prologue

My second date with my husband was, for both of us, more memorable than the first. Not because it was joyful and flirtatious and exciting (although it was), but because as we both tucked into our sesame chicken, I suggested that if his intentions were other than fun, he should forget about a relationship with me. I told him I had no desire to get married, nor have children. Perhaps I might, maybe, in the far-off future, but for now, I was doggedly pursuing adventure, travel and a career in publishing and I was unwilling to compromise or sideline it for the sake of marriage.

Coming from a family in which divorce always followed marriage, I inevitably reached adulthood considering the whole process a painful waste of time. My mother was divorced before she was thirty; my aunt, her only sibling, was divorced, too. Even my grandmother had been divorced, left to bring up two babies at a time—in the 1940s—when a woman couldn't even obtain a mortgage without her husband's signature.

No, marriage was not for me. Too much to do, too much to see, too much to accomplish, too much fun to have. And from what I observed, it was evident my personal agenda and marriage were mutually exclusive.

Then, of course, I fell in love with Martin. We married five years after that memorable second date . . . two years after the birth of our first daughter, Rosie. Martin had assured me that he and my dreams could coexist which, it turns out, is true. But that we are still married, I consider a small miracle.

I tentatively regard my marriage a success story, not simply because it has survived several years (most marriages that fall apart do so before they reach their seventh anniversary). I regard it as a success story because I have continued to pursue my ambitions and retain my identity. I feel that being married has embellished my life and sense of self rather than compromised it.

But my marriage is not devoid of conflict. Although Martin and I share the same sense of humor and values, there are epic differences between us. I'm fiery, he's laid-back; I believe I have power over my destiny, he's more content to allow fate to take its course; I'm impatient, he'd put the pope to shame. What's more, we continually challenge stereotypes. I'm four years older than he. I've always been the major breadwinner, sometimes the sole breadwinner, while he put his successful career on hold to look after our children. The ramifications of this have often taken us to the edge of what's tolerable to us both. From the way my career power and presence affects domestic decision-making to the roles we play in bed, no aspect of our relationship remains unchallenged by our breaking with tradition.

But there's more. Conflict literally abounds—in my head and in my heart. My fear of settling down sits alongside a deep-rooted desire for security. I feel entitled to everything, yet assume nothing. I seek adventure, spontaneity and freedom, yet manically adhere to rituals. I long to be taken care of, yet I clutch firmly to my independence. I said "I do" hoping it was forever, but say "I won't" at least twice a day to remind myself I have a choice. All of this—and more—manifests in behavior which tests the boundaries of my marriage every single day.

So why have I written *The Hitched Chick's Guide to Modern Marriage*? And why now? As well as being a wife and mother of two daughters, I'm a writer and editor-in-chief of women's magazines, from *Cosmopolitan* to *Mademoiselle*. I have spent the majority of my life talking to, listening to and documenting women's thoughts and feelings. Whether they're my readers or my friends, their ever-evolving opinions, style and codes of behavior fascinate me, as they obviously fascinate the millions of women who buy magazines.

Secondly, subjects don't get more provocative than marriage. The vast majority has, has had or nearly had one. If they haven't been married, they'll know someone who has and will definitely have an opinion on it. Marriage has always been a hot topic. Rarely has it been hotter than now. Celebrity Marriages, Lavender Marriages, Broken Marriages, Open Marriages, Marriages of Convenience, Arranged Marriages, Starter Marriages, Death-Row Marriages, Traditional Marriages, Modern Marriages, Gay and Lesbian Marriages, Pet Marriages . . . seems the whole world has gone marriage crazy. Despite the depressing divorce statistics, we all want to exercise our right to get married and heartily believe our marriage will buck the trend.

Every generation believes they can improve on their predecessors, and this generation of marrieds—those born between 1960 and 1980, people who hover between the so-called Baby Boomers and Echo Boomers (or Generation Y)—is no exception. So optimistic that we hold the magic formula, even during the recent recession, we unreservedly splash out an average of $19,000 to say "I do" (source: womencentral.com). Even wedding guests spend up to $1,500 to whoop it up with their peers—more if we are a bridesmaid or best man (source: Barclaycard).

There's reason to believe our money won't be wasted since many *are* making marriage work. Six out of ten. That the remaining four flounder is no cause for giddy optimism, but our modern obsession with and access to data has exposed many of society's long-harbored dirty little secrets as "news." Like perversion within the priesthood and corporate crime, profoundly unhappy marriages have always existed. They *aren't* a current trend or new phenomenon. We have only recently had the courage and means to expose them and, in the case of marriage, had a legally documented escape route via no-fault divorce.

Thanks to our increasingly sophisticated communicating skills and our willingness to learn, even if the lessons are painful or challenging, we are able to grow and, hopefully, improve on the past. That the institution of marriage attracts a receptive and keen audience is a promising start. For despite what we have witnessed within the private quarters of our parents' marriages and continue to observe from the publicly conducted marital brawls of the rich and famous, the majority of us *want* to be married. And the majority of us believe we *can* get it right. (In a 2002 survey of twenty-five- to thirty-five-year-olds conducted by Youth Intelligence, over 75 percent of respondents claimed they believed they will only get married once, with males slightly more optimistic than females.)

Just so long as we can conduct marriage on our terms—

extrapolating the best from unions that have gone before and leaving behind that which made marriage untenable for so many—we
stand a chance of success. Which is why, rather than rushing
headlong into wedlock, we will take our time, find our*selves* as well
as a near-perfect mate and marry them not because we have to, but
because we genuinely want to. We will do the groundwork—have
pre-marital counseling and pre-marital sex, draw up duty rosters
and pre-nuptial agreements—to prevent potential conflicts. We
will learn from the mistakes of previous generations by conducting
ourselves differently. We will not attempt to squeeze ourselves into
a suffocating pre-ordained unit; we will manufacture our own
perimeters, flexible boundaries which do not bind us together as
one, but allow us to flourish as two unique halves. We will succeed
not despite our differences, but because of them. *Vive la dif-
férence!*

It's this difference—between us and our mothers and us and
our husbands—which deserves to be documented. What young
women are doing today to ensure their marriages have a better
chance of success is worthy of note. And celebration. We cannot
continue to clump all marriages and all wives into one big homog-
enous mass. Today they're as individual as, well, individual people, with unique belief systems, motivations and circumstances.
The dynamics of modern marriage are so different from the marriages that have gone before—our mothers' marriages and certainly
our grandmothers' marriages—they need a new, bespoke approach
to advice that reflects the contradictory and complex values and
attitudes toward their status. And one which also reflects the spirit
of the modern married female. The spirit she is desperate to maintain despite her intelligence, despite her accomplishments, despite
her responsibilities, despite being a Mrs.

See, like it or not, we live in a youth-oriented world in which
vitality, freshness, fun and, yes, youth, are marketable attributes.

That we are smart and possess sophisticated skills is even more appealing and coveted when combined with a youthful attitude. The maintenance of these attributes is what keeps us exercising into our seventies and eating low-fat, fiber-rich foods. To enable us to be interesting, good company, employable, we tune into trends, keep a watchful eye on the news, embrace modern technology and emerging codes of behavior. Although our motivation might be superficial, it's paying dividends. The average woman today can expect to live well into her eighties. Therefore, what used to be regarded as old/mature/senior is no longer the case. Hence everything—from styles of dressing to life's cornerstones—have shifted up a decade. Rather than leaving school in our teens, most of us now leave in our twenties. Rather than having babies in our twenties, we're having them in our thirties. What used to be called middle age is now called middle youth. If age-related ill health usually started in our forties, most of us now won't experience the first symptoms until our fifties. Today we don't even consider ourselves to be in our twilight years until we reach our seventies.

It's this *youth*-fashioned, not *old*-fashioned, appearance, conduct and attitude which define this generation of married women to whom I refer throughout as Hitched Chick for that very reason. As one of my recently married interviewees, Amanda, twenty-nine, said, "I didn't want to talk about marriage with my partner because it just seemed so old to me. Kind of old-fashioned, something for old people. I just wanted to feel young and keep on having a good time. I thought marriage was silly and old and materialistic."

Amanda's resistance to an institution which she believes is patriarchal and implies ownership and old-fashioned codes of behavior was echoed by almost every married woman I interviewed. And I interviewed over one hundred between twenty-three and forty-five from America to Australia, the U.K. to Yugoslavia. All of them, without exception, needed to be convinced that once married, they would not have to deny the youthful qualities they treasure. And they believe that although they're married, they display exactly the same qualities they had when they were single girls—fun, interesting, smart, independent, vital, mischievous, sexy. Youthful and unique.

Talking about and to all married women is now more challenging than talking about and to all single women. Helen Gurley Brown's revolutionary 1960s book, *Sex & the Single Girl*, opened the door on single women. It paved the way for a variety of media—from magazines like *Cosmopolitan* and *Jane* to TV shows from *Charlie's Angels* to *Sex and the City*—which exposed, explained and celebrated single women's diversity. What makes them tick, the tricks they play, their dilemmas about every aspect of their singleton life from their G-strings to their pizza delivery guy fantasies, no stone has been left unturned about the rich yet bittersweet life of the single girl. And thank goodness. Laid bare, understood and validated, the "sad single female" stigma has just about vanished forever. But with it, the magical, wonderful mystique of the single girl has disappeared, too.

Not so the mystique of the married woman. For although the single girls we loved to read about, watch on TV, discuss, tear apart over coffee or cocktails are getting married or have already tied the knot, no one's saying much about *them*. Not really.

Maybe it's because society continues to believe the story of life—and all its thrills—*ends* with marriage. After all, that's where our favorite fairy tales—from *Sleeping Beauty* to *Sleepless in Seattle*—reach their twinkling conclusion.

Or maybe it's because, once married, we consider that our feelings and experiences should be treated with more seriousness and, therefore, more secrecy. We have no hesitation in casually asking our single friends, "How's your love life?" Cringe at the thought we'd ever ask a married friend, "So, how's your marriage?" Too intrusive, too bold, none of our damn business. Even if we want to take a peek into their private world, once there, the details might be too challenging for us to hear and accept. Although we long to hear good news, we are inherently competitive and fear another couple may be faring better than we, they might be happier than we are, more in love, more of a team. And we worry that what they have to say will make us confront our own fears, doubts, niggles and insecurities about an institution to which we fully subscribe, but the membership to which we know is not necessarily for life.

It's the almost impenetrable wall of silence that we build around us after our vows that gives marriage its mystical quality but makes us sometimes feel isolated and unsteady. We rarely know whether we've got it absolutely right unless it goes horribly wrong. There are no benchmarks now. Only the lucky few can put hands on hearts and say their parents' marriages conformed to their ideals. We can't compare against our friends' marriages either, since our friends are as uncertain and unique as we are. In this speedily evolving world, our environment changes, and changes *us*, by the day. New rules need to be written, codes of conduct modified, opinions withdrawn, expectations reassessed. Good grief. Little wonder that marriage can seem like so much work that if we decide to embark on it at all, only the very strong survive.

It *is* hard work, of course. The best things in life always are. Think for one moment that you can slip into complacency as soon as the rings are slipped onto our fingers, and it's over before you can say "good night." Hithced Chicks know this. Far from being lackadaisical and focused on instant gratification, they have learned from their parents who, says thirty-five-year-old Terri, "very much rested on the fact that they made a commitment and now they're just driving an automatic car." Instead, Terri (like all the women I spoke to), says, "I really think of marriage as a stick shift—okay, we're in first gear, now we're in second, third, oops, reverse, okay, put in the clutch and go back to first gear. I think we have a stick-shift marriage rather than an automatic marriage and to me that's how I see us as different from our parents."

When women get married today, romantic ideals are underpinned with a healthy dose of realism. Although they love their husbands-to-be (and marry because they want to, not because they should), they know that love is not enough for a successful marriage. Yes, marriage is a warm, reassuring refuge when it seems like the rest of the world has turned its back on us; a sanctuary, a cozy nook in which to collapse after a stressful week. But even paradise has thunderstorms, unexpected torrential downpours which may be unpleasant and frightening, but which give our idyll its lushness and fertility.

We know that marriage, like the dream jobs and perfect bodies we strive for, will exasperate and irritate us. It will challenge us and we will need to challenge it, not in order to destroy it, but to exercise it and make it a stronger and more rewarding place for us. And married women are fully equipped to give marriage its much-needed workout. They are fighters, confident and courageous and with a sense of entitlement born out of feminist principles and post-feminist Girl Power. They already possess all the traditional weapons of their gender (the ability to multi-task, nurture, communicate, tap into their instincts). But thanks to a better educational focus and an increasingly feminized workplace, they now enter marriage armed with the kind of practical weaponry that used to be the exclusive battalion of men—social power, financial savviness, well-formed identity. It's a new and powerful cocktail of attributes, but one which also brings its own hangover.

Yet today's wives lack a wide range of positive marital role models from whom to seek advice when the need arises since, broadly speaking, the women to whom they might have turned have fallen into two hapless categories: those who subjugated themselves and lost their identity to that of "the little wife" or those who swallowed the Superwoman ideal, then collapsed under the pressure of balancing their careers, their kids, their social lives and their relationships. Spending over a decade as an editor-in-chief, I have communicated with millions of young women from every culture and class. I've talked to them face-to-face, over the phone, via e-mail and letters, and one theme comes through loud and clear: women today do not relate to their mothers, nor do they wish to resemble them. Much as they adore their mothers and view them as influential role models, their influence is derived as much—if not more—from what they didn't do as from what they did. How can we turn to our mothers when we are all too aware of their mistakes and witnessed first-hand the price they were forced to pay?

What's more, modern women are experiencing the additional modern challenge of being married to men who will be battling with their own identity issues and values. Yes, husbands and wives have more parity than ever. Yet, despite his outwardly progressive attitudes, conservative and traditional belief systems runs deep which means the modern husband will be as conflicted about marriage as his wife—but for entirely different reasons. As thirty-two-year-old Stella says, "Women looked at their parents' marriages and saw it was their mothers who were getting screwed and they thought, This has to change. The guys looked at their fathers and thought, This is okay, and didn't feel the need to change at all."

Vanessa, thirty, agrees, saying, "Women have evolved so much, but men have hardly evolved at all. So the problem we have is that we're just not in the same time zone. It's like having a conversation with someone who just woke up. Like they're having breakfast and you're having dinner. And somehow you both have to find a way so that you're both having lunch."

"Having lunch," as Vanessa describes staying married when the initial bloom of novelty and romance fades, as it inevitably does, is what *The Hitched Chick's Guide to Modern Marriage* is all about. And how Hitched Chicks go about it will certainly raise eyebrows since it involves more cunning than Clue, more energy than Twister and more strategy than chess. It is a carefully considered operation designed not only to preserve our marriages, but to preserve ourselves.

Don't be fooled by the pretty floral dress, high heels, underwire bra and bed-head hair. Women today have the confidence to display these obvious badges of femininity. In their hearts, however, lurks the kind of iron will and strategic thinking normally associated with facial hair and combat pants.

This book does not profess to have all the answers to a happy modern marriage. It will certainly challenge conventional thinking since many old formulas are no longer relevant (nor have they worked). But I hope that through my observations, interviews and confessions from women who are "having their lunch" and eating it, my documentation does justice to their self-esteem, wit, savvy and determination to make their marriages work. I hope, if you are a Hitched Chick, you experience the rush of delight, reassurance and intimacy, that feeling of "Thank God, I've felt that, too," when you recognize your own behavior in the revelations of someone else. I also hope that while some of the advice may be surprising and controversial, it helps you to choose a way forward that's fitting for your own circumstances. What's more, I hope this book will give you the extra confidence to break the rules that need to be broken and create your own in the pursuit, not of the perfect marriage (since it doesn't exist), but of a marriage that's right for *you*.

1.

Me, Myself and I

Although the word "selfish" connotes negative behavior, I don't think it is. It's a good thing to be selfish, although I prefer to use the phrase "watching out for yourself and taking care of yourself." When you take care of yourself, you're better in your marriage, you're more fulfilled. . . .

—*Sabina, forty*

Perish the thought that a woman could think about herself, be selfish, put I before He, especially within marriage. Giving, devoting, sacrificing . . . these are the actions of a good wife, no? No. These are the actions of a drudge, a sucker, a sap. These are the actions of a woman who sits meekly at a dinner party and feels worthy only of discussing the accomplishments of her husband, while quietly despairing over society's disinterest in her. These are the actions of an intelligent, once-vibrant woman who held so much promise, yet will come to be known as *Whassername* when her former classmates see her at their reunion. These, too, are the actions of a woman who will find herself struggling with her own self-worth and identity issues, fearful for her future, when she discovers the husband, to whom she has sacrificed herself, is having an affair with his dynamic, self-possessed coworker. (How devastating to discover an e-mail from him to his vivacious lover, stating "My wife is such a bore.")

Women have historically been the caretakers of their marriages and husbands, running themselves ragged to appease the moods of a petulant spouse, looking out for *his* needs, squishing their own identities and putting on hold their own aspirations and dreams to allow their partners to pursue theirs. Our mothers were brought up to believe a "good wife" is an ATM of selfless deeds, no deposits required. As a result, when the marriage breaks down, it won't just be her financial well-being that's seriously depleted. What remains of her self-worth will likely be destroyed, too.

It all began even before she floated down the aisle on a wave of dreams. Should she have received a good education and scored academically, her family's expectations for her will doubtless have stretched little further than a husband who would provide for her and their brood of children. She'd take a job to supplement her husband's income until the first baby bounced along, maybe. But it was generally understood that her career would be short-lived, since a woman's defining role was that of nurturer, caregiver, selfless saint whose fulfillment and joy would be derived from the accomplishments and well-being of others. Perhaps she'd be able to resume work—as if looking after a family wasn't work—once her chicks finally flew the nest? A nice little job to get her out of the house, provide a bit of what my grandmother used to call "pin money" . . . you know, pennies she could spend on little treats for herself. Ooooh, like, pretty brooches and stockings? Yes, and, if she saves her pennies up, vats of alcohol with which to drown her pain and fill the sheer rotten emptiness of her soul.

Of course, some of our mothers, Baby Boomer women, did continue to work, even while their children were young. Whether their reasons were rebelliousness, dogged determination to give their education meaning, financial necessity or—gasp—pure pleasure, there was always, *always,* the implicit understanding that husband and family came first since her identity was primarily that of wife and mother. After all, did she not relinquish her own identity when she took her husband's name and vowed to forsake all others, which we know then included herself? *Especially* herself. This was not to be questioned. Hell's bells, it was to be celebrated!

For the vast majority of our mothers, her wedding day was her family's proudest moment. Forget that she was trilingual/athletic/artistic/literary/psychic/academic. It was small potatoes that she was on the way to discovering another life form/cure for cancer/alternative energy source. That she was getting married, had secured a husband, *that* was the accomplishment for which no expense would be spared. Huzzaaah! And aside from vowing to capitulate to her husband forever, her greatest gift to the world at that point was to throw her bouquet to the nearest single female in the hope that another woman would have the great fortune to lose herself to a husband. And soon.

See, even the identity of Mother paled into insignificance against that of Wife. In fact, having a child without also having a husband wasn't just stupid, it was shameful, stigmatized and the only reason to be ostracized by family, friends and society. No, a woman's only true, meaningful identity was that of Wife, even if it meant a life of slavery, submission and suppression. Perhaps *because* it meant slavery, submission and suppression?

But that's enough soapbox ranting. There are plenty of authors who have furiously filled books with historical home truths, rhetoric and self-pity. And although well-meaning and justified, they can be exhausting and dreary to read and, as such, uninspiring. Yes, yes, we know women have had it rough. Yes, yes, we know many women continue to suffer. But what's the whole story now? What lessons have we learned and how do we regard our role today? How are we preserving our identities in the midst of an institution we uphold, but which continues to challenge our sense of self?

Finding Myself

M y generation is marrying much later. And one of the benefits of getting married later is that we've had time to try things on our own, make our own friends, have our own successes and failures," states thirty-year-old Lena, who's been married to Andrew for two years. "Once you feel grounded in who you are—once you like yourself—and understand your own goals, values and dreams, only then are you prepared to share them with someone else. The only way a woman can keep her identity when she's married is if she has forged an identity *before* she got married. A lot of people think that finding a life partner is about finding someone to complete them. You have to be complete on your own and look for someone who complements you instead."

The average Western woman today marries (for the first time) at the age of twenty-eight (source: One Plus One). She will generally be five years older than her mother and three years older than her father was when they (first) skipped down the aisle. But there's been very little shuffling miserably on the infamous singles' shelf for today's women. If the shelf is groaning under the weight of unmarried women, it is because the shelf is considered a good place to be today. Contrary to Sylvia Ann Hewlett's panic-mongering book, *Creating a Life: Professional Women and the Quest for Children*, every woman I interviewed believed the so-called shelf to be a viewing station for all the options before her, somewhere she can take stock and experiment with life choices. (And as Emily, thirty-three, says, "Having so much choice can make it hard to choose!") From here, she can dip her toe in the workplace waters before either plunging in headfirst or drying off until she decides to try something new. From here, she has the time to ponder who she is, what she wants and whether these would be complemented or compromised by marriage. And deciding they could be complemented, the shelf is also an exciting as well as comfortable (if not downright luxurious) place from where she can view candidates and make her final selection.

Who's writing those volumes about fraught single women, panic-stricken at the age of twenty-five that they'll never get married? Pontificating over the elusiveness of a smart, generous, progressive male maybe. But that's simply part of the joy and pain of today's selection process, and no more sinister than the discussions we have over the shortage of well-cut, perfectly tailored black pants. It may make us miffed, but it doesn't make us desperate or pathetic. In fact, it simply prolongs the time we have to relish in the search for a partner. And ourselves. For many, that time isn't long enough. The growing and forming of identity during those single years is taken so seriously today that when the ideal man makes himself known, it's perceived as too soon even at the age of thirty.

Thirty-two-year-old Pia, who's been married one year to Michael, says, "I loved being single and had a lot of reservations about giving it up, which is why our engagement was long. My reservations weren't about Michael, but at thirty, I felt very young and I was still in the realm of growth and possibility. I think of life as split into stages of being and becoming. I always enjoy the becoming stages rather than the being stages because I'm just not interested in status quo. I'm interested in passion and excitement and I felt nervous about giving that up and having something solid. I enjoy longing and desire and the feeling that anything is around the corner, so I never had the urge to settle down, have a husband and kids and a diamond ring. It wasn't in my field of desire."

Terri, thirty-five, says she felt the same when she met her husband five years ago. "My father's African-American and a southern patriarch in that he is one of these iron-fisted men who likes to dominate. It had a profound effect on me. I spent many years working through the effects of my childhood and I felt I didn't need the validation of marriage. So when I met Chad and he said, 'Hey, let's get married!' I said, 'Hey, let's not!' I was so nervous that I'd lose what I'd fought for."

And Rachel, twenty-eight, remembers meeting her husband at the age of twenty-four. "I was so young. I wasn't planning to get married. I'd only known Patrick for four months and he was telling me how much in love with me he was and I'd say, 'No, no, no . . . ' I was going away for the summer to work in a boys' camp so there'd be lots of wonderful men there, too. Right before I left, I said to my mother, 'Mom, I'm falling in love with Patrick and it's so inconvenient.' I just didn't want to be settled. I wanted to be young and free and great."

Few women today immediately step out of their graduation cloaks and into their bridal carriage. But we're not whiling away the years between school and marriage just thinking about what we want from life. We're working, playing, evaluating, experimenting, reconsidering and fine-tuning. From our moral values to the direction we wish our lives to take, from the challenges we face alone to our ever-evolving modes of conduct, we rely on our single-years experiences to form and celebrate our identity. Once established (though never fully complete, we know, until the day we die), it's only then that we wholeheartedly embrace marriage.

I couldn't even entertain the idea of getting married until I had edited my own magazine. My life plan was pretty much this: junior writer, features editor, global travel, buy own home, become an editor-in-chief, get married and have kids. Incidentally, I was prepared to take or leave the final two and, if they happened, I didn't much care about the order of arrival. No question, I'm thrilled to pieces that I did get married *and* have children, but the point is, they were last on my list of priorities. Top of my list: me.

It's for that very reason that thirty-three-year-old Jo retracted her decision to marry Aaron when he first proposed just three months into their relationship. "He was the kind of guy who, when we'd be walking through Washington Square Park, would literally sweep me off my feet, swing me around and kiss me. I became swept up in this incredible romance, so when we were on line for sushi in the East Village and he turned around and spontaneously said, 'Will you marry me?' I said yes! Then we went and got drunk on saki. But the whole mood shifted when I woke up the next morning. I realized I just couldn't do it. I was in a job I hated and I wanted to leave that job to pursue my own thing. I felt like I needed to do that before I got married. I wanted to get married when I was wildly confident in my own life. Yes, I was wildly confident about this man in my life, but I wanted to be as confident with my own direction. So I told him, 'Listen, I think I've made a big mistake. I do love you and I want to be with you for the rest of my life, but I don't want to get married yet.' He didn't talk to me for three days."

Says thirty-two-year-old Gabrielle, married for two years to Murray, "I came into my marriage having traveled, I'd earned my own money, I'd been through crises and got myself through them. I'd been left and betrayed and I'd betrayed others. I'd had the experience of knowing that I wouldn't die if someone stopped loving me and those things enabled me to go into my marriage feeling whole and good and complete and that I didn't need Murray to complete me."

Stacey, thirty, is one of an increasing number of women who enter their first marriage as a mother already. Fear of losing her identity was the main reason she *didn't* marry the father of her child. Fiercely independent, Stacey never felt the need to have a husband, either to make her complete or to secure the well-being of herself and her child. "Although we had a baby, I just didn't see myself going down that path with him. He wanted me to be someone I'm not. And he was controlling. If I wanted to go out, he'd say, 'Why should I baby-sit?' Whereas if he went out, I'd have to stay at home and look after our son. So it would be termed 'baby-sitting' for him, but for me, it would be doing my motherly duty. My worst scenario would be to wake up at forty years old and realize that the last twenty years of my life had not been what I wanted, married to somebody just because I had a child with him. I'm selfish like that."

Having forged a career, single-handedly bought and furnished a home and established her sense of self (as well as that of her son, Harry, for ten years, with whom she also took a trip around the world), Stacey is more protective of her identity than ever. "I am my own person and I certainly didn't need to compromise who I was for the sake of companionship. I could get what I needed from Harry." Now married to Ben for two years, Stacey says, "I don't see myself *just* as Ben's wife. I'm very much me and it was important that Ben understood that. I love Ben and feel lucky to have him, but he's also very lucky to have *me*."

So Long, Sainthood!

Hel-o-oh? Are these *women* speaking? It's a stereotypically male attitude toward marriage that has emerged, though why men could ever have held these attitudes is anyone's guess. For Pete's sake, proof that marriage is good for men doesn't get more positive than this: married men live longer than single men, even if their marriage is well below par. What's more, according to Steven L. Nock, a University of Virginia sociology professor who has interviewed six thousand men every year since 1979, "The research shows that marriage per se increases men's achievements as reflected in earnings, labor force and occupational prestige."

If anyone needs to worry, it's women. Statistics show that single women are generally healthier and stronger than their married counterparts (source: American Heart Association). Could this possibly be due to the fact that when a man marries, there are two people looking after him (three if you count his mother, but more of her later . . .), caretaking *his* nutritional/emotional/physical/social/dental/ psychological well-being? Whereas there's only half a person caretaking *hers?* If that. Most women recall their mothers deteriorating into empty shells, shadows of themselves, unrecognizable when compared to the smiling, hopeful, supremely confident young women they were in their college, even wedding, photos.

Observing the behavior of our fathers, our mothers' responses to it and the impact that had on both of them and their relationship has struck terror into today's women. Although our mothers married at a time when you could hardly hear the church bells over the sound of burning bras and feminist rhetoric, few of them truly practiced what they felt, at last, free to preach. For the overwhelming majority of women, even if their mothers continued to work outside the home, even if they maintained separate interests from their husbands, the ideal Disney marriage was the reserve of celluloid. For many women growing up, marriage had all the components of a horror film, where the weak, despite their feeble protestations at the start, are swallowed up by the strong, spit out and left for dead. Happy endings? *Pah!*

I'll come to the subject of money and power later in the book. And for sure, a severe lack of both were key factors in keeping our mothers married to our fathers long after the "best before" date had expired. But what most women claim to lie at the root of their mothers' marital problems was lack of identity. (Or, more specifically, the problem of *imposed* identity.) Suppression of her own feelings, desires and needs if, indeed, she was able to define them at all. She didn't have a whole heap of convictions, never mind the courage to see them through. How could she when she hadn't taken the time to discover what they truly were, what *she* was, before she got married? In vowing to be totally committed to her husband, she was pledging to become devoid of commitment to herself. Says Emily, "In our mothers' generation, there was a clear definition of what a woman was supposed to be." She was, she felt, put on the planet with the sole purpose of serving her husband and to hell with what she wanted. As it happened, hell was what she ended up with.

Says Niki, thirty-five, "I saw my mother being tired, stressed, muffled. My father had a terrible temper and she was always appeasing. She was always doing what she could to prevent the outburst. I remember being a kid and we had a thing called 'Daddy napkins.' The rest of us, including my mother, used paper napkins, we used the cheap ones, while he had to have the nice napkin. He had a special *every*thing. And we had to be quiet even if he chose to work in the middle of the living room. We'd have to tiptoe around him. She was our role model in that, she was the one who taught us to do that, otherwise the consequences were just too unpleasant."

And Suzannah, thirty-nine, recalls, "I have this very distinctive image of my mom when I was about fourteen. I came home from school and she was at home looking absolutely awful in this horrible track suit outfit. Her hair was a mess and I remember thinking, God, she looks terrible. She just doesn't care how she looks. So I grew up thinking, I'm never going to be this. I'm never going to be stuck in the house, waiting for my husband to come home, bringing up my kids who spend their whole time daydreaming about when they can leave home. I'm never going to do that. But my mother wanted her own identity and life. She just didn't know how to get it."

Even if Suzannah's mother had been possessed with the certainty of who she was, what she wanted and equipped with the skills to make it happen, it's likely she would have still subjugated her identity to her husband's. It's what many of our mothers did. Their identities were inextricably linked to their husband's. And based on *their* mothers, our grandmothers', behavior, they had few role models to show them the benefits of an alternative. Moreover, since their mothers were even less likely to complain, never mind remove themselves from their unhappy union, they grew up believing that self-sacrifice was the only mode of behavior.

Gina, thirty-four, says, "I watched my mother do everything for my father. She didn't just have a good heart, she genuinely wanted to make him happy even at the expense of herself. She'd abandon her yoga night class when he'd suddenly call her and tell her he wasn't coming home, he was going out after work. She'd go to enormous lengths to make every Christmas perfect for him to make up for his miserable childhood. She'd go camping because *he* liked it, when really she preferred hotels. God knows, camping with four kids was no vacation for her, especially as my father would spend all day fishing on his own. And how did he treat her? Like trash. He'd talk to the dog more respectfully than he talked to my mother. I hated him for it. And, strangely, I despised my mother, too. And because of that, I treated her very badly, like he did. I'd come home from college, leave my clothes in a heap, expect her to fetch and carry, have a meal ready in case I felt like eating. I got away with it because she allowed me to. And that was obviously my father's attitude. She died suddenly from cancer seven months ago. Even at her funeral, my father made jokes about my mother. He said, 'You'd think Janet would have stocked the freezer with pastries before she went.' I was almost sick. I haven't spoken to him since that day. My mother was a saint and look where it got her."

The tragedy of Gina's mother is echoed by many. Says Lena, thirty, "My mother adored my father. She did everything. Even though he didn't do a thing, she never bitched about it. Then my father met someone else and he left her. It was very painful."

Bettina, thirty, says her mother's lost identity manifested itself in obsessive and destructive behavior. "She became retentive. She spent four hours making dinner every night and every little thing my sister and I did was hyperscrutinized. If I left a quarter in my jeans pocket, she said I did it on purpose and it would become a big fiasco that had to be analyzed. It's because she invested everything in being a housewife."

Says forty-one-year-old Rae, "That happened to my mother. She developed OCD—Obsessive Compulsive Disorder. That thing where you have to check twenty times whether you've switched off the lights? The hand-washing thing, too. She was classic. I'd say, 'You've got to see someone about this.' I mean, I know a lot of doctors. I'll never forget what she said: 'It doesn't matter. I'm a nobody. Who cares?'"

Says Sara, thirty-five, "They say that suppressing your emotions causes cancer. There's absolutely no history of breast cancer in my mother's family, yet my mother got breast cancer four years ago. She didn't drink, she didn't smoke, she ate healthily, kept herself in shape. I think it was because she just bottled up everything inside for the entire duration of her marriage. She was so smart, she could have been anything she wanted to be. But she put everything on hold for my father and for her kids. My father would criticize her in front of us and she'd never put him straight. I'd say, 'Mom, why don't you tell him to shut up? He shouldn't speak to you like that,' and she'd say, 'Oh, you don't know. He doesn't mean it.' But I knew it got to her. See, he was her everything. Without him and without us, she had nothing. Then when she got breast cancer, he left her anyway. He had this fucking ridiculous mid-life crisis. Now, he wants to come back to her . . . yeah, now that she's more or less recovered. But she won't go back. She's taken up classes, started traveling. It's like she's suddenly discovered herself, who she really is. I just wish it hadn't taken her so long."

It isn't accurate to say that all the women I talked to recall unhappy marriages between their parents, but a majority of those whose mothers did have an identity away from the home acknowledge it was secondary to their primary identity of wife and mother. They describe their mothers putting their real selves "on hold," "fitting in" around kids' school schedules and husbands' work commitments, and only finding herself once everyone else had fulfilled their imperatives, mainly when the kids had left home. If her mother and father don't then go on to divorce (which is extremely common, on the increase, and, more often than not, at the woman's behest), their marriage will certainly be challenged by the wife's newly discovered identity and her desire to "make up for lost time."

Naiela, thirty, says, "When my sister and I left home, I think my mother wandered around the house for a year. She had no idea what to do with herself. I'd phone home and my father would say, 'I'll go and get your mother, she's in the garden talking to herself.' She was desperately lost, even though he was there. But my mother had always been good at languages. So one day, I called home and my father picked up the phone. He said, 'You'll never guess what your mother's gone and done. She's enrolled herself into college.' I said, 'Wow, that's great.' So my father said, 'I'm not happy about it at all. The woman's fifty-six. Who does she think she is?' That said everything. They argued about it for months, even though she still performed her wifely duties, cooking his dinner, keeping the house clean. Now I think my father's quite proud of her. But it caused a lot of upset for a long time."

Irrespective of their family backgrounds, today's brides are under the spell of powerful forces. For many, it is the combination of witnessing their mothers' nightmare and the prevalence of empowering messages from the media. For others, positive role models and mentors have instilled in them the importance of seeking and keeping their identity. But there's one more force which cannot be ignored— the positive effect of our mothers' sacrifice on our own sense of who we are. That she was always there, taking an active interest in our development, encouraging us to fulfill our potential, focusing all her attention on us, stroking us, bolstering us, willing us on, making us feel like we were the center of the universe, none of this support should be undervalued.

"I have a lot to thank my mother for," says Tyler, thirty-one. "She was there for every recital, every sports day. Even if I didn't win, she told me I was the best. I was bullied for a short time at school and although my mother didn't really get involved, I remember her saying, 'Don't let anyone belittle you. Stand up and fight for who you are.' The next day, I kicked the shit out of that girl. I got into trouble at school for it, but my mother was right behind me and I never let anyone walk over me again. It's bizarre because my mother didn't fight for who *she* was. I guess she didn't want me to end up being like her."

We're all too aware of the contradiction. Says Rachel, twenty-eight, "My mother was a full-time mother. I don't disrespect what she did because I benefited from it in so many ways. I'm so glad I didn't grow up with a nanny. I know I'm more confident because my mother was always there. But," she continues, "I saw my mother throwing things. The strain for her of just being a wife and mother was too much. She made me aware that you *have* to be selfish, so I will get a nanny when I have kids. I don't want to be like my mother."

Neither do I. "Learn from my mistakes. Work hard, have a career," my mother would say over and over. "Be yourself." Thanks to her constant presence and affirmations, I went on to develop a huge—at times obnoxious—sense of entitlement. Although I wobble at times, I'm able to draw upon the enormous reserves of self-confidence and self-belief that she stocked and continues to replenish, if not daily now, certainly on a weekly basis. So while I (and what I have accomplished) can in many respects be attributed to my mother's sole focus, despite it *and* because of it, I am unwilling to do the same for my children.

Our mothers were so influential and effective in making us feel important—often to the detriment of themselves—we still believe the world revolves around us and cannot, *will not* entertain the idea for one second that it does not. So whether we want to be like our mother because she proved the importance of identity or, more commonly, we don't because she had none of her own, the end result is the same. Identity is to be preserved at all cost. It will not be compromised for anyone. Not even our children. But especially *not* for someone we regard as an equal. *Especially* not for our husbands.

"I Do" Not ID

When I got married," says Niki, thirty-five, "I was already thirty-two years old. So I was used to my name, it's *my* name, and I never wanted to take Ron's name. I used to make a joke that it just makes it easier so I don't have to give it back later. I don't mean to be so cynical about it. It just never occurred to me to take his name. Anyway, my two names together are very short. People tend to call me Niki Dean like it's all one word, 'Nikidean.' And if I'd taken his name, I would have sounded like a soap opera character, which was also a problem. So I never wanted to, I never thought about it."

The days when a woman automatically, unquestioningly took her husband's name are becoming a distant memory. Even the hyphenated compromise now seems laughably outdated, pretentious and nonsensical. Today, the refusal to be invisible and relinquish our identity when married manifests itself within seconds of saying "I do." When the paperwork is presented and she holds her pen over her marriage license, the newly hitched chick isn't simply scrolling her signature, she's making a statement. And one which, very often, her husband will oppose. *Ding, ding!* Round one!

Says Stella, thirty-two, married one year to Martin, "He said to me years ago, when we were first dating, 'I will never marry a woman unless she changes her name.' And I said, 'We may as well split up now because there's no way I'm going to change my name. What would happen to Stella Reece? What's going to happen to that person?' I won't change and I felt like if I changed my name, I would change or would have to change. But he wanted me to change my name because he comes from a very conservative family. Even on our wedding day, his mother turned to me and said, 'Oh, Mrs. Latham!' and I said, 'Who's that?' I said to my mother, 'Goddammit, you'd better not ever put his last name on my mail because there is no Stella Latham. She does not exist. If I do get mail with Mr. and Mrs. Martin Latham, it makes me mad. It's like I am not a person."

Lola, thirty, gulps back her wine and shrieks, "That happened to me! Even though Tommy is so contemporary in many ways, he even said, 'I will not marry somebody who does not take my name.' In fact, that's one of the reasons we broke up years ago. I said, 'Tell me why? I can tell you fifty reasons why I will not change my name, you tell me one good reason why I should.' He said, 'Tradition.' I said, 'You can stick tradition up your ass!' "

"Cheers to that!" eight of us girls around a table hoot.

Lola's still on a roll. "Who made up this rule? Who the hell said it has to be this way? In the past, women had to change their names because they thought they belonged to somebody. You couldn't own property. But today is a different day. The fact that he said 'tradition' is appalling to me. I was born with my name. It represents my family, my culture. It represents who I am."

Thirty-one-year-old Julia says, "I will never be Mrs. Julia Broadbent. That's bizarre. I'm Julia Pisani. This is my identity, and why would I forsake that for someone else? But it's funny because, of course, you have your father's name anyway and that's the primary contradiction of being a modern female. That's our bugbear, it's never our name. But it's become your name long enough that to give it up is devaluing. Also if people see me as married, am I suddenly going to seem less cool, not as adventurous, less of a good friend? Am I going to seem like this anachronism? Compromised in some way?"

"But," says Bettina, thirty, "my family name was changed at Ellis Island so I didn't feel particularly attached to it. One of the reasons I decided to keep my name was for professional purposes."

"Me, too," says Vanessa, thirty. "That's the person people know. I've been practicing law for five years and everything in my office says Vanessa Thomas. That's the person who went to school, that's the person who got the degrees. That's who has accomplished so much."

"Also," says Bettina, "even though I was still of two minds about it, I finally decided to keep my name because my grandmother said to my aunt in my mother's presence, 'Thank goodness you're having a boy so he can carry on the Levin name.' When I heard the story, I said, 'What about me? *I* can carry on the name.' "

"That's another thing," says Lola. "I'm the one who's going to be freakin' carrying the child for nine months. I'm the one who's going to go through labor. I can't even imagine that this child does not have my name. I have more right for that child to have my name than my husband. I want my child to have both at least. In Spanish culture, a child has both names, then drops the mother's name when he or she gets married, but that's their choice then. It really upsets me so much. Women weren't important fifty years ago, so her name didn't mean anything. It does now."

Julia, twenty-eight, "Of course I kept my name. I love my name. Also I have a little eagle tattooed on my butt, which means 'von Eichel' in German. It's me, it's who I am."

It's society's on-going stubborn desire to preserve the status quo which makes even a thoroughly modern women finally surrender her name. When children enter the scene, most women feel it necessary to start using their husband's name, if not for their own sake (God forbid anyone might think they had a child out of wedlock!), but for their children's ("Good Lord, has the child no father?"). This was certainly the case for me, particularly once we were attempting to get our daughters into the best school in the district, which happened to be a church school. Like many, I refused to surrender completely, so grudgingly opted for hyphenation. But it's a right old mouthful, especially for a four-year-old, which is why, to my husband's quiet delight and my simmering irritation, our girls are usually referred to by his name alone. *Grrr.*

When Suzannah's children entered their first school, she says, "I felt like I existed in two spheres. When I was being the wife and mother, I called myself Suzannah Forest. I didn't call myself Suzannah Pearson, my birth name, on anything to do with the kids. The people at the kids' school didn't understand me. Even the way I'd say hello to them, nothing gelled. I didn't even try to be my normal self. I had other areas of my life, like when I'm with my friends or at work, when I could be the true me."

But Suzannah's strategy did not sit comfortably with her. Now that her kids are off to another school, she says, "I've said I'm Suzannah Pearson because, at this school, I feel like I can be her. And already, I'm pulling faces during parent meetings at the other mothers as if to say, 'For fuck's sake' and they're pulling faces back as if to say, 'I know . . . Jesus Christ!' And that's fantastic. There *are* other people in the world like me. So I feel like I've reclaimed a part of me."

Suzannah's right, there are many people just like her. But there are still a surprising number who won't accept a woman's identity outside of the confines of Mrs. And many of them are women.

Mary, thirty, says, "We hadn't been married long and had to move back to Tom's hometown while he was doing his Ph.D. In a way, it was a very academic crowd, but they were also very conservative. I met a woman on that first Sunday we went to church and since I was new to Tom's family, I didn't know whether she knew of us or not. So

I said, 'Hello, I'm Mary Sharpeton' and she turned and said, 'I don't trust any woman who doesn't take her husband's name.' I didn't know what to say to that!"

Says Alice, thirty-five, "It's not just men you have to watch, it's older women. Many of them are so bitter and so repressed, they take their bad choices out on younger women because their husbands won't listen to them. I've met some nasty pieces of work and they're always older women." Thirty-year-old Chloe agrees, "They want you to join their club. It validates what they have done."

THE HITCHED CHICK'S GUIDE TO
"I DO" ID

"With a name like Iacoviello, who wouldn't take their husband's name?" laughs thirty-five-year-old Beth, who's been married ten years, but adds if she was getting married today, "it's quite possible I would keep my name." Says Joely, twenty-six, "Some of my friends changed their names because their husbands wanted them to so badly, but many of them now regret it. It's stupid to change your name. I don't understand it. Your name and identity are very important." About to make your decision? Regretting the decision you made? The modern choices aren't restricted to two . . . and you can *always* change your mind.

- ✦ You both keep your own birth names (Mandi Norwood and Martin Kelly).
- ✦ You take your husband's name socially (Mandi Kelly) but keep your own name professionally (Mandi Norwood).
- ✦ You take your husband's last name (Mandi Kelly).

+ You hyphenate your name and your husband's name (Mandi Norwood-Kelly).

+ You use your birth name as a middle name (Mandi Norwood Kelly).

+ Your husband takes your name (Martin Norwood).

+ Both you and your husband hyphenate (Mandi Norwood-Kelly and Martin Norwood-Kelly).

+ You use your husband's birth name as a middle name and he uses your birth name as a middle name (Mandi Kelly Norwood and Martin Norwood Kelly).

+ You both pick an entirely new name (Mandi Kennedy and Martin Kennedy).

I Work, Therefore I Am

Women comprise an increasing share of the world's labor force. In America and the U.K., around 44 percent of the labor force is female, up from just over 40 percent in 1988. In fact, the percentage of adult women who work increased from 26 percent in 1940 to 60 percent in 1997. The higher she's educated, the greater the likelihood a woman will work. And not just for the financial rewards. While the $$$$ are important to meet her standard of living expectations, and she greatly values the impact of her economic power, there's another, equally important reason the hitched chick needs to work. Her identity.

For many, it's the sole reason she works. The additional income is terrific, wonderful, great. But according to today's wife, no amount of money stacks up against the contribution of work to her identity.

"Work is the one area you can be yourself more than anything else," says Amy, thirty-two, a journalist. "They really aren't interested in whether you're a wife or whether you have kids. Generally speaking, if you're good at your job, that's what you're judged on."

"What I like about work is that sense of individualism," says Mary, thirty, who now attends medical school. "When I worked in a hospice, even though I was working with a group, it was something that was all mine, it had nothing to do with my husband."

Says Tyler, thirty-one, a fifth-grade teacher, "Like all couples, Dez and I have our ups and downs. When I go through those moments of worrying whether we're really compatible after all—will we get divorced?—I thank God I am not just a wife. I thank God I have my work. Not just because I would be able to take care of myself if we did split up, but also because I know I wouldn't fall apart and have nothing. I'd still be me."

Rachel, twenty-eight, agrees. "I want to be something, I want to be a known artist and that means I have to be pretty selfish and self-absorbed. I have to take time for myself and my art. If I didn't, it would make me feel inadequate, like I was a nobody. By taking my work very seriously, I'm a success to myself."

Since modern brides tend to be higher educated, they can afford to pick and choose their career path and do so with their identity at the front of their minds. Unlike many of our mothers who, if they did work, rarely regarded their jobs as a career. Knowing it would come to an abrupt end once babies arrived, to most a job was something they did to bridge the short gap between school and marriage. If it lasted longer than that, supplementary income was their primary motivation. Identity-related? Are you kidding? So many women had no idea what their identity should be beyond the boundaries of marriage. Those who did and determinedly pursued fulfilling careers were glorious (if not exhausted) exceptions. In the main, the jobs our mothers had were either low-paid, low-status or low-satisfaction. Probably a combination of all three. The only bonus: no-hassle employment termination when her "higher calling" of wife and mother demanded it. Who'd *do* such a job? Certainly not her husband. His identity was far too closely linked to his work for such drudgery.

Having been educated first and very likely exposed to a vast array of experiences and possibilities before she marries, a woman knows who she is and what kind of career will complement her by the time she gets hitched. And since she will have been in the workplace for at least five years before she becomes a wife, the layers of her identity will be well-established and as tightly knit as a pair of Wolford tights. Her work and who she is will be one.

Says Suzannah, thirty-nine, a screenwriter, "I don't feel like I am primarily a wife and mother. I feel primarily that I'm a creative person, that I'm a bit edgy. So my work is all about me, establishing my identity and confirming it. It allows me to think about who I am and what I feel. I've always worked. It's who I really am."

Denise, thirty-six, a human resources consultant, agrees. "I hate cooking. I hate cleaning. I hate all those traditional female pastimes. I'm terrible at sewing and decorating. And when you're bad at things, you hate doing them. What I'm good at is clarifying, motivating, organizing, problem solving. That's why I love my job and why my job loves me. I can't conceive of giving it up. Maybe I'm a freak, but I wouldn't even give it up if I won the lottery. Okay, maybe for a year. But forever? No way."

Says forty-three-year-old Wendy, a writer and publishing consultant, "I would never sacrifice my career. It's too much a part of who I am. I couldn't sacrifice that."

Sally, thirty-one, a lawyer, admits her work frustrates and stresses her, but agrees with Wendy. "Give up work? For what? I sometimes think I'd like to spend weeks and months just doing my painting and going shopping, but it would kill me. I'd eventually die of boredom. If I didn't work, what would I be? Nothing."

Sam, thirty-six, has experienced both sides of the coin. Before she married Ray and moved from Manchester, England, to New York, she ran her own marketing and advertising firm. She remembers the agony of making the decision to give it up. "When Ray asked me to come to New York with him, I said, 'I don't know. I'll have to think about it.' I summoned my girlfriends 'round for spaghetti and a bottle of wine and I told them I didn't know what to do. Even though I loved Raymond, I was very proud of myself and my business. I was in a real quandary. But they said, 'What do you mean, you don't know?' One of them said, 'If you don't go, *I* could learn to love Raymond! Manchester or New York? You go!'"

Initially overwhelmed by the excitement of her move, it didn't take Sam long to realize what she'd given up. Unable to work until she receives her visa, she says, "When people say, 'I'd love the life of Riley,' I say, 'You wouldn't.' Waking up and not having anything to get up for . . . I was going nuts. That's why I started doing the voluntary work and my website, Spraggworld. My biggest thing during the day was 'What shall I cook for Ray tonight?' I'd go out shopping and make all these amazing meals for him. Ray eats like a pigeon, but he'd come home to these amazing five-course meals every night and the poor thing would have to eat them all up. And as soon as he'd get in, I'd start, 'How was your day? What did you have for your lunch? What have you been up to?' I felt like I'd lost my identity. I'm a very social person and I just hated that."

Who does this remind you of? Surely not your mother? If not your mother, then your friends' mothers. Most Hitched Chicks don't walk in Sam's (or their mother's) shoes until they have children and, albeit temporarily, take time off work for maternity leave. Until such a time, they enjoy a certain amount of wallowing in the stay-at-home fantasy. No stress, no deadlines, no expectations, no brain strain. . . . In our dreams, it's eternal bliss. In reality, however, the contentment is short-lived.

Anabelle, thirty-five, a copywriter, says, "I love being Willi's mom and looking after him, but having him has made me feel quite out of control, so I have become much more anal about tidiness in the three months since I've had him. So if someone said I couldn't go back to work, I'd freak. In fact, I think doing my work and being apart from Willi makes me a better mother. Feeling like I'm still Anabelle is so important to me. When you work, you're doing something for yourself, it's yours."

Says Amy, thirty-two, who has two children, "After the birth of each child, I immersed myself in the mom's role and spent little time on me. During each period, I felt like I lost my identity. When that happens, you become more vulnerable to other things, such as thinking you're fat or unattractive, which in turn makes you vulnerable to approaches from other men."

Ruth, thirty-eight, empathizes. She has resumed her career in the fashion business, but clearly recalls her crossroad. "I'd just had my youngest son and I'd been at home eight months. One week, we went out to Martha's Vineyard with a whole group of people and I remember sitting at a table with all these women and men, all of whom were executives or had their own businesses, and they were from all parts of the country. So I was just sitting there and nobody talked to me because they thought that as a mom—and only a mom—I was uninteresting. In fact, I *didn't* have anything to offer to the conversation and I remember thinking, Oh my God, I'm just a mom. I mean, I love my kids and know I'm a good mom, but that's *all* I am. My whole self-esteem is connected to what I do besides being a good mom and a wife and a friend."

So, I ask Ruth, you didn't return to work simply because of the way other people regarded you? After all, social pressure to quit your role as wife and mother is as bad as social pressure to be just that. "Not at all," counters Ruth. "Staying at home is not enough for me.

My husband did say, 'I think you should go back to work because you're starting to count the blades of grass.' He was right. It has nothing to do with how much I love my children or how much I want to be with them. Nothing. Without work, I just felt invisible. It isn't my personality."

I wasn't counting blades of grass, but I know that feeling. I remember being at home after the birth of my littlest one, Daisy, and turning into an absolute nutcase. My most vivid memory involves a cake. I'm no cook, so it took me all day to bake that cake . . . what with breastfeeding, changing diapers, vacuuming and washing.

Come teatime, I carefully placed the cake on the table. Within seconds, my husband had sneezed, not a little *schnift* into his hand, but a bloody great *airchoooo!* Granted, he'd turned his head away from the table, but I was convinced droplets of God-knows-what were, nevertheless, cascading over my precious cake. Screaming hell fire (along the lines of "And why don't you just fucking well stab me in the face while you're at it?!"), I scooped that cake off the table, slammed it in the trash and stormed out the front door. As I sat in the park on my own, weeping and trying to de-blotch my nose, I realized my whole identity was wrapped up in that cake and Martin had had the gall to sneeze on *me*.

Lunatic? You bet your life. A month later, I flew back to work faster than a starving dog heading toward a sausage factory. Finally, I rediscovered feisty, difficult, creative, selfish, fabulous *me*. For sure, the stress of juggling family and job almost blows my head off at times, but it's infinitely preferable to being a cake. Even if it is chocolate.

Domestic? *Moi?*

Anabelle's husband, Pete, leaves his clothes on the floor. Now, I know Pete. He's smart and fit and hysterically funny and, like Anabelle, he has a demanding job. Pete's inability to pick up his clothes is not a symptom of any physical impediment. Nor is he chronically forgetful—he'd have been fired from his job donkey's years ago if he'd truly lost his mind. No, Pete leaves little heaps of pants, socks and T-shirts everywhere because, like most men, he loathes the domestic imperative of civilized life. But here's the thing: like most women, Anabelle loathes it, too. But unlike her mother, she does not see herself as her husband's domestic sidekick, known more commonly as "the wife." And as such, will not meekly shuffle around after him, dutifully picking up his clothes, washing them and, like a little ghost in the night, returning them to his closet. This is *not* Anabelle. *This* is Anabelle:

"A couple of weeks ago, as usual, Pete left his clothes on the floor. So that day, I just said to him, 'Oh, Pete, I'm just going to tell you that the next time you leave your clothes on the floor, I'm going to throw them out of the window. So I'm just telling you. Okay? I'm not telling you aggressively, I'm just warning you that that's what I'm going to do.' And I then threw a few things into the garden and made sure they landed on the garden path so that when he came back, he understood I meant it."

Servant, domestic help, cleaner, picker-upper . . . this is not the Hitched Chick's identity. And with every fiber of her being, she is refusing to make it so. The statistics paint a damming picture of her attempts. Although research shows that wives have halved the number of hours they spend doing housework compared with the 1960s, married women still do twice as much as their husbands. Hot damn. But what those grim stats reveal is that, albeit slowly, the tables *are* turning.

Says Niki, thirty-five, married three years, "If I don't buy the cat food on the way home, it won't get bought. It's the same with toilet paper. Ron still has the idea that somehow these things miraculously appear. He only realizes when he's in a bad position and there isn't any there . . . otherwise he'd have no idea. And it's funny because when he is in that position and he does remember, then he does get it, he's like a little puppy. He'll say, 'Look! I got it! I got it! And you didn't even ask me!' It's surprising."

The trouble is if our mother was being a positive role model to us, even by simply complaining about her domestically focused identity, chances are our husband's mother was too busy ironing his underpants (and loving it, who knows?) to reveal the colors of *her* true ID. Result? Even the most progressive man still, even in the twenty-first century, associates a wife's identity with housework. Little wonder newly Hitched Chap feels confused and surprised when after the first few weeks of slovenly bliss, the sex kitten he married turns into a tiger and snarls, "I won't tell you again, pick your dirty shit up off the floor!"

"I soon put a stop to that," says Melanie, thirty, referring to the imposition of a domestic identity. "I'd be running up and down stairs doing laundry, which is one of my peeves, and he'd see me going back and forth, *while* I'm cooking dinner, *while* I'm trying to clean the kitchen. And he'd be sitting there, flicking over the television. So then I just dropped everything right in front of him and I said, ''Scuse me! Do you not *see* me?' And then he said, 'What? What did I do?' So I said, 'What? Are you a fuckin' *retard* that you don't see me running up and down stairs?'"

Are you effective? I ask. "Most of the time," says Melanie. "He might start giving me attitude and then I'll say, 'Listen, I'm asking you for help, so listen to me and stop your bullshit.' And then after he has his little episode, he'll say, 'You know what? I'm sorry, you're right, I promise to help you.' And then he does. But I'm very verbal, so if I don't like something, you're gonna hear it. I don't give a shit if you don't want to hear it. I'm not passive-aggressive, I'm *very* aggressive. It's the better way to be."

Emily, thirty-three, and her husband of six years had a similar baptism of fire. She says, "We had a very difficult first year of marriage. I run a company and I work harder than he does and I can't be 'the wife.' He'd say, 'It's not a talent, it's not a talent. I'm just not good at washing up,' and I'd say, 'You know what? *I'm* not good at washing up either. We're just *both* going to have to do it.' "

Says Tracy, thirty-four, married for twelve years, "I saw my mother hold it in. It was a different age. You just didn't talk to your husband like that, but I don't ever want to be my mother."

Joely, twenty-six, married for one year, offers this advice to friends who don't want to be their mothers. "Just stand there and start screaming, because that's what I do and it works. Some of my friends say, 'I just can't stand there and start screaming because then I'd be like the mean wife.' Then I say, 'Mean? *Mean?* No, no, you don't understand. It's completely unacceptable.' If you stand there and scream long enough, someone is going to realize that you're standing in the middle of the room screaming. They're going to come over and say, 'Why are you screaming?' My mother didn't confront. She'd get silent and I'd see that having a detrimental effect on her."

Joely describes the detrimental effect of her mother's silence as a buildup of frustration and misery, which resulted in each of her parents retreating into their own disconnected worlds. Joely's resolve to behave differently—to shout and scream—works effectively in her marriage. But others concede this aggressively vocal approach achieves little, saying their husbands "switch off" and "become defensive." They have learned to sit down and discuss calmly but firmly the ramifications of the inequities in their relationship.

Take Lena, thirty, married two years. She also witnessed the detrimental effect of a silent domestic identity. "My mother," she recalls, "would come home at night, throw on her leotard and tights, run out to her aerobics class, come home and cook us a full meal. People would say, 'You're always eating late,' but we ate late because no one—including me—would pick up the slack. I don't ever remember my father making a meal. I remember feeling resentful when he'd say, 'Do the dishes' and I'd say, 'I've got homework, you do the dishes,' and he'd say, 'I went to work today.' "

When Lena saw a familiar pattern emerging in the first few months of her marriage, she started to seethe. "I was furious and exhausted, just like my mother always was. The difference is my mom never said a word. And I do. The conversation that finally worked was when I sat him down and said, 'Andrew, I'm desperate for this to change. We're childless now and I'm coming home, wiped out, and there's a meal to be made, I'm not in bed until midnight and you're not helping me. We need to come up with a schedule of who does what, because if we have the same setup when we have kids, I'm going to implode. I can't do this by myself and I won't. It's not going to be 'Mommy makes the meals and does this and Daddy gets the fun stuff.' That finally resonated with him."

But for many Hitched Chicks I talked to, they didn't even let a few weeks of marriage pass by before establishing that a willingness to do domestic chores is not part of her identifying personality. "I made it clear from the start, even before we started living together six months prior to our wedding, that domestic work was not me," says Lou, thirty-one, married three years. "So we drew up a list of all the chores and took turns putting our initials next to the chores each one of us would do. I chose to cook because I actually enjoy cooking.

Vaughn chose the laundry. It got tricky when it came down to who would clean the toilet. But I chose that, only because I prefer cleaning the toilet—especially now that you can buy those lovely toilet wipes—to changing the cat's litter tray."

Was it important to shake off a domestic identity before marriage? I ask. "Oh yeah," says Lou. "It gave us—me especially—a head start on enjoying our marriage. I could be me from the get-go."

Says Laurie, thirty-nine, married seven years, "I still see myself as sexy and young and fun. Housework is just not sexy and it's certainly not fun. You have to start as you mean to go on. I've always just done my own washing and ironing and Jerry does his. I cook when I want, but otherwise Jerry does the bulk of it. Otherwise, we eat out. The cleaning's done on a we-can't-live-in-the-mess-anymore basis, then we both spend half a day madly tidying and vacuuming. It's a chore, but so long as you both do it, that's as good as it gets."

Albeit gradually, the traditional and imposed identity of wife and mother *is* chugging off into the distance. Some women do the domestics of their choosing. Some draw up lists of who does what—and stick to it vehemently. Some bite their tongues until they can contain their fury no more. For others, a total reversal of traditional male and female identity is emerging. Says Becky, thirty-five, "Rupert does everything. He looks after the kids, cleans the house, buys the groceries, everything. He quite likes it, but being a housewife just isn't me." In Mary's case, her husband of six years does everything while she studies. "Although," she says, "I have to work very hard to make him feel like I'm not taking him for granted."

And increasing numbers, refusing to even have a discussion, simply seek outside help. Says Ruth, "I have a live-in nanny who does all the cooking and the cleaning and all the food shopping. And she cooks dinner every night." Thirty-four-year-old Patti, who has taken extended maternity leave, tells me her cleaner still comes twice a week "to do the beds and the bathrooms and give the kitchen a good clean." Says Sam, who doesn't have children, "I like to cook, but we have a cleaner to do all the other stuff."

Whatever their setup, it's a far cry from the stereotypical female identity. Says Stacey, "Ben and I lived together before we got married and we almost split up over the domestic issue. I got serious cold feet for about a month. I hate the whole domestic thing—I even do my ironing in private as it really leaves a bad taste in my mouth. It's not who I am. So Ben went out and bought a dishwasher and employed a cleaner. Then I felt fine about continuing our relationship. It took the pressure off me to be something I'm not. So we did get married. It was funny, because my brother, James, stayed with us last weekend and he said, 'Ben and Harry [her son] are really quite lazy, aren't they? They don't do anything.' And I just said to him, 'James, neither do *I*.'"

I Before We

The way my parents got their marriage to survive when I moved out," says Simone, twenty-nine, "was to have their own and separate places. So although they still see each other—they're exclusive, it's not a 1970s free-love situation—and they go out together and go on holiday, my parents don't live in the same house. They're still married, but they have their own space. My mom lives on the left bank of Paris and my dad lives on the right bank of Paris. So if my dad wants to play poker on a Wednesday night and my mom just wants to eat her sandwich in front of the TV, watching stupid programs, she can do it. It was separate living that salvaged their marriage."

It was a cautionary tale for Simone. "There's this TV image of a married couple who does everything together. They take up golf together and go to the gym together. But it's very important to do things for yourself outside of the famous 'we.' I think women have traditionally felt guilty for being selfish, but you're not saying, 'I don't love you anymore.' You just have to make time for yourself to feel comfortable and special," she says, admitting that while she is a naturally very giving person in her relationship and at work, she also needs her own space and time—badly.

For Simone, her "me time" is spent at the ballet and opera, pursuits her husband dislikes intensely. "But it can also be me stealing an afternoon and watching VH1's *Behind the Music*, just flicking channels and eating potato chips." It doesn't matter, so long as she can, Simone says, "have time just for me."

Much has been written about the time famine women face. The most up-to-date stats were featured in a British Social Trends 2000 report, which revealed that the average woman has fifty minutes less leisure time each day than the average man. I'm not disputing these findings. I'm justifiably horrified by them. But what I do know is that every Hitched Chick I interviewed, without fail, in a career right now or not, with kids or without them, possessed of a cleaner or otherwise, made "me time" a priority. And I'm not talking about a solo dash to the supermarket for choc-covered pretzels or a once-a-week glass of wine in front of *Sex and the City*.

Today's wife pursues her own time and space as ruthlessly as men have been doing for centuries. Without seeking permission, without asking forgiveness, she is steadfastly digging in her stiletto heels and being "selfish." "My attitude is that Murray can't expect me to be home on a Saturday night all of the time," says Gabrielle. "Sometimes he has to book me in advance. I need to do things for me that don't involve him and I need to do them during times that might be considered 'our time.'" For instance? "I do yoga," Gabrielle says, "and there might be a class I want to do and I can only do it at night, so I do it. It means he has to think more about his life and realize that I'm not always, one hundred percent, going to be there. I really believe in being selfish, particularly when it comes to activities which focus on personal health issues. By doing this, I'm a better person and better able to be in this relationship. Being a wife is not enough."

Says Melanie, "I go to the gym religiously, Monday through Thursday. When we got married, I had to quit my gym because I moved into his house so I couldn't travel to my old gym. He said, 'Join my gym and we can go together.' But this is one thing in my life that I want to keep separate—it's just for me. Honestly, I get peace of mind, I don't have to talk to anyone, it's my time to unwind from work. It replenishes who I am, it replenishes my mind so that when I come home, I'm just a nicer, happier, better person."

For Emily, thirty-three, a frantically busy self-made entrepreneur and mother of one, her "me time" takes place at the nail salon every week. She also does yoga and pre-corps. "It's a kind of elliptical machine, like a StairMaster, just less harsh. I do that four times a week. Afterwards, I feel more in control, more accomplished. It makes me feel I've done something for me and my body, so I can check that off the list."

For Ellis, forty-three, it ranges from her "spooky dance practice on a Friday night" to simply reading a book alone on the couch. She says, "If I don't get a certain amount of time to myself, I do go mad. I need it to refresh myself. I do find myself being quite judgmental about couples who do everything together and can't be apart. I think, Don't you know who you are? I can't imagine not wanting to be with my own company. I get so much out of it."

Says Petra, thirty-seven, "I go for a bike ride by myself on the weekend. I go to the gym. I run four times a week. I play on a softball team once a week." *Sheesh!* Plus she holds down a career and has two kids, which is, she says, precisely why she needs to have her own time. "It's good to be selfish and it's in everyone's best interest in the end."

Anabelle gets her "me time" swimming twice a week. The piano is

Sabina's thing. Horseback riding is thirty-eight-year-old Paulette's. Painting is Sally's. Tennis is thirty-two-year-old Lottie's. For April, forty-three, it's her photography. For Lou, DJ'ing reminds her of who she is.

Lena goes to the theater almost weekly and attends a book club on a Saturday night. "It makes me feel balanced in my marriage," she says, "because it's time just for me."

Says Rachel, "I go to museums by myself. I really need time alone and I can't have time alone when I'm at home. Even Patrick is a distraction. Last week, I went to the Met, I went to the Museum of Modern Art, I also went on a long bike ride. It makes me feel inspired."

Mary's "me time" comprises "volunteer work. I get a lot out of it emotionally. It's outside of my work, it's outside of my marriage. It's very important to me in terms of my identity."

When the frenzy of juggling it all—work, love, children, friends, in-laws—threatens to consume us, the pursuit of "me time" is not just a pleasure, it's a necessity. Women I talked to believe much of their mothers' unhappiness and frustration was as a direct result of their denial of "me time." Alice D. Domar, a leading stress-management expert at Beth Israel Deaconess Hospital and Harvard Medical School, seconds this notion. The Boston-based psychotherapist and researcher says, "Women older than fifty still cling to the idea that a husband should be everything to them." As she says, it's as unrealistic as it is old-fashioned.

It's a lesson Fiona, thirty-seven, learned the hard way. After five years of marriage and two children, she teetered on the brink of divorce. She felt like a single parent anyway, she says. "At the start of our marriage, George seemed like a modern man. Although he carried on playing sports very heavily and going out with his friends, I had my own hobbies and interests so it didn't bother me much. But after our first child was born, I knew within weeks he wasn't going to be around at all. So I took it all on myself. At the time, I was too exhausted to feel anything, but it was a nightmare because he was never around. He worked all hours, his life didn't seem to change at all for this baby. I should have realized then that I had made a rod for my own back."

Fiona soon became pregnant again and despite continuing with her career after her second child was born—albeit on a part-time basis—her husband stubbornly refused to accept she needed "me time." "When he was around at the weekend," Fiona says, "he was not involved. He was bad-tempered and no fun. And if I wanted to go shopping for myself at the weekend, it would be a nightmare. The kids would be screaming, there were dirty diapers . . . and he would say, 'Just go if you're going' and he'd be in a foul temper and wouldn't speak to me. Then I wouldn't go because I couldn't leave the kids in such a state. And if I was going out at night, he'd always say, 'I can't get home to see to the nanny.' It was impossible."

Finally, Fiona could take no more. "I was compromising everything about myself too much. I told him I had decided to leave him and move back to the city where I'd get an apartment and resume my life. But," she says, "his reaction was really shocking. He said he really loved me and I think he did. He gave up a lot of his sports, a lot of his friends and he concentrated on me. Plus, I said, 'I need regular time on my own, to be able to go out without there being fights. I need time to reestablish myself, spend time with myself, time to figure out who I am and where I want to go and I can't do that when you or the kids are around.' I fought hard to give myself that time away and I've now got back in touch with myself. He started to respect that if I wanted to go out on a Saturday, I was going to. If I want to curl up with a book on a Sunday afternoon, I do. I've always loved cutting up things and putting them in books. It sounds crazy, but it's what I'm like and I feel all that coming back. You cannot live a lie, denying who you are. And you have to keep at it if you want a happy marriage."

Me, No Kids

W hen the research and marketing company Youth Intelligence asked 3,440 Generation X women (i.e., twenty-five- to thirty-five-year-olds) what indicated success in the year 2002, only 20 percent said "having children." Children as a success indicator lagged behind "pursuing one's passions," "having good friends," "having a good relationship with family," "having a happy marriage" and "having a balanced life." Although the majority of women today do regard children as a happy bonus, they are adamant their identity and success is not dependent on being a wife and mother. For increasing numbers, it's to the exclusion of children.

Here are some facts:

+ Population projections suggest one in five women who are now of childbearing age may never have children.
+ Census figures show that in 1976, 35 percent of American women between fifteen and forty-four were childless. In 1996, the rate was 42 percent.
+ According to the U.K. Office for National Statistics, two out of three women born in the 1970s have yet to have children, compared to those born in the early 1960s, half of whom had children by the time they were twenty-five.
+ Women with less than a bachelor's degree recorded the largest increase in childlessness since 1980, according to the U.S. Census Bureau.
+ Among women who are married or have been married at some point, the levels of childlessness of white women are the same as black women (U.S. Census Bureau).

✦ Regardless of marital status, Hispanic women had lower levels of childlessness than non-Hispanic women (U.S. Census Bureau).

Experts agree that the reasons behind remaining childless are as diverse as women themselves. But the unifying fact is that choice is the reason women are opting out. (Although we can't ignore its existence, decreasing fertility due to delayed procreation is not at the root of the data.) Says Rosemary Gillespie, a leading researcher from the School of Social and Historical Studies, University of Portsmouth, England, what we are witnessing is "the emergence of a radical feminine identity, distinct and unshackled from motherhood."

Unshackled from motherhood? Yikes! It's difficult for us (female or male) to imagine being shackled to anything—neither friends, family, work nor marriage. We have grown up in a "free to be me" environment where the only expectations that really matter are our own. That we should feel we have to be something we are not is untenable to us. Yet, the fact that so many column inches exist on the subject of voluntary childlessness among women—the fact that I am including it, too—proves society remains challenged by its presence.

When a woman makes the decision to preserve her childless identity (or "childless femininity" as Rosemary Gillespie calls it), it hardly seems to matter that she feels content with it. Others are not. Like retaining our names, it's perceived as one break too many with tradition, it's unnatural, or even a sin. As thirty-five-year-old Shelley says, "Someone—a woman—said to me, 'I understand if you can't have children. But if you can and you don't want to, it's just plain wrong.' And this woman thinks she's modern." What's galling, says Shelley, is "no one would ever question a man who didn't want children."

She's right, of course. Men's identities have never been linked to children. Even if a man does take an active role in child rearing, he will rarely be described first and foremost as "Joe Bloggs, father of two." Shelley, like most women who don't want children, generally responds to questions and comments with little more than a roll of her eyeballs. "You want to turn around and say, 'Mind your own damn business,'" fumes Shelley, "but most of the time they don't mean any harm, they're just intrigued."

However, some women object intensely to being in the line of fire. "I don't want kids because I was sexually abused as a child," says Pauline, thirty-six. "I have enough of my own issues to contend with. It's not fair to bring a child into the world just because you feel pressure from ignorant people. I have very personal reasons I don't want to discuss with strangers, yet they feel they have the right to pry. You know what it says to me? That women are still regarded as public property. It gets on my nerves."

What gets on my nerves is that the general attitude toward women who choose to be childless is that they're somehow irresponsible—which is, as we know, something women should never be. Freewheeling men are one thing. Freewheeling women? Freaks of nature. Yet many Hitched Chicks do want to be and are freewheeling. "Why should marriage mean you have to settle down and wear carpet slippers for the rest of your life?" demands Shelley. However, it's not because they lack a responsible attitude to life. The decision not to have kids and freewheel, from what I have experienced, is based on a consuming desire to *be* responsible.

One of the strategies of successful business people is prioritizing. Making a list of your priorities is responsible and effective business practice. Since many wives today are successful businesswomen, they know they have to delete tasks which are not a priority. Having it all, we now know, is not what it was cracked up to be. What's better is having what's right for us.

The choices women have today are so enormous, exciting and demanding, having children is often just not high enough on their list of priorities. Says Shelley, "When you have kids, you can't just sling them over your shoulder and go. Have you seen all the crap parents have to carry around with them? Don't get me wrong, I like kids. But I just like other things more, like traveling, adventure, I love my job and I just don't want kids enough to give that up. What could be worse than bringing a child into the world, then resenting that child? It's irresponsible."

Says Niki, thirty-five, "Yes, I like to stay out at night and not worry about it, so I guess I'm selfish. But I also look back on my childhood and see how at various times I was unhappy, so I have this massive fear of scarring somebody else. But really, I just don't have a biological clock. I figure that if I did, all the warning signs would have started flashing. But I don't have the longing for children."

Neither does Sabina, forty, who says she has "no maternal feelings. I'm just not very comfortable around children." I ask her whether she's ever been called selfish. "Hmm, I might have been. But I think it's selfish when people have them when they don't really want them. Matthew and I talked about it before we got married and neither of us said we wanted children. Sometimes it bothers me that I haven't had maternal feelings. But it's who I am, so I either accept it or be very unhappy."

THE HITCHED CHICK'S GUIDE TO
Putting Me Before We

Compromising who we really are, always putting ourselves second, detaching ourselves from the feelings, responses and actions that make up our unique identity, as any therapist will agree, is not only classic female behavior, it's classic *dangerous* behavior that will ultimately destroy us and detonate our marriages. Even before our mothers said "I do," they were programmed to believe "I should." Witnessing the disastrous consequences of this self-sacrificing behavior, smart women now know being selfish is not bad or shameful, it's actually good for our well-being—and our relationship. So when the urge to succumb to "we" at the detriment of "me" threatens to overtake you, photocopy the following and stick to it—if not for God's sake, then for your own.

◆ *Know your feelings are normal.* Just because you feel or respond to a situation differently than your husband, it does not make you mental. Says Rae, forty-one, "Sometimes Louis will say I'm crazy just because I react differently than him. *That* drives me crazy. I tell him if I feel it, it's valid." Rae's right. Human beings are not all wired alike. Do not allow yourself to believe that just because you feel or behave differently than how your hubby feels or behaves that *you* are wrong. You're just different. And you're different than other women, too. Not happy/angry/ excited/maternal? You're not a freak of nature. There is no standard behavior. What's wrong is ignoring your feelings.

Wronger still, having no feelings at all (good-bye feelings, hello depression).

+ ***Yell, scream, laugh, lose control.*** To do otherwise is not self-discipline, it's self-destructive. Men have scoffed at women's display of emotion for so long, we think it's bad or immature to cry, shout, stamp our feet, even giggle. Hey, to hell with that. Containing our emotions always backfires. Says Rachel, "I saw that happen in my parents' marriage. That buildup, buildup, buildup . . . and then it explodes. It's a positive thing to let somebody know what you're feeling right there and then, even if it makes them uncomfortable. Now that I'm pregnant, I'm even more of that attitude. Last week, I said to Patrick, 'Look, I've tried being polite, but when I'm hungry, I am so *fucking* hungry I'm about to pass out and I'm about to *kill* you unless you get me something right *now*!' Sometimes you just have to get mad." Sally, thirty-one, agrees: "If I try to keep a lid on my anger, it just comes out in other ways. I turn into a sarcastic bitch." If sarcasm's all Sally suffers from, she's lucky. Containing emotions eventually manifests itself in many ways, from illness to chronic anxiety, even alcoholism (heard the phrase "drowning your sorrows"?).

+ ***Negative feelings are not bad.*** Angry woman? "She should control herself." Feeling hurt? "Oh, get a grip." Unhappy? "Pull yourself together." Disappointed? "Don't be a baby." Frightened? "Be brave." Any of these sound familiar? Women are professionals at putting on a happy face. Although it isn't just a female habit to chirp "I'm fine" when someone inquires "How're you doing?" women do draw extreme distinctions between feeling happy, optimistic, confident, brave ("good feelings") and feeling miserable, insecure, fearful, angry ("bad feelings"). Says Lottie, thirty-two, "My mother used to say, 'Don't let Ed see you're upset. Your father couldn't cope when he knew I was miserable.' I said, 'Mom! Being angry doesn't make you a criminal or a crazy woman.' I just can't play the role of happy wife if I'm not. I think our generation is much more emotionally literate." Remember, every feeling has merit. If you don't value sadness, how can you truly value joy?

✦ *Keep tabs on your debits and credits.* Even the humblest financial investor expects a return. Why should we expect anything else when we invest our emotions? And while every deed doesn't need to be matched within minutes, it's fair to expect a deposit sooner or later. Okay, enough banking comparisons. But as Simone, twenty-nine, says, "Being married is not always immediate tit for tat. But women make the shift from 'I' to 'we' much more quickly than men, and if you're not careful they can start to take you for granted even at the beginning of your marriage. So I said to my husband—he's a doctor—'I'll pick up the slack while you work thirty-six-hour shifts, but when the time comes that I have longer hours, you have to pick up the slack.'" Una, thirty-seven, agrees with this. "My husband, John, was going through a very tough time at work. It lasted over a year and I was supportive and patient and sensitive. I didn't mind as he was under so much stress. But when my boss left and a new one started who I absolutely hated, John just didn't reciprocate the support. We were both in the habit of putting his feelings first; mine just didn't seem to count anymore. I won't make that mistake again. Neither will he. I haven't stopped asking him how he feels, but I expect him to ask me, too." And if he doesn't? Says Una, "I just say sarcastically,

'Thanks for asking, this is how *I* feel . . . ' and he gets the message." Gina, thirty-four, goes one step further: "No one—not even your kids—will think more highly of you if you give, give, give. Certainly, men don't. Most of them don't possess the guilt gene. So this is my rule of thumb— take two for every one you give. It's the only way to keep respect and preserve yourself."

♦ *Celebrate your imperfections.* No, please don't gag. Listen, our mothers were always trying to be "the perfect wife" and berated themselves (if their husbands or mothers-in-law didn't do it before them) for not achieving top marks in cooking, bed making, child rearing, sewing, time management, multitasking. But in many respects, there's even more pressure on women to strive for perfection. "Christ Almighty," says Alessandra, thirty-four, "you're expected to be the perfect wife, the perfect mother, the perfect sex kitten, the perfect daughter-in-law, the perfect boss, have the perfect body . . . it never ends." I know, I still have to squish the urge to say to dinner guests, "Sorry, I'm no cook," despite the fact that I enjoy mucking about in the kitchen. I don't ever recall any man apologizing for his lack of expertise in the kitchen or anywhere. That he's doing anything at all is a cause for celebration. But women still fall into the trap of believing they have to be perfection to all people. As Shelley says, "You just have to be yourself, warts and all." And says Suzannah, "We're only human beings. I'm willing to accept other people's humanity, so they have to be willing to accept mine. You can't expect everyone to be perfect, but they can't expect you to be perfect either."

2.

Lust or . . . Bust!

Good sex with Danny was a prerequisite for marrying him. I wouldn't have married him if the sex hadn't been good. Nope. No way in hell. I want it all the time. I need it. I love it. Before Danny started his new job, we'd have sex three or four times a week. Now, he's got this job, he's tired. But being sexually compatible with him was one of the main reasons I married him—and then the son of a bitch goes and turns into a woman!

—*Melanie, thirty*

The old cliché about the wife who constantly refuses to have sex with her husband because she has a headache? Grab a cloth and wipe that myth clean away. Doesn't exist. Hitched Chicks love sex. We want it. We need it. It isn't a chore. It's a necessity. That's the truth.

Women today are proud of their sexuality. They are self-aware sexual beings—and they're in lust. And that lustiness doesn't disappear when they marry. Heard the one about the young, married female executive who rents porn movies to watch alone when she's away on business trips? She exists. Heard the one about the three-year-married illustrator, Rachel, twenty-eight, who books herself a Brazilian bikini wax every four weeks so oral sex is even more intensely pleasurable for her? She's real. And how about Tina, thirty, who insists she meets her husband in a nearby hotel for a twice-a-week lunchtime make-out session? No, she isn't fictitious. You just never hear about these women because lust is something only single girls admit to during imposed periods of celibacy, right? Wrong, wrong, wrong . . .

You may be excused for assuming Hitched Chicks don't demand or expect pleasure if magazines that purport to target married women are anything to go by. "The Six Sex Secrets He Wishes You Knew" screams one. "His Five Hot Spots He Wants You to Touch Tonight" declares another. I mean, what *is* this? Do married women not want their hot spots touched? Do married women not have any sex secrets they wish their husbands knew? Apparently not, according to these "respectable" magazines for married women. But they're chronically misjudging them. Because the reality is, married women are saying "yes, yes, oh yes" more than anyone knows.

Even today, even now in the twenty-first century, women's sexuality confuses and scares the hell out of society. It's dark and mysterious. It's hidden and impenetrable. On the one hand, it's the stuff of fantasy; on the other, it provokes fear. The contradictions of fifty years ago still abound and conspire to make women feel guilty about their desires and experiences, even when they're married.

I'm thinking of Skylla, twenty-nine, who arrived for our interview in a pair of the most daring, pubic-skimming low-rise cord pants and a cropped asymmetrical top. She looked fabulously sexy—and she knew it—and I watched when every male eyeballed her up and down in admiration as she swung through the bar. Yet could she bring herself to tell me she'd slept with over twenty-five men before she met and married Carl? Hardly, for fear she'd be judged as "loose."

I'm also thinking of a brunch at the Park Café in New York with a group of late-twenties women who had attended the same college. They told me about a fellow student who loved sex and indulged in lots and lots of it. Problem? No problem . . . not really—except she was unfemininely *vocal* about it and, as a result, was practically ostracized.

And I'm also thinking about the movie *Unfaithful*, starring Diane Lane and Richard Gere, which was creating a stir in New York while I wrote this section of this book. Not because it's sexy and explores the controversial issue of adultery, but because—gasp!—it portrays a married *woman* who has sex with another man simply because her sexual desire for him overwhelms her. At a dinner party at the time, one of the guests hadn't yet seen *Unfaithful*. When her husband left the table to go to the bathroom, another woman hissed at her, "You've gotta see this movie . . . but don't take your husband. He'll *hate* it."

Society has always accepted male sexuality without question or judgment. And while our comfort level with women's sexuality is at an all-time high, it remains laughably out of step with how modern women really feel, think and behave. Today women know and experience all too well the benefits of sexual pleasure and regard an active sex life as a barometer of a healthy relationship. But sex also makes them feel good. It has a significant and positive impact on their self-esteem, their feelings of happiness, satisfaction and productivity. Without sexual pleasure, they feel deprived, anxious, unfulfilled. And that they should compromise their sexual enjoyment for the sake of "pleasing their husband" incites resentment, if not outright fury.

It makes sense. Today's Hitched Chick has grown up on a diet that spans MTV to Madonna, *Cosmopolitan* to *Playgirl*, sexy feel-good Lycra to super-low-rise jeans, *9½ Weeks* to *Sex and the City* . . . all of which extol the virtues of being and feeling young and sexy. The messages ring loud and clear: expression is good; repression is bad; sexy is great; guilt is sad. Having taken on board these messages and discovered they liked them when they were single, their

sexual expectations for the future are greater than any other generation of marrieds. Long live lust!

Touched for the Very
First Time . . .

Not one Hitched Chick I spoke to was a virgin on her married day.
Premarital sex is alive and kicking and screaming for more. The
more, the better. In fact, women describe the notion of saving yourself
for a husband as "ridiculous," "insane" and even "irresponsible."

And yet, the most up-to-date statistics on premarital sex make
gritty reading. The average American woman has sex for the first
time when she's 16.4 years old, with nearly one in ten losing her virginity before the age of thirteen (source: Centers for Disease Control
and Prevention).

Losing It

Average age for first-time sex:

America	16.4
Brazil	16.4
France	16.8
Germany	16.9
Canada	17
Britain	17.1
Holland	17.4

(SOURCE: 2000 DUREX GLOBAL SEX SURVEY)

Now, you can argue until you're blue in the face about the land-scape of teenage sex. And for the record, the idea of my own daughter having sex at the age of thirteen gives me the skweebs. But it would give me the skweebs if I had a son, too. This isn't a gender issue. Whether kids should be taught how to have sex safely or how not to have sex at all until they're married is a hot topic right now. And sure enough, it makes intense dinner party conversation. It also makes intense political rhetoric.

The debate about sex education in America reached its height in 1996, with a companion bill tacked on to the Welfare Reform Act. The WRA budgeted $440 million over a period of five years to support abstinence-only sex education programs, but the cash came with some provisos: programs would only be funded if they abided by the federal eight-point definition of abstinence-only education. Among those points: "that sexual activity outside the context of marriage is likely to have harmful psychological and physical effects" and "a mutually faithful monogamous relationship in the context of marriage is the expected standard of human sexual activity." What's more, a proposed amendment to the act, calling for "medically and scientifically accurate sex education programs," was rejected. I mean, hel-lo-oh! What planet do these people inhabit? Clearly a planet that no one I know will be going to on vacation in the next hundred years.

Sending out the message that sex is bad out of the context of marriage will not ensure people don't have sex. Nor will it guarantee happier, more successful marriages. What it *will* guarantee is the nudging of sexuality back into the closet and the practicing of unprotected sex. In *U.S. News and World Report*'s May 2002 lead story on the subject, seventeen-year-old Elizabeth Marchetta from Rutgers University in New Brunswick, New Jersey, bemoaned the fact that teen staffers on the *Sex, Etc.* college newsletter have to deal with kids who come looking for answers that they're not getting from parents or in school. Many of these questions, she says, revolve around contraceptives which their friends seem to know worriedly little about. "Abstinence-only programs aren't going to stop teen sex by not giving information about how to use contraceptives. They're trying to take away the one thing that could possibly keep kids safe. They're numb to reality." Out of the mouths of babes . . .

To those ideological, political or clerical old duffers who claim to uphold the institution of marriage, modern wives say this: Premarital sex *protects* the institution of marriage. Without it, there would be many more unhappy marriages and many more divorces.

Sexual compatibility and the presence of lust in marriage is essential to its success. Any and every marital survey and relationship expert will concur with that. Yes, good sex can occur in a bad relationship, but consistently bad sex in a good relationship? It's practically unheard of. But how do you know if you are sexually compatible before marriage unless you've had premarital sex? Even then, how do you truly know you're sexually compatible unless you've had sex with someone with whom you are not? And how do you know what good sex is unless you have experienced degrees of pleasure with someone else? You can't. Premarital sex is no guarantee of a successful marriage. Hell no. But if you can strike the possibility of just one future conflict from your list, isn't it wise to do so?

The *Janus Report on Sexual Behavior* states that around one in ten women are virgins when they marry. This doesn't correspond with my own research, but *Janus* goes on to concede that the more educated a woman is, the less likely she is to be a virgin. There are dozens of potential reasons that this should be the case. But since increasing numbers of women today experience some level of higher education (they haven't tripped straight out of high school and into marriage), their learning curve undoubtedly takes place below the belt as well as above the neck. And do they regret it? Are you kidding?

Not one woman I spoke to regretted having had sexual experiences pre-marriage. Oh, for sure, some admitted to regrettable sexual experiences, but the majority were no more devastating than a regrettable hairstyle, regrettable shoe purchase or, at a push, a regrettable quantity of cosmopolitans in one night. Back in 1993 when *Janus* shocked the world with its findings, almost 60 percent of twenty-seven to thirty-eight-year-old women felt it was important to be sexually experienced before marriage. Now I'm willing to stake my mortgage on it that those numbers are even greater.

If marriage is such a precious institution to be entered into wholly and committedly and good sex is known to be one of the prerequisites of a successful long-term union, should we not attempt to sample all its different dimensions before we take our vows? It's preposterous to think otherwise.

Thirty-two-year-old Gabrielle observes, "Our parents got married because they fell in love and had all these lustful feelings. Often they'd get married because they just wanted to have sex. Then when they did get married, they were totally disappointed with what they ended up with. And it wasn't just the sex that was bad. Because they'd rushed into marriage so they could be respectable and have sex, they didn't realize they weren't only sexually incompatible, they were incompatible in other areas of their relationship, too."

Says Rachel, twenty-eight, "I'm pleased I didn't enter my marriage as a virgin because I really don't feel you trust that you know what good sex is until you've had sex with a few people." She adds, "Sex wasn't so great with some of those people, but it taught me that passion is very important and there are so many men who don't know how to be passionate."

When I repeat Rachel's advice to Tyler, thirty-one, she shrieks. "That's so true! I slept with about twenty men before I met Dez. Some of them were so selfish in bed. It was all about them. And the longer I stayed with them, the more I realized that if a man is selfish in bed, he's selfish in other areas, too. It's rare to find a man who is selfish in bed and generous in every other aspect of his relationship. Forget it. I might have married a couple of those guys if I hadn't slept with them first and started to see how that selfishness infiltrates other ways they behave. Dez is one of the most generous men I know, in bed and out of it. And because I experienced how giving he was sexually, I had a pretty good idea that he'd be fair and giving in our marriage." Turns out, she was right.

Patti, thirty-four, also reveals her lucky escape from a disastrous marriage thanks *to* premarital sex. "I had been engaged to a guy called Adam before I met and married Tim. On paper, Adam and I seemed like the perfect match—similar backgrounds, our parents were good friends and we were like brother and sister. But that was the problem. There was absolutely no passion between us. We hardly ever had sex. But I was so inexperienced, I didn't know whether this was normal. And I certainly wasn't going to tell anybody, because if we *were* going to end up together, I didn't want them to know we hardly ever slept together. At that time, I was working at a company where everyone was young and having fun, drinking and making out and sleeping together. And here I was, engaged and not even having sex. I hated it. So even though I was supposed to be marrying my fiancé, I also started dating other men. I realized that this was the time I should have been enjoying single life, so I started cheating on him and it was actually then that I slept with Tim who later became my husband. At that point, I realized that my relationship and sex life with my fiancé wasn't normal. It wasn't good and, chances were, it never would be. So, three weeks before the wedding, I broke it off. I went crazy for the next two years and just had the greatest time. I really felt like I got it out of my system and I have never looked back."

So, How Many Men *have* You Slept With?

Heard about "the lover's knot"? Believe me, this has nothing to do with saucy lingerie or creative lovemaking. No, no, nooooo. I'm referring to a surgical procedure. And it's only two generations ago—ask your granny!—that women felt compelled to have it done to fool their new husbands into thinking they were virgins. Involving a few small stitches in the labia, a sexually experienced woman could piously show off "the bleed" associated with losing one's virginity on her wedding night. It's hard to blame the women. They were simply safeguarding their future. But what of the double standards of men? It may have us all spitting enough feathers to fill a duvet, but here's what I've learned: double standards still exist. It's way more subtle, but it's out there. Men still battle—poor things—to come to terms with a woman who is as sexually experienced as they are. And if you've had *more* sexperiences? Oh man . . .

Trouble is, savvy women know that, like her, men desire a certain amount of sexual confidence and experience in their prospective spouse. Even in *Janus*'s 1993 report, 40 percent of men claimed it was important to marry a sexually experienced woman. But there's the finest of lines between the responsibility of too little and the emasculating effect of too much. I asked a few male friends how men view female virginity now and their responses ranged from "No way, I don't want the task of breaking in a woman" to "I wouldn't mind, but I'd wonder what was wrong with her and worry she might be frigid when we got married" (from Pete, twenty-eight, hitched to

Naiela, thirty, who definitely was not a virgin when they met or married).

However, this is how a friend, Isaac, thirty-two, sums up the general consensus: "You want to know your wife has had sex and that she enjoys it. But you don't want to think she's been with every guy in the state of Texas. If you know she's had more experience than you, you may think you haven't had enough and question whether this is the right time to settle down." Neil, also thirty-two, adds, "You want to learn something from a woman sexually. It's dull if you're the one always saying, 'Do this, do that.' But you don't want to know *how* she learned it and who she learned it from, and you certainly don't want to imagine her doing it with hundreds of guys. Bottom line: A man always likes to think he's considerably more sexually experienced than his wife."

So, what's the ideal number? A quick straw poll among my male friends reveals they're comfortable that their wives have had up to five lovers. "But I want to know I'm the best," states Richard, thirty-eight, elbowing Mel, thirty-seven, who swiftly reassures him. "Yes, you are, sweetie. Of *course* you are," she coos, and we all fall on the floor in fits.

I asked women the same question: How many men do you think a woman should sleep with before marriage? And guess what? A woman's ideal is significantly greater than a paltry five.

"At least ten," says Leslie, thirty-four, who had sex with double that number of men before marrying.

"Ten to fifteen," says Stella, thirty-two, and then adds, ". . . maybe a few more."

"Hmmm, about twenty. Yeah, that seems about right," says Alice, thirty-five, who married her twentieth. Thirty-four-year-old Dawn agrees. She had sex with twenty-three men before marrying Kenneth, and still refers to them by affectionate nicknames: Red Ferrari, the

Snail, Superman, Anal Pete, the Artist, the Poet, the Builder, the Student, Snake Hips, Greg the Head, Six-Fingered Simon ("Now there was a guy who'd just touch you and you'd come like a bastard!" Dawn says loudly in the very crowded wine bar).

Says Sam, "Me and my girlfriends counted and it's under fifty, but over forty. I was just fascinated by sex. But I think forty is a good number. I'm pleased I slept with so many men before I got married. When I met Ray, I was spent. I'd been there, done that, shagged *him* and *him* and *him*. . . . I knew I would get married someday so I thought, I'm going to have fun while I still can."

"Sleep with as many as you can! I must have had sex with, oooh . . . seventy guys," claims Jenny, thirty-six, who practically had to be frog-marched down the aisle two years ago by Stephano. "I loved being single. I don't regret my sexual encounters at all. I say to my single friends, have as much sex with as many men as you can before you get married because you'll be sleeping with this man for the rest of your life."

It's a far cry from our mothers' generation when a woman's "reputation" was to be protected at all costs. I even remember my own mom wagging her finger at me and saying, "Mandi, it takes years to build a good reputation and just one stupid night to blow it." And that was in 1982, for crying out loud! She didn't know then that my so-called reputation had already been well and truly blown. *Tut-tut.*

The discrepancy between what the sexes regard as the ideal number of sexual partners before a woman marries is still causing conflict for those brave enough to be candid with their husbands. Take Melanie, thirty, who had sex with nine men before she met and married Danny. "He didn't want me to be a virgin, but it definitely bothered him that I'd had as many men as I did. It bothered him because, in his mind, I was only for him. When we would fight in the beginning, he would sometimes make me feel like I was some kind of cheap whore, but I ended that real quick. I told him, 'My past made

me who I am, just like your past made you who you are. If you can
say to me you have not had sex with anyone else, okay. If you have
led a pure life, then you have the right to judge me. Other than that,
fuck you!' I have no regrets. I never had one-night stands. I have to
have affection for someone. He wasn't Mr. Pure, so he had nothing to
say to me after that. He knew I was right."

These double standards are the root of thirty-five-year-old Shelley's divorce proceedings. Married for three years, she instigated a
split not because her husband disliked her lustiness—"far from it, I
taught him how to be a fantastic lover," she says, ruefully—but
because he dared to use it against her in a fight.

"Matt and I had a great sex life when we were dating and it continued throughout our marriage," she tells me. "We'd have sex four
or five times a week, maybe more in a good week. But he'd always
been weird about the number of guys I'd slept with before we met.
Let's say, my sex partners outnumbered his three to one . . . at least.
Hey, I like sex! Then one night, we had a huge argument over
olives—I like them on pizza, he doesn't. It turned nasty. An hour
later, he accused me of being easy, a slut. The implication was that I
was dirty and immoral."

Shelley and Matt's fight lasted into the wee small hours. "He
brought up so much intimate information I'd confessed to him about
my experiences with past boyfriends. It was as if he'd harbored this
grudge all the time we'd been together. Obviously he resented my
sexual past. But I certainly wasn't going to apologize for my behavior
before we'd met—why the hell should I? And, God knows, he'd
reaped the benefit of my experience many, many times. Yeah, we
finally made up, but our relationship was never the same. I still
wanted sex, but from that moment, I felt inhibited when we were
making love, as if Matt were judging me and wondering where I'd
learned my technique. To me, sex is as important as eating. Some
couples like walking in the park; I like spending all day in bed

together. It's a vital part of my life. Now something was getting in the way of my lust and I started to feel resentful and angry. We tried a couple of counseling sessions, but gave up. I just couldn't forget how Matt tried to make me feel during that fight and, sadly, our marriage deteriorated faster than I would have ever believed possible. He still calls and we continue to talk—he hopes we can patch things up, but we can't."

Shelley's story is infuriating, all right. But it demonstrates how women today simply will not tolerate the hypocritical residue and stereotype of a past generation . . . even when they marry *into* that generation, as thirty-nine-year-old Generation Xer Connie did after dating fifty-five-year-old Baby Boomer Keith. Marrying older men is nothing new. But what is new today is that the roles of sexually accomplished husband as teacher and sexual novice wife are often reversed.

Connie laughs at the notion of herself as a virginal bride. Like many Hitched Chicks, Connie didn't even think about marriage until she had achieved her professional ambitions as a travel correspondent and, until such a time, was content to indulge in the responsibility-free world of dating. Totally unlike her husband of two years, Keith, who met his childhood sweetheart at seventeen, married her at twenty and remained married for over twenty-five years. The result? Keith had had significantly fewer lovers than Connie when they met and married. In fact, aside from one brief affair, Keith had only had sex with his former wife and, even then, their sexual relationship had come to an abrupt end after the birth of their second child, almost twenty years ago.

Connie says, "I had many boyfriends and had sex with a lot of guys. In fact, I used to keep a list . . . until it became too confusing. How many men? I would easily say one hundred . . . easily . . . it might even be one hundred and fifty. Although Keith has never been offensive about my past, he did go through an intensely jealous phase about the men I dated before him. But he just has to accept that I'm not going to be my age and have remained a virgin. As I see it, I've had fun, great, wild sex, a lot of passionate love affairs, so I feel like I got my ya-yas out. When I married him, I really felt ready to settle down."

Yes indeed, the norm has certainly changed and continues to change and some men at least are starting to view women's increasing premarital sexuality as a good thing . . . for *him*. Take twenty-eight-year-old Alexandra's husband, Stewart, twenty-nine. It was he who was the virgin when they met seven years ago. Has it been an issue? Maybe just a little, but it has had its benefits. "Stewart hadn't been saving himself," Alexandra points out. "He's a very confident person and a late bloomer. He'd kissed some women before, but he'd never had a sexual relationship with anybody. He felt very excited about it and I thought, Wow! I get to create the ideal lover from scratch since he has no preconceptions of what sex means and how it should be. Luckily, Stewart had great instincts about sex, so sex has always been wonderful, but I know he has wished sometimes he could somehow, in a parallel universe, taste the other offerings. I respect that. In fact, we talked about whether it would be possible to create that freedom for him, but decided that we couldn't do it without damaging our relationship. Sometimes I wish he'd had more experience. Sometimes I wish I'd had more experience, too. But we've talked openly about being attracted to other people. Although we've chosen this monogamous partnership, it doesn't mean we don't have a range of sexual feelings."

Today, when a woman marries, she's as much used to receiving pleasure as giving it. Chances are, she'll have mirrored a stereotypically male pattern of premarital behavior: that of a sexual predator, systematically seeking out lovers with the sole purpose of no-strings-attached sex, relishing the variety, valuing the experience, and, more often than not, having the self-confidence to retain control over her sexploits. Recalls Sam, "I went to bars and clubs, but always took them back to my place, shagged them senseless, made them breakfast in the morning and then asked them to leave. And I'd always get their numbers. They'd say, 'Why don't you give me *your* number?' But I'd always say, 'I'll call *you*.' "

Today's bride will, on average, have had more than a decade of sexual experience and, therefore, will have absolutely no problem instigating sexual relationships, taking a dominant role and showing off her sexual skills as previous generations of women may have done with their culinary talents. Ta-*daaa*! That tantalizing lustiness she undoubtedly displayed when single will keep her husband wanting to remain married to her. It will provide the scaffolding when the inevitable challenges of modern married life threaten to send tremors through its foundations. But, by the same token, that her husband keeps up his end of the sexual deal is crucial for the Hitched Chick to continue wanting to stay married to him. Hitched Guy, listen up.

What She Wants: Quality and Quantity

While our mothers may have been content to let their husbands take the driving seat in the bedroom as well as out of it, we are not. We have our foot firmly on the sexual accelerator at least as often as our husbands. But, also unlike our mothers, we are deciding *when* we have sex and whether we take the scenic route or a quick hop around the block. Says thirty-nine-year-old, Suzannah, "After ten years of marriage, David and I are still very sensual. But I dictate the terms of when we have sex and how we have sex."

We're all familiar with the stereotypical scenario of married sex:

husband makes overtures, wife complains of headache, husband presses on regardless, husband clambers on top of wife, two minutes later the mutually unfulfilling experience is over, wife pulls down nightdress, husband snores, the end. Yes, it's a cliché, but like most clichés, it's derived from truth. Yesterday's truth.

Now, here's the truth today.

My interviews reveal that Hitched Chicks—newlywed or not— expect sex at least twice a week. Preferably more. A considerable number of us want sex every day (it's certainly not reserved for *night* times), exploding the myth that once married, women turn off and turn over. The ideal lies somewhere between two and five times a week once married life settles into some semblance of routine.

Most women complain they don't have sex as often as they'd like. Sam says, "I'm begging on hands and knees, '*Please* can we have sex?'" Says Petra, thirty-seven, "Me, too. I definitely wish we had more sex." And Emily, thirty-three, confides, "We just had a huge fight because I want more sex than he does." Which is why all wives wistfully recall the first heady months of their relationship with their husbands when they literally couldn't keep their hands off each other. "We'd just fuck and fuck and fuck," says Amie, thirty-three, married for five years to Otis. "We'd fuck before work and we'd fuck immediately after work. And weekends? My friends thought I'd fallen off the face of the earth! But we'd just lie around eating and fucking all weekend long. It was fantastic."

"Us, too," says Carmen, thirty-seven, married ten years to Michael. "I remember our first Christmas together, just three months after we were married. We told our parents we wanted to enjoy the holidays alone and we spent the entire time in bed. We had a tiny apartment so we pulled out the sofa bed in front of the TV and had sex solidly for three days. We even had sex in between opening our presents. And . . . hee, hee, hee . . . I ate my Christmas lunch off Mike's tummy. The peas were rolling everywhere; I even poured gravy over him, which totally ruined the sofa bed. But we just didn't care, we were so in lust, it's all that mattered."

The rule of thumb states that the frequency with which we have sex halves over the first twelve to eighteen months, but the slower sexual pace isn't and shouldn't be perceived as a signal that the relationship is heading downhill faster than Eddie the Eagle (infamously bad British skier). "So long as you are *having sex*," says Carmen. "If we haven't had sex for a week, I start to worry. In fact, I worry about it more than Mike does. I really miss it. I miss the closeness. And I miss the sensation."

"Yeah, I really value our sexual connection," says Gabrielle, thirty-two. "And I get very upset if, for some reason, Murray and I don't have sex at least once a week. There are certain times when I'm feeling fat and I realize that I'm not really fat, it's just that I haven't been sexual. I start to feel really lost, like, 'What's happening?' I feel this more than Murray. And I monitor if we don't have sex for two weeks. I think, This can't go on because if we don't have sex for two weeks, then it'll be three weeks, then it'll be four, five and six. And then we'll be divorced. So I tell him, 'Get in there and take all your clothes off!' "

A woman has good reason to worry if she isn't having regular sex. Two snippets of research you should know: women who frequently have sex without condoms (that's the majority of Hitched Chicks for whom the Pill is their preferred contraception choice) are less likely to be depressed than those who have sex with condoms and those who abstain. According to New York University researchers, it's due to mood-changing chemicals that are transferred by the man. (*Woo-hoo* for sperm!) And the second? Research has shown that couples need regular shared and enjoyable activities to keep their relationship on an even keel. Yet our lives are becoming increasingly busy. Not only are we juggling the demands of work, family and friends, there's the pressure to work out at the gym, keep up our art classes, schedule appointments at the hairdresser, nail salon, dentist, homeopathist, gynecologist, aromatherapist and every other "ist," which means that fewer and fewer daily activities are shared between modern wives and husbands. In fact, for many married women, sex may well be the *only* thing she still does with her hubby.

In fact, when counselors attempt to determine how happy a couple is together, their conclusion is often derived from simple mental arithmetic: deduct the number of arguments the couple has from the number of sexual events over a particular period of time. If sexual events outnumber fights, the couple will rate as happy.

This is what thirty-nine-year-old Suzannah tells me over a drink. "When we don't have sex for a while, it manifests itself in our whole relationship. David and I get really distant. We lead pretty separate work and social lives as it is, but I notice we start to drift even further apart and we might start to argue more about really silly things. Like, I might get riled that he never rings me from his office. I'll suddenly realize, Hang on, he hasn't called me from work for ages. However, I'll only get mad about that because we haven't had any physical closeness. And I'll pick on him. I'll say, 'You're not interested in the children, you haven't read them a story for weeks.' But I know it's because we haven't had sex."

After the first couple of years, research shows that among happy couples, sexual frequency takes another twenty years to halve again, not including the temporary sexual droughts that occur due to having a baby, illness or other major life events. Until such a time, the Hitched Chick regards sex as the glue that not only holds her marriage together, but keeps it alive and well. It's what also enables spouses to continue seeing each other as sexual beings despite the mundanities of day-to-day marriage. The more sex you have, the more likely you'll see your husband as a sex god, rather than "the guy who takes out the trash and snores in bed."

"Bill and I have an agreement that we'll always say yes to sex even if one of us may not exactly feel in the mood," says Natasha, thirty-one. "Even if I haven't been in the mood beforehand, I'm always pleased I did it afterward. So if Bill doesn't want sex when I do, I'll just put my hand down his pants until he can't help himself. I don't want to be a nag about it, but without sex, what have you got?"

"Just friendship," says Melanie, dipping her banana chunk into the chocolate fondue. "And that's not enough for a good marriage. I've got plenty of friends, but I don't want to be married to them. Hell no! Sex is right up there with trust. You've gotta have both. If I don't have sex, I'm moody and miserable. I might be sick for a week or five days and I'm blowing my nose, I'm coughing up a lung and I'm like, 'Do you wanna have sex with me?' And he'll say, 'But you're sick.' And I'll say, 'But I'm not dying.' He's really sweet when I'm sick because he won't try anything, he just holds me and won't even mention it. Meanwhile, I'm saying, 'Hel-lo! I'm not in the coffin. Let's go! Just let me be on top because I can't breathe if I'm lying down!'"

"She's right," says Natasha. "And I've noticed the more sex I have, the more sex I want. And the better our relationship is."

I've noticed it, too. Sex is the ultimate libido arouser. And while a burst of hot, passionate sex is fantastic, the benefits can be fairly short-lived if it isn't supplemented with regular bouts of tender, less frantic sex. In fact, here's something you should also know: it works the other way, too. The chances of having hot, passionate, hang-on-to-your-hairnets sex increase when, at other times, we have lazy sex or, get this, dutiful sex, sad sex or even angry sex. Biological fact: It's all to do with oxytocin, a super-powerful hormone that's produced by sexual arousal. Oxytocin encourages us to form strong emotional bonds which make us fall deeply in love with our partners all over again and experience the sexual rushes we adored at the very start of our relationship with him. . . .

Sex o'Clock!
Time for Ecstasy . . .

If she thought she was starved for time when she was single, she's truly caught in the middle of a time famine now that she's a Hitched Chick. So you might imagine that with so little time on her hands, she may prefer a bubble bath and time alone with a book when she has a spare second. Granted, she enjoys that. But if you think reading about sex is enough to satiate her, you're so out of the loop.

Remember at the beginning of this chapter, I mentioned Tina? She starts work at 8:30 A.M. in a frantically busy marketing department for a big clothing store in New York and often doesn't leave work until after eight o'clock at night. Her schedule, she says, is so frantic that instead of going to the gym, she walks speedily to work. Instead of spending her free time doing domestic chores, she's just hired a cleaner. And instead of having tired, unsatisfying sex at night with her husband, Billy, who happens to work five blocks away from her, they book into a hotel on a regular basis for a lunchtime make-out session. (Luckily, Billy knows the manager—apparently he does a lot of corporate entertaining with that particular hotel chain, which helps secure a swift reservation.) Says Tina, "I'm sure my boss would think I was a sexaholic if she knew. I'm not a sexaholic, but I do like sex. And I find that sex in the middle of the day when I'm high on nervous energy is better than sex at night when I just want to sleep. Some people like to beat a punchbag at the gym at lunchtime, I like to have sex with my husband. What's wrong with that?" Uh, nothing at all.

"Sex is my way of unwinding," says Lottie, thirty-two, a commercial Realtor. "I have a stressful job and work long hours and, you know, often there just isn't the time to sit and have a romantic dinner and talk. When I get home from a fourteen-hour workday, I'm so wound up, I want sex, *then* I'm happy to talk."

What Tina, Lottie—and many Hitched Chicks—experience today is stress-induced sexual appetite. The more stress she's under, the more she craves satisfying sex. (A 2002 study by *Good Housekeeping* magazine in the U.K. revealed one in six women claims sex significantly helps to relieve her stress.) But I'm talking about a certain kind of stress. Not the sort of stress our mothers may have experienced when their fairy cakes flopped or the washing machine flooded. No, that's wearying, irritating, *dreary* stress; the kind of stress that makes nipples shrivel away from touch and buttocks slump down to the knees; the kind of stress that makes sex seem like just another tiresome chore.

The stress that differentiates us from our mothers is the kind that makes our eyes flash, our complexion glow, our heart skip, breasts heave—and our self-confidence and libidos leap into the stratosphere. It's the stress derived from a demanding situation, an unpredictable environment, competition, triumph, danger, even disaster. Researchers at UCLA discovered that major disasters and war can trigger feelings of danger that stimulate our libidos, which is why some even predict another baby boom after the trauma of September 11. But in this context, I'm talking about the adrenalin-based stress from the kind of challenging work environments in which married women are carving out successful careers and which can best be rewarded (or alleviated . . . up to you) with sex: deliciously soothing, reassuring, calming sex that restores feelings of safety and harmony or sex-plosive, pressure-cooker sex that releases tension via passion.

Lottie confides that her sexual appetite delights her husband, who compares notes with his bar buddies. "He tells me some of his friends complain their wives are too tired for sex," says Lottie. "These women are my friends, too, and believe me, they're not too tired or stressed. They want sex as much as they've ever wanted sex. The truth? They just don't want sex *then*, or maybe they're using exhaustion as an excuse for boredom. Many men today are either too tired themselves to make an effort in bed, or they feel so emasculated by their smart, successful wives, they *can't* make the effort. Or their husbands just aren't tuning into their wives' schedules. But lust is still there."

"Oh yes, lust is still there," says Elizabeth, twenty-nine, a web designer. "And I notice it's higher than ever now that I'm working full on. In fact, when I was made redundant last year, my sex drive plummeted, which was weird as I spent three months hanging around at home, just going to the gym and wandering around the park, so you'd think I'd feel more up for it. As soon as I returned to work, I was like, 'Wey-hey!' And a heavy day at work makes me even more sexual than a slow day. I jump on Leon's bones sometimes the minute I get home from work. He might be cooking, and I'll pinch his ass and that's it! See, it's not the stress that kills my sex drive. What kills it is if my self-esteem is low, if I don't feel like I'm a success in myself. Being busy at work? No. Na-ha."

So it's not about appetite, it's about timing? "That's right," says Sonja, twenty-four, a nurse, who's been married to Jackson for three years. "I'm up at five o'clock in the morning. He's a store manager so he doesn't get up until eight o'clock, so he has more energy at night than I have. But I'll often push my butt into him before I get out of bed to show him I'm in the mood for sex. I love sex in the mornings, it makes me feel good for the rest of the day. I'm not going to wait for the weekend. I'd go mad."

Thanks to the sexual confidence they gained during those single years, the Hitched Chick has the balls to call the shots when she's married. The majority of women are not sacrificing their sexuality for their busy schedules, they're more likely to be incorporating their sexual needs and desires *into* their schedules by making creative use of their time. But it's on their terms. Sex is not reserved for when the sun goes down. In fact, it emerges that many Hitched Chicks *least* like sex at night—"too exhausted," says Suzannah, thirty-nine— preferring to have sex when they walk through the door, "straight after work on a Friday night," says Alice, thirty-five, when adrenaline's coursing through her veins, just before they're due to go out (again, when adrenaline's high or they're feeling sexy and fabulous), in the middle of the day, or on a Saturday. In fact, the consensus is that Saturday afternoon sex is pretty much the best sex of all.

With two lively children, a demanding work schedule and a whirling social life, Suzannah says, "Having sex for me at bedtimes is never or hardly ever. It's more likely to be in the afternoon, when the kids are playing downstairs, or in the morning, when we first wake up. But it can happen at different times during the day when the moment comes upon us. It's never, ever when we get into bed at night and that's at my insistence. I like to bring my tea up to bed and I read a book. Now, we openly say, 'Oh, never at bedtimes' . . . or very rarely, unless I've had a drink and we're smashed, then we might do it at bedtime."

Paulette, thirty-eight, also has two children and although she's put her career on hold for now, is as busy as ever, juggling her role on the Parent Teacher Association with her own, as well as her daughters', hectic social life. "It's important to keep your sex life spontaneous and that can be difficult when you have children. But often, I'll say, 'Okay, right now, right here!' and Simon will say, 'Are you kidding?' . . . because by bedtime, we're just too tired. We might be in the bathroom and the girls are off watching a movie and I'll say, 'Come on!' and then we'll do the 'Oh no we can't, oh yes we can, let's do it' thing. So while I still like two-hour marathons, often there just isn't the time, so we do the five-minute event, which is really fun. You feel like a kid doing something naughty because you might get caught."

Although Amanda, twenty-nine, and Larry, twenty-eight, don't have kids—yet—her preference is still for Saturday afternoon sex. "We almost always have sex on Saturday afternoons. It's the best time for me. It's not about stress, it's about being tired and I don't like having sex when I'm tired. We do have sex during the week, but it's more like getting-into-bed sex. On a Saturday, we're in the house together and it happens very often before we leave the house. We're playing, napping, talking, laughing . . . and it happens in any room, any place. We rarely have sex in the bedroom on Saturdays. We'll either have sex on the couch or on the floor or on the chair . . . and that's really nice."

The rule-breaking element of any-time-but-nighttime sex is surprisingly common among today's marrieds. "Naughty sex," spontaneous sex, get-it-while-you-can sex, sex with an element of risk, danger or forbiddance adds the frisson and fun synonymous with dating sex. That it's manufactured doesn't deter them; it pales into insignificance next to the benefits. "Sex can become rote," says Jo, thirty-three. "If you're not careful, it becomes, 'Okay, you get on top, flip your legs over . . . ' The challenge is to constantly be reaching new

When Hitched Chicks Have Sex . . .

HOT	Saturday afternoon
◆	Friday night
◆	Sunday morning
◆	Early evening
◆	Weekday mornings
◆	Saturday and Sunday
◆	night
◆	Middle of the night
Cool	Weekday nights

heights . . . *eww*, bad metaphor. But you have to be always rediscovering one another in new ways, otherwise sex becomes ritualistic and boring, like brushing your teeth. Then you don't want to do it."

"The best sex Aaron and I have ever had," continues Jo, "is when he's literally on his way out to work. When he's getting dressed and he's buttoning up his shirt, just standing there in his shirt and boxers, there's nothing more fun for me than being blatant and just pulling down his underwear and starting to kiss his penis. It's just so unexpected. I can't stomach the idea of going to bed every night and reading a few chapters of my book and then saying, 'Okay, dear, do you want to get on top . . . ?' That, for me, is so depressing. Sex should be a surprise, unexpected."

Says Jess, thirty-four, married to Bob, "The latest thing we've started doing is having sex in a cab. We went out one night and had a few margaritas, hopped in a cab to go home and I gave him a blow job. But you can only do it if he's behind the driver's seat . . . ! Ha ha! Now it's gone further and further. It's so funny, it really makes me laugh."

"I like that feeling of danger, that we're doing something we shouldn't. I'd much rather have sex on a Sunday morning in Central Park than at night with the lights out," says Lottie. "It's not always possible if it's busy, but the risk of getting caught reminds me of when I was a teenager. Although I'm married, I still want to feel young and fun."

"The thing is, I think our parents' marriages suffered because sex was something you did either as a chore, when every other chore like putting out the trash and walking the dog was done," opines Claire, thirty-two, a makeup artist. "Or it was a luxury that had to wait until the necessities were out of the way. I mean, it makes me wonder how my parents had the inclination to conceive me! But I think women today, couples today, make their sex life one of their priorities. So they do it when they feel like it, irrespective of the time or place. In fact, there's something very old-fashioned about bed sex. If I was just having sex at night, in bed, with the lights out, I'd feel pretty pissed about the state of our sex life. It would make me feel like I had my parents' sex life and I definitely don't want *that*."

In fact, not having sex at night, in bed, has positively transformed thirty-four-year-old Tracy's sexual relationship with her husband Jeff. When her mother moved in with them due to ill health, Tracy was forced to alter her sex schedule. "Her bedroom's the next room to mine," she says. "So we don't have sex in the house anymore. We have to take rides to have sex now and if we don't, I bitch about it. We have sex in the car, we go to hotels, we have sex in the parking lots of hotels without checking in. . . . We have sex at drive-ins. If someone comes over and asks what we're doing, I just feel, They don't know me, I don't know them, so I don't care. It's really enhanced our sex life. It's the best now that it has ever been. And afterward, I feel great. I feel like a big stress has been relieved. It's like a long drink at the end of a stressful day."

"Waiter!" I hoot. "I'll have what she's having. . . ."

Coming . . . Ready or Not!

I like a conclusion to everything I do," says forty-year-old Sabina, married for seven years to Matthew. "It's very important for me to have an orgasm during sex." Sabina's not alone. For every Hitched Chick I know, orgasm is the ultimate goal. Yet it was less than half a century ago that the female orgasm was no more than a footnote to the male sexual experience. The world into which my mother married seems light-years away from the one in which Married Girl exists. The sexual one-way street of a generation ago has undergone dramatic reconstruction and evolved into a sexual superhighway where both sides expect to reach their climactic destination. My mother would no sooner have talked breezily about the benefits of clitoral stimulation and the deep penetrative style of the doggie position than hack off her toes with a butter knife. Back in the days when she was a bride, words like "clitoris" and "masturbation" were never uttered and unsatisfying sex was the norm. Today's bride not only freely (and often loudly) pontificates over the merits of clitoral stimulation versus penetration, but she is much more likely to insist on an orgasm even if the bridegroom doesn't come, and will, if necessary, help things along herself to achieve her goal.

Modern women are totally clued in to the intricate mechanics of their own bodies, and we know darn well we are biologically built to experience orgasm regularly. In fact, although women do conceive without having an orgasm, research from London's Hammersmith Hospital indicates that the uterine contractions during orgasms greatly increase a woman's chance of becoming pregnant, by propelling sperm from the uterus into the fallopian tubes, where eggs are fertilized. Yet familiar with this knowledge or not, women rightly expect orgasm and know how to achieve it. They do not subscribe to the view that they should simply serve and gratify men in bed. And the word "frigid" has been erased from Hitched Chick's vocabulary. Historically used to define a woman who couldn't, within minutes, achieve orgasm in the missionary position, the so-called frigid female belongs in the dark ages when women—and men—didn't know any better. The pressure for a husband to significantly understand his wife's body and fine-tune his performance accordingly is greater than ever. Because the truth is that while few women consistently reach orgasm during intercourse without additional manual stimulation, a cursory rub on her clitoris during the horizontal mambo isn't going to suffice either. The more women talk to each other—and, man, are they now talking—the more we know that there is a myriad of ways to experience ecstasy.

Simply concentrating on the clitoris may well be better than ignoring it entirely, but we know today that our erotic potential extends even deeper, and to realize it, demands a high level of creativity, patience, energy and generosity from our partners. I'm referring in part to the ubiquitous G-spot, that small but gloriously sensitive area a third of the way up on the front wall of the vagina. But I'm also talking about the less cutely named AFE (Anterior Fornix Erotic) zone, a highly charged area between the G-spot and the cervix which, when stimulated, practically guarantees orgasm. For over a third of women, count on multiple orgasms.

But, as many women have told me, we are not as genitally dependent as men are for our gratification. Our entire body is a potential erogenous zone. Reveals Lottie, "I can climax from nipple stimulation alone." Alice, thirty-five, confesses, "I can come just having my back and neck caressed." In fact, tests at the Center for Marital and Sexual Studies in California discovered that in a space of one hour, a woman's orgasmic potential can be as much as eight times a man's. The research, conducted by Drs. William Hartman and Marilyn Fithian, established that at least 75 percent of women are multiorgasmic. Put this into the context of history. Only fifty years ago, the Kinsey Report declared that just 14 percent of women were multiorgasmic. Now various surveys have upped that figure to 50 percent. Are we to believe that women have evolved physically in that time? Of course not. Says Dr. Hartman, "What has changed is their expectations of sex, of men and of themselves in all sorts of ways."

My belief is that if I expect to get what I want in business, why should I not expect to get what I want in bed? Elaine, forty-three, and married for two years, shares my view. She says a woman needs to be as demanding in bed as she is when she's having a salary review meeting with her boss. "If you don't ask, you won't get. And when you don't get, you feel like shit."

Yes, women crave the intimacy of sex. And of course they see the impact of the shared closeness and fun on their moods, sense of well-being and marital harmony. But sex without orgasm?

Says Shelley, "It's like when you pull a party popper and it doesn't bang. Everyone groans. It's such a disappointment. You feel cheated. Even if every other party popper in the box goes off with a bang, there's still that sense of deflation when that one party popper just goes *phoof* . . ."

Shelley has a right to feel deflated and disappointed if she doesn't have an orgasm. Experiencing an orgasm with your partner is more than just a selfish desire or an emotional impulse. Evolutionary psychologists say it influences bonding and mate selection. It's been found that a woman is more likely to form the most lasting tie of all— parenthood—with a man with whom she can orgasm, rather than with one she can't. (Remember? Orgasms help you get pregnant. Yay!)

In fact, Rosa, twenty-six, married George because he was the first man with whom she'd been able to come. "It wasn't the only reason," she adds after listing gorgeous George's innumerable positive attributes. "But, yes, it was a huge factor. I just felt this intensely animal connection."

Melanie also says, "I met Danny in a bar and we started talking and before I knew, we started making out. We went outside, my legs were wrapped around his waist, we were up against a wall, literally, we were like lunatics. I was grabbing his ass, it was animalistic. But what was important, even then, was that it wasn't all about him. It was about me, too. Still is. I love sex, but I want an orgasm, too. And Danny makes sure that I come. He's very unselfish. It's really important that he takes care of me like that. I wouldn't have married him if my pleasure wasn't as important to him as his."

I put the orgasm/marriage theory to thirty-one-year-old Sally, who agrees and adds, "There's something about having an orgasm— whether it's a mind-blowing orgasm or a series of those little fluttery ones—that differentiates married sex from the sex I had when I was single. When I was single, I'd sleep with some guys who only wanted to get their rocks off. It made me feel empty and dissatisfied afterward. On the rare occasion that I don't have an orgasm with Jed, it reminds me of being single. It's still nice, but I don't feel as connected with him. Being married is about being a team and in a team, you should both win."

Says Sara, thirty-five, married to Ken for eight years, "For me, not just having sex, but having an orgasm during sex is a sign that my marriage at that time is better than good, it's great. I notice when I'm feeling resentful or angry with Ken, it's difficult to be orgasmic. Nor do the orgasms flow when I know I've pissed him off. It's as if I won't allow myself to give myself fully to him or abandon myself to our pleasure." She makes a good point: having an orgasm in front of another person is an intensely emotional moment, isn't it? I mean, it isn't just about raw pleasure, it's about trust and feeling utterly comfortable in your husband's presence. Having an orgasm means you truly get naked, take off your mask and reveal the core of your being. No surprise then that surveys always show the frequency of mutually satisfying sex—where you both experience total pleasure—is the strongest predictor of marital happiness and success.

But for many Hitched Chicks, orgasm is an important stressbuster, too. Their lives are so frantic, they describe often feeling like a pressure cooker that's about to explode. They talk at length about the struggles of overwhelming responsibility and the expectations modern life imposes upon them. They even confess, guiltily, to feelings of violence. Says Julie, thirty-six, a busy creative director for a leading advertising agency, "There are days that I fear I'm going to lose control and trash my office. If someone looks at me or says something I don't like, I want to slap them." This is in stark contrast, Julie says, to her mother's life. "She had nothing going on. All she thought about was how she was going to redecorate the bathroom or what to buy for our dinner if she couldn't get her hands on any decent steak. My father *had* to eat steak. But she just cooked and cleaned, cleaned and cooked. That didn't make her a calm person, it just made her depressed, which is far, far worse than feeling wound up. But, still, I hate that feeling of pent-up emotion and energy, so it's crucial I have a release."

It doesn't matter whether she's having quick mid-week sex— "like on a Wednesday night even when you're both tired," says Julie— or on the weekend when she has the time and energy to indulge in more leisurely lovemaking, the purpose of sex for the modern wife is in equal parts emotional intimacy *and* the physical release of an orgasm. "Being intimate is very soothing, but that in itself isn't enough sometimes. It's having an orgasm that actually keeps me from losing it the next day."

Lola, thirty, a lawyer, agrees. "I can't imagine not coming through sex. It's a waste of my time. If I don't come, I'll say to Tommy, 'I'm going to be a bitch now all day so you've got to finish me off.'"

Twenty-six-year-old book editor Joely says this: "I don't see the point in having intercourse if I'm not going to have an orgasm. I really don't. Especially during the week, I just don't have time for it. I have everything scheduled down to the last fifteen minutes. That's my personality and my life. I mean, I only had one night this week when I came home and sat on my ass and watched TV. So I want to get down to it, have an orgasm and be happy."

Says forty-one-year-old Rae, a dentist and mother of one, married to Louis for nine years, "Louis and I have sex at least twice a week, even if we're tired or upset about something. I get so much from it." Like what? I ask Rae. "Reconnection and intimacy between us. But as important, an orgasm, of *course*, because I love orgasms and that amazing *whoosh*! It's a great release. It's like jumping on a big, fat watermelon! Like I've burst open a tightly packed suitcase of emotion. It's fantastic. I know that over the following days, I'll feel happier about myself and life in general. I have more confidence so I'm able to be more assertive and productive at work. Funny, but I'm better at dealing with the bank manager or car mechanic after an amazingly good orgasm!"

Rae and I practically hang on to each other howling after this final revelation. God, it's so true. Forget that hideous sense of sufferance and obligation previous generations of women had regarding sex, which is why I practically choke when I pick up a copy of *Redbook* and read its main coverline: "Best Sex of His Life! The Ohhh-So-Simple Move He'd Love You to Try." *Bleurgh.* I wish they'd get with the program. Do they not know modern married sex is not about servicing your husband, for freak's sake. 'Course, you want him to enjoy sex. You love him so you want him to be happy and fulfilled. But having sex and experiencing orgasms is about self-entitlement, too; doing a service for yourself. And society.

Twenty years ago, ex-madam Cynthia Payne came out with the immortal words, "Men need regular de-spunking." Popular wisdom has it that the physical release of ejaculation makes men calmer, less prone to outbursts, even less aggressive, which is why, in sporting circles, wives and lovers are kept well away from them before a game. Now women's lives are equally, if not more in many cases, charged than their husbands', we have woken up to the de-stressing benefits of sexual gratification and are demanding to be de-spunked, too. Yes, women derive increased feelings of love, tenderness and self-esteem from sex, the value of which can't and shouldn't be underestimated in marriage. But the physical release of lusty sex and orgasm is just as important for women as for men. Women who rarely have orgasms with their partners often regard both their sexual relationships and their relationships in general as dissatisfying. So given the increasingly high-profile role and expectations of women in society, regular satisfying sex is a global as well as matrimonial concern. Orgasms? Bring 'em on . . .

Come Again!
Ten Good Reasons to Have an Orgasm Tonight

Photocopy this, stick it on the fridge and don't stop till you get enough . . .

1. It alleviates the pressure to go to the gym. Having an orgasm is a great cardiovascular workout, briefly increasing your heart rate to levels comparable to those you achieve during a sprint.
2. An orgasm reduces your chances of a panic attack by helping you breathe fully and effectively. As your breathing increases to maximum levels, residual air is cleared from deep in the lungs.
3. Headaches and menstrual cramps are relieved thanks to the increased blood flow and levels of natural pain-killing endorphins in your body.
4. Vaginal and pelvic muscles expand and contract during orgasm. Result? The toning effect helps prevent urinary-stress incontinence.
5. Your chance of a good night's sleep is dramatically increased as feelings of well-being flood through your body.
6. During orgasm, your metabolism increases momentarily and helps you burn calories and shift stubborn fat.
7. Having an orgasm temporarily improves your complexion and removes fine lines and wrinkles. As blood surges through your capillaries, the surface of your skin plumps and tightens and develops an attractive rosy glow.

8. Forget creams and pills, having an orgasm boosts breast size, albeit temporarily, by increasing chest muscle tone and the engorgement caused by heightened blood flow. So have an ecstatic session before a party . . . or job interview! Why not?

9. Your marriage will instantly be enhanced and revitalized. You'll feel calmer, more compassionate toward your beau and more focused about what you want from him. You'll also feel a darn sight sexier, too, because . . .

10. Having one orgasm increases your chances of having another . . . and another. And, whoops! There goes another! Orgasms help develop strong nerve pathways from the source of stimulation to the brain. If those pathways become weak from under-use, your orgasmic potential is decreased. Having come tonight, you can practically guarantee that tomorrow you'll come again.

Hitched Chick's Favorite Sex Positions

Every woman has an opinion on what gives her pleasure. None I spoke to were ambivalent. Yes, she's likely to take into consideration what turns on her husband, but since most men can come in most positions, the one—or two or three—they have sex in will more than likely be her choice. But out of the 243 *Kama Sutra* sex positions, which will most press her joy buttons? Here, in order of popularity, the top four sex positions guaranteed to give us maximum pleasure . . . and three not so common, but it-works-for-me positions you may want to try out tonight:

Coming in at Number One:

Woman on Top

Since this position practically guarantees orgasms, it's no wonder the Queen of the Castle scores top marks. By moving her body just so, women can control both the angle of penetration and exactly which erogenous zone is stimulated. Says Melanie, "Being on top is the only way I can have one of those mind-boggling orgasms where I'm like, 'Okay, my clit is hurting, don't touch it! Don't move!'"

And so say most of us. But there are other advantages, too.

"I like to be in control," says Rachel, twenty-eight. "I'm a control freak in every area of my life."

Says Rosa, twenty-six, "I love the feeling of deep penetration, especially when I bring my knees up and I'm squatting."

And Sabina, forty, admits, "He can get a better view of me and is able to touch other areas."

Vanessa, thirty, agrees, and adds, "There's something very adoring about this position. I feel very Adonis-like. All my necessary parts are in place. And then once I'm taken care of, I'm willing to do what he wants."

Jess, thirty-four, says, "I like being on top because that's the only position that gives me multiple orgasms." It wasn't always the case, however. "It's the big difference between having a husband and having a boyfriend. Before we were married, I felt a little bit awkward or embarrassed when my tits would be flying everywhere! It's not always what you see on the movies, is it? When you're on top, you have to be really comfortable with your partner."

And often there are practical reasons for preferring this position. Says Stella, thirty-two, "I can't do the missionary thing because my husband's very tall. He's six feet six. But I do love this position because it's the only way I can orgasm, it's about control and I also love the intimacy. I like being able to look down at his face and see his reaction."

For max pleasure: Your husband lies down and you sit in a kneeling position on top of him with your legs on either side of his body. Begin slowly moving up and down on his penis. As you rise, pull your pelvis up and backward so his penis rubs more firmly against your vagina. When you feel excited and on the edge of orgasm, switch positions until you lie on top of your husband, placing your legs together inside his. The tightness of this final position will bring you to orgasm. Wriggle your body down his so you can feel his penis inside you for final orgasmic sensations.

Straight in at Number Two:

The Doggie Position

When you're crouching on all fours and your husband either crouches, too, or stands on the floor behind you, this position allows for the deepest penetration of all, which is why it emerges a firm favorite. "There's something very animalistic about him banging into me from behind," says Lottie, thirty-two. "And when he reaches and touches my clitoris, I feel like I'm going to explode. This is the only position I've ever ejaculated in."

Further testimonials for position number two:

"I'm more likely to have an orgasm when he enters me from behind," says Amy, thirty-two. "I think it's because he's hitting my G-spot."

Rae, forty-one, says, "Y'know, I'm so strong and in control during the day, I like the feeling of losing control when I'm in bed. I like that Louis is doing most of the work and taking charge for a change."

Mandy, forty-three, claims, "Christopher just has easier access to my clitoris when we're having sex doggie style. It's difficult for him to get his hand in the correct place when we're in the missionary position or if I'm on top of him, so he gets what I call 'spastic hand,' where his hand looks like a claw and it really turns me off."

Laughs Tyler, thirty-one, "It's frantic and fun."

And from Juliene, thirty, "I like the doggie because he can kiss the back of my neck."

For max pleasure: Position yourself next to a mirror while you're having sex so you'll be stimulated visually, too. Then once you're in sexual rhythm, place the V of two fingers over your clitoris, pressing on your labia. Squeeze and knead in rhythm and watch your reflection as orgasm takes place.

A Very Close Number Three:

Missionary Position

Since her husband's pelvis can rub against her clitoris in a similar way to the stimulation she enjoys from masturbation, the missionary position remains popular with the Hitched Chick, despite its associations with male dominance and traditional, boring sex. "I love the pure missionary position . . . on my back, legs stretched. You can get the perfect amount of friction to achieve a really deep orgasm," says Joely, twenty-six. "But it's not about drilling. I'm always trying to explain this to my friends. For me, it's about riding. Like the ocean. We usually have an orgasm at the same time."

Why others like to lie back and enjoy it:

Says Dee, twenty-nine, "It goes pretty counter to everything about my personality, but it's also because I'm more selfish and I don't want to be the one who's doing all the work. I just want to lie back and enjoy myself."

"It's my opportunity to take on a more submissive role for a change," says Chloe, twenty-nine.

"This position is so intimate, I love it. I feel like he's consuming me," says Naiela, thirty.

"I just get more pleasure from the missionary position, especially when I tuck pillows under my pelvis area to lift me slightly. That feels great," says Lena, thirty.

Dawn, thirty-four, claims, "I've tried every position in the book and I always come back to the missionary position. No, it isn't boring because there are so many variations—like when my legs are hooked over his shoulders—but the key thing is still happening, that he's rubbing on my clitoris and that's going to give me an orgasm every time."

For max pleasure: Turn the basic missionary position into the Waterfall. In other words, lie back *across* the bed so your waist nudges the side of it and your body falls over the edge. Try putting cushions on the floor to rest your head on if, like me, you have hard wooden floorboards! As your husband lies between your legs and enters you, the stretch of your body will cause a tightening of the muscles around your vagina, increasing the sensation for both of you. Ask him to use long, deep strokes ("Riding not drilling!" insists Joely), pulling the tip of his penis out to the edge of your vagina and by moving his pelvis slightly forward, he can use his penis to rub against your clitoris. I'm telling you, it works.

And Bringing Up the Rear, Number Four:

The Reverse Cowgirl

Best performed wearing your diamante-backed G-string, this back-to-front variation of woman-on-top works wonders for both of you, according to many. (Interestingly, a recent *Cosmopolitan* survey asked men which position haven't you tried that you'd most like to and 33 percent answered "her riding me backward." Perhaps the majority of men surveyed were single, since it's my theory that married women have the confidence in themselves and their relationships to blatantly take care of their own pleasure by not choosing the more emotionally connected face-to-face positions.) As you kneel over him facing his feet and ease yourself onto his penis, he receives an unobstructed view of your glorious butt, which will have him coming in no time (great for middle-of-the-day quickies). And since it's likely he'll be able to hit your G-spot, and your clitoris can be easily stimulated, there's a pretty good chance you'll orgasm simultaneously. "This position is fantastic for me. I look great from behind, I know it. I can control the pace. I can control how deep he goes. I come every time," says Alessandra, thirty-four. "Plus," she adds, "I feel like a whore doing it, which all adds to the pleasure."

More rear-guard action praise:

Says Skylla, twenty-nine, "This is definitely the one for me. My husband can't move too well because I hold on to his ankles, but it doesn't matter. He can see everything . . . *everything*, even when I come."

And Beth, thirty-five, says, "I just can't imagine my mother doing this. She may have done, I don't want to know, but it's so risqué, I love it."

For Carmen, thirty-seven, it's all about "control. That's the great thing about this position. I'm totally in control."

And for Alison, thirty-three, who's six months pregnant, "Many positions just don't work when you're pregnant. Sex becomes quite uncomfortable, but this one's easy. Plus, my belly doesn't get in the way!"

For max pleasure: Once you achieve a rhythm and you feel waves of pleasure rising, slide your hands down to his ankles until your breasts are almost resting on his legs. Ask him to caress your buttocks or hold your hips, then by grinding your pelvic bone in rolling motions and rubbing your clitoris against the shaft of his penis (or by hand . . . up to you), *Eureka!* is only a shriek away . . .

S.E.X.

The following positions also come with the Married Girl Stamp of EXcellence . . .

Standing in the Shower

Says Joely, twenty-six, "Sex in the shower is very sensual. Sometimes, you try all these different positions and it feels almost clinical. Sex in the shower is different, it feels organic somehow." Her advice? "You have to angle yourself properly so put one foot up on the side of the tub and one foot in the corner. All that water and steam? Fabulous."

Hands up!

This one's best performed in very high heels. Most Hitched Chicks have what they call FMBs or Fuck Me Boots, which were bought because they looked fabulous with a suede skirt, but it turns out they look even better with nothing more than a garter belt. "Face a wall and stand with your palms pressed against it, high above your head as if you're under arrest," instructs Karen, thirty-four. "Bend your body slightly, push your butt as far out and up as you can and let him enter you from behind. He'll probably need to stimulate you with his hands, but the combination of high heels and rear entry does it for me."

The Scissors

Okay, this one's difficult to describe, but bear with me. Having tried it myself, I know it's worth it. This is how Sandy, thirty-one, describes it: "Start by sitting on top, then lean backward until you're also lying on your back. Both of you stretch your legs out and rest them on either side of each other's body so you form an X position." Just think of two pairs of scissors cutting into each other, hence the cutesy name. What I love about this position is that effort and pleasure are equally shared. Plus, if you want those small fluttery orgasms, they're yours. And for that final ecstatic blast, a few seconds of stimulation is all it takes.

Anally Yours?

Just a few words about the most taboo sex position of them all: anal. If tons of wives are into it, they're keeping their preference a closely guarded secret. Many did disclose they'd given anal a go, but less than a handful admitted they enjoyed it.

Says Melanie, thirty, "I like anal sex, but I don't love it. If we're just heading out and he says he wants to do it, my ass automatically says no and clenches. But when we have more time and he gets me going and he's fingering and licking me up there, I'm like *ptheur* . . . You can stick a bar up there. But he knows how to make me want it." How Melanie's husband makes her want it is through reassurance, trust and lots of attention. "I had anal sex with an ex-boyfriend and I didn't like it at all. But with Danny, he gets me lubed, ready and wanting. Begging for it. If I think about me begging for it, I can't believe it, but I just trust him so much. I trust that he's going to stop if it hurts."

Thirty-four-year-old Alessandra's in absolute agreement. "I never had anal sex with anyone before Stephan. I didn't trust anyone enough before to do that. Even now, it only tends to happen if I've been out and had a few drinks. Then I'm relaxed enough. And I must admit I enjoy it. But it's only because I trust Stephan implicitly and I know that he loves it so much."

It's the prospect of pain that puts off most women. Says Tracy, thirty-four, "One time we were going at it and he missed the spot he was supposed to go in and he sent me flying across the room. I yelled, 'I hate you, I hate you, I hate you. Don't talk to me!' and ever since then, I just go, 'No, no, no, no, *no*!' I've heard too many stories about people who have anal sex having to go to the bathroom for a week after. No thank you."

Suzannah's the same. "If David goes anywhere near my bottom, I tell him to clear off!"

On the other hand, anal stimulation is acknowledged by many to be highly erotic and arousing. After all, it's an area alive with nerve endings which, when stimulated during sex, can make orgasms even more intense. "If I'm really wet, I like when Bill massages me there," says Natasha, referring to the perineum, the spot between her vagina and anus. "Sometimes, while we're having sex, he'll then put his finger into my back passage and move it in small circles. And I'm like, 'Wow!' It's incredible. But you have to be really wet or get the lube out."

For whoever is doing the stimulation, lubrication (as well as *short* nails) is essential to avoid tearing. "When I put my finger in his ass," says Alessandra, "my hand's practically dripping in lube." How far does she penetrate him, I ask. "A couple of inches," she says, "then I press." This part is essential, according to the experts, since his G-spot is located there. Final tip: wash hands (or penis or sex toy) before and after anal stimulation. It's the only way to prevent infection or the transfer of bacteria to other body parts.

Eat Me! Eat Me Goood!

Everybody loves oral sex. Women declare that if they had to choose between intercourse and oral sex, they'd take a good licking any day of the week. Says Melanie, thirty, "One thing my mother said to me when I was engaged to this guy who only went down on me once in seven years, 'If he isn't eating you out now, he isn't going to when you get married.' Eventually we broke up. Then the prerequisite for the person I was marrying was you need to go down there and give me a long, good lick around."

Sam, thirty-six, couldn't agree more: "Men who wouldn't muff-dive were a big no-no for me. If they weren't prepared to muff-dive, I'd get rid of them. I'd say, 'Fuck off then!' No, I wouldn't have married Ray if he didn't do oral. It's so fantastic!"

We all agree—no orgasm compares with the orgasm we have during oral sex. Oral sex orgasms, say Married Girls, are awesome.

"They're prolonged and intense, it's more out of my head," says Joely, twenty-six.

Freya, thirty-five, agrees: "And it lasts twice as long as an orgasm from regular intercourse."

"Oral sex orgasms are deeper, like they're going through my entire body," says Rachel, twenty-eight.

Says Alexandra, twenty-eight, "I don't have an orgasm during intercourse, only through oral sex. So I love oral sex!"

"Oral sex is this incredibly open thing," says Amanda, twenty-nine, who has way more oral sex than intercourse with her husband Larry. "You're totally exposed usually, you're so . . . open. You're just out there doing something really exciting and you have a sense of freedom, so we have lots of oral sex instead of sex."

In fact, pushing pleasure aside (just for one minute, please!), there's something about the trust required between a woman and a man that makes oral sex so wonderful for the married girl. "I had regular sex with many guys, but I'd only allow a select few to go down on me," says Tonia, thirty. "When a woman lets a man down there, she's really showing him that she trusts him one hundred percent. And when you trust someone fully, you can totally let yourself go, which is the key to really good oral sex."

So it's about trust, but it's also about confidence. I've never had a conversation with my mother—or anyone else's for that matter—about oral sex. But it strikes me that oral sex is only just coming out of the closet. I remember going on a trip about ten years ago with a group of other journalists. I forget why twenty of us had schlepped to Scandinavia, but I haven't forgotten a conversation in the hotel bar one night when we were all a bit tanked up. One old buffoon was especially merry. "I was with this woman," he regaled a bunch of us. "And she says to me, 'Let's try the sixty-nine.' So I said to her, 'Let's try sixty-eight. Go down on me and I'll owe you one!'" *Haw-haw-haw!* Now, I like a laugh with the best of them, but what struck me as really funny was the way three female journalists, average age forty-eight, reacted to this so-called joke. Sheer horror. Stomach-churning mortification. Faces like beetroot. Clearly, they were leftovers from a generation of women who had genitalia issues, who stocked up on freesia-scented "feminine wipes" and probably spent as much time attempting to scrub their natural odors away as wiping down their countertops. Unlike the five of us younger women who proceeded to talk loudly about encounters with rimcheese (technical term: smegma) and stinky penises, which sent the aforementional old buffoon scurrying back to his hole in seconds.

See, women now won't put up with that crap. They have wholeheartedly bought into the idea that no one can give you pleasure if you're not willing to accept it. They subscribe to the view that they have a right to be pleasured and to revel in the moment. We have not been trained to give pleasure to others without at least expecting the favor returned. "It's about reciprocity," says Alexandra, twenty-eight.

And as for genitalia "issues"? Basic hygiene is simply a sign of self-respect, but no modern girl truly believes she should whiff like her bridal bouquet. Acceptance of our bodies, complete with its unique odor, hair and texture, is one critical manifestation of the increased sexual confidence with which our generation is blessed.

And the idea that men only perform oral sex out of an exaggerated sense of fair play is finally being laid to rest. In a 2002 issue of *Cosmopolitan*, seven thousand men were asked: If you could spend foreplay doing only one thing, what would it be? Giving oral sex was their top answer. Twenty-eight percent said they loved "giving her oral sex," 2 percent more than those who said "fondling each other" and 5 percent more than those who said "receiving oral sex."

Says Jess, thirty-four, "Bob is very good at oral sex and sometimes he'll stay down there for ages. I feel like saying, 'Okay, see you in a while!'" And nothing, *nothing*, stops Noah from going down on Kath, thirty-three: "He'll do it when I have my period. He'd do it even if I didn't take a shower for six months. I like that a lot." Clearly, our capacity to enjoy oral sex is as much about what's going on up here (head) as what's happening down there (crotch).

So now we know what's going on up there (i.e., not much other than, How can I make this last for*ever*?), what *is* going on down there?

THE HITCHED CHICK'S GUIDE TO
Getting Great Oral Sex

Feel the need to turn your well-meaning husband into Slick Lips? Read on, thanks to Hitched Chicks Freya, Sam, Rachel, Tonia and Joely . . .

+ Concentrate on the clitoris—sucking, nibbling very gently, twirling it with the tongue. Since there are few nerve endings just within the vagina, unless your husband has a tongue the length of the I-95, probing inside it is nowhere near as satisfying as when he's playing around outside it.

+ Take time to revel in the sensations. "I prefer when Jon starts kissing my neck, then my breasts, then down over my stomach, before he zones in on my clitoris. It's a gradual build-up," says Tonia. "You can't hurry oral sex."

+ Gauge your sensitivity. "The best oral sex happens when you're lying back," says Tonia. "Your clitoris is exposed more." But Freya says, "I'm so sensitive, if I stand up, I can last a lot longer. Anyway, I feel like a goddess when I'm standing, like he's worshiping at my altar!"

+ If you want to max your sensitivity, get a Brazilian wax, advises Rachel, referring to the bikini wax which whisks *everything* away. "I have one every four to six weeks. When there's no hair down there, oral sex is amazing."

+ Don't flick. "Ooooh no!" shrieks Tonia. "I was with this guy who used his tongue like a barbecue prong. Stab, stab, stab! It was terrible. No, his tongue has to be more like a paddle, soft and wide." Says Sam, "They should never do that around-around thing. It's up and down, nice and slow, boys, not around and around."

+ A bit damp won't do. Wet to the point of slurpy works best, so get him to use lots of saliva.

+ On the point of orgasm, for goodness sake, don't allow him to stop. "Sometimes I've been gasping like a fish so Jon has stopped, which is the worst thing he can do," says Tonia. "He's got to keep his rhythm going until just when I come. Only then should he stop. In fact, afterward, I'm like, 'Stop! Ow!'" Says Freya, "Me, too. But if Michael stops licking before I come, I'll lose the orgasm like *that* (snaps fingers)!"

Vids, Toys, Cuffs and the Whole Nine Yards . . .

The fun element of modern marital sex cannot be underplayed. Spontaneous moments and unconventional locations certainly create a gulf between the stereotype of married sex and what takes place today. But it doesn't stop there. Sexy fun comes in many shapes and forms for the Hitched Chick and she's just as likely to introduce playful pleasure boosters as her hubby. In fact, since her spouse still often associates erotic stimuli with covert gratification (the idea of the naughty boy under the bedcovers with his "dirty mag"), today's wife is the one confidently suggesting it and bringing it into the bedroom . . . or living room, kitchen, bathroom . . .

Dinner and a Movie . . .

That women don't get off on hard-core porn is no news, but what is newsworthy is that porn is no longer a feminist issue. Generally, we don't feel degraded, devalued or disgusted by pornography. In fact, 70 percent of the women I interviewed felt porn positively enhanced their sex lives.

They see it for what it is: voyeuristic fun. Says Freya, thirty-five, "I think that's a big difference between us and our mother's generation. We don't look at the women in porn movies in a political sense. I mean, the majority of women in porn today are in it because they want to be and they're earning a very nice living, thank you. Yeah, there are girls who do porn to feed their drug habits, but I know plenty of people with city jobs who spend all their salary on drugs. And no one can ever condone child porn. But the porn Michael and I watch is your basic doctor-and-nurse set-up. No one's getting hurt, no one's being denigrated."

Says Jess, "I like porn, but I'm not into the hard-core stuff. I prefer a bit of a story. It's sexy watching a man running his hand up a woman's leg. I like the seduction aspect rather than the *bang, bang, bang!* Sometimes I'll say to Bob, 'Go and get a video and we'll have a night in, have dinner and a couple of drinks and watch a movie . . . ' "

Sam has no problem suggesting it either. "When we lived in Manchester, we had boxes of videos. And because it's always bloody raining in Manchester, we'd just stay in bed all day, and I'd say to Ray, 'Go on, put one of the dirty films on.' I don't care what anyone says, as soon as you see someone at it, you're like, 'Oh right, shall we do what they're doing?' It's dead normal."

And Amy, thirty-two, says, "We watch the *Playboy* Channel movie together—the quality's rubbish and I tend to be really critical, but there's sex going on and I find that erotic."

Sabina, forty, agrees. "Porn is something different, you get a different sort of arousal. Also, they're good for new ideas. I enjoy watching straight sex between the woman and the man although when I see two women together, it's a turnoff."

Dee, twenty-nine, disagrees. "It's the women I find *most* arousing. The men are so unappealing. Women are something you wouldn't necessarily try, that's what's so exciting and adventurous about it."

Kath, thirty-three, says, "I like watching lesbians. The men are so gross, and a penis on a man you don't love is gross. I'm not a lesbian, but the female body is just so much more exciting to look at."

Lesbian scenes are popular with Melanie, too. "A regular fucking scene does nothing. But a lesbian scene will turn me on because it's not something I would ever do. It's just a fantasy. Or like an S and M scene—not bleeding or whipping—but something out of the ordinary that I wouldn't normally see or know."

As for specific movies that women enjoy? Most claimed the porn industry still doesn't cater to a female audience. "But there *is* one that's really wonderful," says Rachel. "It's called *The History of Porn*. It's a collection of short films, some of them five-minute silent films from the turn of last century until the more explicit ones today. In many of the clips, you don't actually see them having sex. But the unknown is often sexier."

Make Believe . . .

Gender politics have crept into every aspect of our lives and marriages. Smashing stereotypes, breaking with tradition . . . the bedroom is just about the only place where we can let our guard down and, on occasion, flirt with roles which normally make us wince. What's forbidden behavior in the real world becomes tantalizing in the bedroom via elaborate fantasies and dressing up. We're scornful of the meek, submissive bride in real life, but we find it arousing to play the overwhelmed virgin in our fantasy life. We may pity the demeaned woman who is forced onto the street to charge for sex, but pretending to be a prostitute in our bedroom is strangely empowering—and fun. Playing naughty nurse, wild cowgirl, strict schoolmarm while your beloved assumes the role of straight-laced doctor, laid-back cowboy or naive student is a sexy novelty for many. And whether it's due to men's lack of confidence or imagination (or that he's out of the habit of exercising it), shyness or laziness, I find women to be the instigators and directors of fantasy.

Says Gemma, thirty, "Peter loves it when I say, 'Are you needing some treatment?' That means I'm going to play doctor and he'll be my patient. Or we play this game where he's a virgin and I'm teaching him how to have sex. That's a great way to get him to do stuff that I might have read about. Acting out scenarios is an excellent way of telling your husband what to do and what you like without actually saying, 'Listen, I really, really want you to try this or that.' You know how men can take requests as a criticism of their performance?"

Agrees Pat, thirty-eight, "Yes, acting out a fantasy is a great way of experimenting. You can kind of hide behind the fantasy if you feel shy about suggesting something new. My favorite is the slave fantasy, where Mike is examining me—my hair, my back, my breasts— to see if he wants to buy me." We both laugh convulsively when Pat tells me Mike says to her, "Let's rub this nipple and see if it goes hard. I won't buy a slave who doesn't respond to my command!" *Hilarious.* But that's the thing about fantasies—they sound so ridiculous in the cold light of day, which is why few women confess to them. Yet, those who admit they indulge say they're an important part of their sex life.

Says Eve, thirty-four, "I don't particularly like porn, so role-playing helps shake things up when you've been having sex the same way for a few weeks. I don't usually have a plan to begin with, but if I talk dirty to David, a little scenario will unfold. My favorite is the one where he's a burglar and he comes into my apartment and discovers me asleep. When we did this about a month ago, David said to me, 'Keep quiet, don't move or you'll pay.' I'm normally pretty noisy during sex, so this was a real novelty for me."

Gabrielle, thirty-two, says, "We role-play quite a lot. I take responsibility for starting that quite early on in our relationship. Now we're both adventurous mentally. My favorite fantasy and the one that always works is the prostitute fantasy, especially when I'm a bit premenstrual and I want that connection but my body doesn't feel that sexual because I feel all bloated. My boobs get swollen and sore, so I imagine I'm a stripper or prostitute with *huuuuge* breasts and I've been ordered to go to this house and whether I want sex or not, I have to have it. It's kind of a functional fantasy in the sense that I only need it for five minutes and then I can come back to what's really happening."

But Gabrielle isn't confined to play-acting the prostitute to get her beyond the pain of her premenstrual breasts. Her repertoire is colorful and varied. She says, "Sometimes Murray is the professor and I'm the student and I have to go to his office to see him about a paper that's late and provide sexual favors. He likes that one. Or we've done the one where he's the client and I'm a girl at this expensive nightclub and I've come back home with him. Or hitchhiking. He really likes being the hitchhiker. He hiked across America when he was twenty so he's got this real thing about being a hitchhiker. So I pretend to be a businesswoman on a cross-country sales trip. I'm by myself in a nice car and he's a young hitchhiker who I've picked up at the side of the road and he wants to get in my pants."

Toys4Us . . .

Although women regularly use vibrators for masturbation (see Chapter Six), they're not selfish about sharing their toys. Says Melanie, "We have such a good time when we get out the toys—we have big vibrators, little vibrators, skinny vibrators, thick vibrators. It's not saying Danny isn't good enough. He's secure enough to know better. We have fun with them. He uses them on me, I use them on him." Melanie even shares her most favorite sex toy. "I love my Matador," adds Melanie, who bought her special sex toy, the El Matador, accessorized with horns, from the Adam & Eve catalogue. "But I also use it with Danny—if you put the cock ring part on him, as he penetrates you, all the little beads go onto your clit. It's so powerful, but it's wonderful."

Says Tracy, "My husband loves toys as much as I do."

In fact, thirty-two-year-old Stella's husband enjoys them so much, "Every so often, he'll surprise me with a new purchase," she says.

A survey of 7,700 adults between eighteen and ninety (eh?) conducted by the University of California in 1996, revealed that 10 percent of sexually active adults use vibrators and/or other sex toys in partner sex. Hmmm . . . not as many couples as my own poll suggests. However, further reading reveals a reason for the discrepancy. Those over fifty—our mother's generation—are most *un*likely to use sex toys. A-ha! In fact, my findings closely correspond with a survey conducted by mypleasure.com, in which 32 percent of couples said they sometimes used sex toys.

Thirty-year-old Lena's husband introduced her to the idea of toys. "It was always my biggest fear that I'd start to think I couldn't have sex without the damn battery!" (This is a big fear among the uninitiated, so choose a toy which gently vibrates, to stimulate without desensitizing.) "But," continues Lena, "when he came home one night and said, 'I bought you a toy,' I was intrigued. When he first pulled it out, I said, 'Oh my God, oh my God, oh my God,' then when we tried it, I was like, 'Oh my God, oh . . . oh! Wow!' Now we use it together." Chloe, thirty, shared Lena's reservations in the beginning, but after a friend gave one to her, she now claims, "The way you stretch a relationship is to stretch what you are willing to do."

However, which sex toys Hitched Chicks play with during partner sex differ from those she uses during private masturbation. Much as she adores the added variety of vibrators, she's conscious of hurting her husband's pride when the two of them get up to their tricks. (Who says we're selfish *all* the time?) For instance, Gabrielle, thirty-two, says, "I'd been to this famous dildo shop in California and I came back with an all-singing, all-dancing, throbbing vibrator. I said to Murray, 'We should use this in our sex life and see what happens.' So Murray said, 'Do I use it on you?' and I said, 'Yeah, and I use it on you, too. But I purposefully bought one that wasn't bigger than you!'

He said, 'Thank you for that!' When I was single, there was always that sense of 'Well, if he doesn't want to wear the cock ring, that's okay,' but now that I'm married, I feel that if I really want to try something, like a double-ended dildo, I have the freedom to ask for it now in a way that I didn't have when I was single. I've broken personal barriers."

Although they don't buzz, whir or vibrate, handcuffs are also popular Toys4Us. Says Petra, thirty-seven, "My mother would be shocked if she knew I sometimes used handcuffs, but doing something like this unexpectedly keeps sex fun."

Tina, thirty, agrees: "Billy loves when I handcuff him to the bed and dangle my boobs in his face. And when he handcuffs me and gives me oral sex . . . oh man!"

Says Sonja, twenty-four, "I don't like any of that S and M stuff"—she's not alone, for nearly all women I spoke with, pain remains a turnoff—"but I got a pair of pink, fluffy handcuffs from my girlfriends at my bachelorette party. They stayed in the drawer for months. Then one night, Jackson used them to tie me to the bed. We didn't have sex, he just spent ages kissing and stroking and licking me all over. I almost went out of my *mind*."

Lights, Camera, Erection!

Thirty-four-year-old Alessandra tells me about her favorite wedding anniversary of all time. She and her husband, Stephan, were celebrating five years of married bliss and had gone to the restaurant where he had proposed in Palm Beach six years earlier. But it wasn't the complimentary bottle of champagne from the maître d' or the white gold Tiffany bracelet Stephan gave her that made the evening so memorable. No, her most vivid memories of that evening will never, not *ever*, be shared with Mom and Dad . . .

"Stephan and I are pretty crazy and we've tried just about every-thing in bed," Alessandra tells me. "I knew he'd make a big fuss of me for our anniversary, but I just couldn't think what to get him. A nice tie wouldn't excite him. I mean, what *do* you buy a guy when it's your fifth anniversary? So I had this idea: a video camera! You should have seen his face when he unwrapped it in the restaurant. He was really pleased, but couldn't understand why I was laughing . . ."

A bottle of champagne and a seafood dinner later, however, it dawned on Stephan. "I'd been teasing him under the table with my feet," Alessandra says. "We'd talked about times in our marriage when the sex was really mind-blowing and I said something like, 'Wouldn't it be great if we'd videoed us having sex?' You could actu-ally see him put two and two together and from that moment, he couldn't get out of the restaurant fast enough!"

That night, Alessandra and Stephan made a film of themselves making love. Hey, technology creeps into every aspect of Married Girl's life. Here's what happened:

"The video camera stood on the dresser, pointing toward the bed. I pushed Stephan down onto a pile of pillows and while he was propped on his elbows watching me, I did a striptease. I made sure I kept my sandals on . . . Stephan loves me having sex with my shoes on. Me, too, it makes my legs look longer. But by the time I got on top of Stephan, he was so excited, he couldn't contain himself so the action was pretty much all over and I was laughing so hard, I just fell on top of him. Even now, when I think back, I laugh to myself. It was just so much fun."

Since then, Alessandra and Stephan have videoed their lovemak-ing over half a dozen times. "It isn't something we do *every* night," says Alessandra. "It takes time—and planning, which is fun, too, fig-uring out the scene and the outfit. But even if we don't have the time or energy to make a film, sometimes we'll just watch one we've made."

THE HITCHED CHICK'S GUIDE TO
Sexy Filmmaking

While Alessandra doesn't profess to be a professional producer, she's delighted to pass on some tips she's learned. I've added my own ten cents worth, too. *Action!*

+ Get the position of your video camera just right. You'll need a stable base away from the bed or sofa or wherever you're having sex. Filming from above, rather than below, is far more flattering.

+ Turn on the lights! Two figures fumbling in the dark does not a sexy film make.

+ Clear away clutter from the action scene. Blinking clocks, photos of the kids, used tissues have no place in your sexy video.

+ Wear makeup. You don't want to look like Tammy Faye Baker, but equally, there's a good reason why Casper the Friendly Ghost is not a sex symbol. And all skins look even sexier on celluloid when slathered with oil. Don't forget to baste your beloved, too.

+ Don't fixate on a wildly complicated plot (far too stressful), but a few pre-determined ideas will give your vid structure and help if you feel self-conscious. Alessandra's favorite: "He's a virgin and you're the sex instructor." Command him to caress you and insist he brings you to orgasm "just like *this*!"

+ Speak loudly; the louder the better. Talking to the camera about what you're doing and how it feels makes the viewing extra-raunchy.

✦ Smile—you are, after all, on candid camera!

You think *that* requires tech-savvy? Take twenty-nine-year-old Diane, who I'm talking to on the phone from Chicago where she works as a sales rep. She's usually traveling so, like her husband, Brandon, I'm lucky to catch her. "Since you're on the road two weeks out of four, how does the traveling affect your sex life?" I ask after she reveals sex is crucial in her relationship. "It's always been something we've had to deal with, so you just find ways around it . . . ," she says.

Now, Brandon is an IT consultant and in a fit of missing Diane more than usual, he invested in a couple of devices which completely turned around their times apart. Diane calls them their "his and her" webcams and, she says, you can pick them up for around eighty dollars each. (P.S. It's true, I checked.) "They're little cameras you can plug into your laptop or desktop PC so you can hear and see each other over the Internet," says Diane. "His idea was that we could talk and strip for each other while I was away!" Result!

Diane continues, "When I'm in my hotel room, I just attach my cell phone to the PC in one port and the camera in the other and we have this NetMeeting software to just call each other—it's like instant messaging, but much better—and there he is, on the screen! The picture's not great at times, but it's better than nothing. Now we have these scenarios where we pretend he's the difficult client who won't close the sale until I take off an item of clothing, then another, then another. . . . It's fantastic and hilarious, too. I still miss Brandon—it's not the same as *touching* him, but our times away from each other are less frustrating. Actually, sometimes I now look forward to going away . . ."

Lust and Found

The most ardent sexual advocates accept that in any marriage, there will be sexual droughts. Managing the sheer logistics of life, especially modern life, can sexually paralyze even the most passionate and lustful couple. Shift work, extensive travel within the global business community, recent childbirth and the juggling of parenthood, marriage and career, dramatic changes to daily routine or environment . . . there are many elements of twenty-first-century life conspiring toward making us turn over or turn off.

Most should be viewed for what they are: inevitable blips, obstacles to the day-to-day sexual status quo. In general, a sexual hiatus from such events can last anywhere from a week to three months. Maybe a bit longer. But the point is, they're temporary and shouldn't be regarded as a signal that your relationship is in permanent decline. Couples who, in that time, have not lost their fundamental liking and respect for each other either make a conscious effort to work toward a passionate reunion (and it doesn't make it any less valid simply because it's been manufactured), or it happens quite naturally, almost unconsciously—once hormones or body clocks begin to stabilize or the practical logistics of synchronizing physical and emotional schedules have been figured out and put into effect.

While lust is undeniably important to women today, we live in a world in which we are active participants rather than protected bystanders. Our participation is one previous generations fought for and we embrace and celebrate it. However, this exciting, demanding free world is also one in which, as Shelley says, "Shit happens."

Sometimes events are bigger than we are, beyond our control, remote, global even. But that they are not taking place on our doorstep does not alter their potentially negative effect on the most personal and intimate aspects of our life. As an example, Amanda, twenty-nine, says, "Larry and I were on our honeymoon in Mauritius on September 11 and when you're on your honeymoon, you're just hanging around having sex. But we didn't even hug that night. We were in total existential despair. We just didn't feel comfortable having sex because what happened was so terrible, there's no comfort in it, it's meaningless in the face of what's happened."

Monica, forty-two, empathizes with Amanda. She says, "Many members of my family live in Israel and I'm terrified, every day, that we'll receive a phone call to say one of them has been blown up or killed. I think about it all the time and I fret and worry to the point where, some days, I can't eat a thing. As for having sex? Forget it. I just feel too guilty for some reason. Except I have days when I think I'm going to do something *positive* about it, do my bit for Israel. And then I feel like having sex. But generally, I feel hopeless, like worry is paralyzing me. Like it's just too big for me to make any difference, which is crap. Everyone can make a difference. But on those days when I've been consumed with the news and I think there's nothing anyone can do to achieve peace, I feel empty and depressed, so sex is the last thing on my mind."

Sometimes, however, a tragic or traumatic event is local and only poignant to us. The death of forty-year-old Lynn's mother three years ago, for example. The collapse of Helen's small business, for instance, only eighteen months after she quit her lucrative city job and struck out on her own. But the magnitude of such experience is nevertheless devastating in the way we feel about our life, love for each other and ability to relate to our husband.

Some women, irrespective of what is happening around them, are never affected sexually. They're extremely fortunate and, having met a couple of them during the course of researching this book, appear to be the better off for it, ever feeling confident and grounded in themselves and their marriages. But they are rare. For the majority of us, a profoundly life-changing event sends our sex lives spiraling downward so fast, we wonder whether we can ever experience lust, desire or intimacy again. Whatever that life-changing event is, however (and, let's remember, it's all relative), that lust, desire and intimacy returns to previous levels will ultimately determine whether your marriage succeeds or flounders. It's *that* important.

I heard many stories of lust that was lost and found while talking to women for this book. But none epitomized the effect of tragedy on the desire and lust we feel nor the profound benefits of sexual intimacy on our marriage like the story you are about to read. And I thank Lucy, Joe, Harriet and Thomas (whose names I have changed in respectful accordance with their wishes) from the bottom of my heart for allowing me to share their experience with you.

Lucy, thirty-eight, and Joe, forty-two, had been married for eight years. With a home and lifestyle most of us would envy and two gorgeous children—Harriet, six, and Thomas, four—they felt truly blessed. "Both kids were the spitting image of their father . . . blond, blue-eyed and beautiful and very, very similar to each other, not only in looks, but in personalities as well. They were extremely close and never fought. I was lucky," says Lucy. When Thomas came down with a heavy bout of diarrhea and vomiting, he was admitted to the hospital. But anxiety turned to horror when, within a couple of days of being in the hospital, he contracted meningitis. "Thomas died within five days of his admission," says Lucy. "What's more, Harriet also contracted meningitis two days after Thomas died and spent the next seven days in the hospital where they treated Thomas."

Recalling the first few days after Thomas died, Lucy says, "We didn't really cope with the tragedy then of losing Thomas because all our energies were focused on Harriet and keeping her spirits up. I was in the hospital full-time with each of them, sleeping at the foot of their beds. Besides caring for Harriet, we also had to plan Thomas's funeral, so the week after he died was just a tornado of tiredness, fear for Harriet's welfare and ghastly funeral administration.

"It was only really when we eventually got Harriet home that it all began to sink in. We were all exhausted, shocked, traumatized, terrified, conflicted with feelings of how unlucky we were that this bombshell had hit our family and how lucky we were at least that Harriet survived it. Joe and I operated in two completely separate units, secure in the knowledge that the other was seconds away. No need to talk or communicate with each other, we moved around like zombies, keeping an eye out, I suppose, that the other wasn't floundering too much, comforting each other as best we could. But, basically, if I had to describe the overall instinct, it would be survival. To some extent, we avoided intimacy because of the danger of letting those barriers down. Also, remember, Harriet was with us all the time and she was, of course, our main priority. I couldn't sleep, couldn't bear to close my eyes for the thoughts that came crowding in, but Joe found sleep a great comfort, a great way to keep his thoughts at bay, so we met at the kettle, checked one another was okay-ish, kissed and carried on by."

Only half a mile away, one of Lucy's best friends, Catherine, was trying to cope with the complexities of grief within her own marriage. Her mother had died on the same day as her husband's father died. Remembers Lucy, "She came to see me a few weeks after Thomas's funeral and we were talking about the problems and dangers in grieving at the same time. I was going to say 'grieving together,' but it's not like that; you actually grieve apart because you are grieving a different thing. In our case, we were grieving the same child, but a different loss, a different relationship, different expectations and memories and regrets. Catherine and her husband had fallen into a dreadful trap of a kind of grieving contest: an 'I'm upset' . . . 'You can't be as upset/tired/desperate/lonely as I am' sort of thing. They began to hate each other and resent their own grief being diluted.

She couldn't bear for him to touch her, she thought that she'd explode. And she focused all her anger at her mother's death onto her relationship. It went downhill, the sex fizzled out and now, sadly, they are getting divorced."

Says Lucy, "Catherine asked me if Joe and I were sleeping together again yet. I said I couldn't bear the thought of relaxing in that way, letting my guard down. I thought if I did so, I'd start to cry and never stop. That was when she told me that if only she could have managed to keep the sex going, she believed the rest would have fallen into place. She told me that whatever else, even if we were too desolate to speak to one another, we absolutely must have masses of sex. When all the other communication fails, sex says it all."

Fortunately, Lucy immediately recognized the enormous value of her friend's empathy and advice. "As soon as she said it, I knew how true it was and, strangely, I wanted to cry with relief, almost as though I had license for such indulgence, as though I'd felt guilty at the prospect of abandoning myself to such pleasure. But it wouldn't be pleasure per se, it would be for comfort and reassurance and togetherness, which we both desperately needed. We couldn't bear to talk, but some physical gratification, some reminder that we were real, alive, loved, supported would say it all."

I ask Lucy about her initial, tentative steps toward reclaiming her sexual relationship with Joe. "To be honest," she says, "once I'd talked to Catherine, any fear or reticence I had about resuming sexual relations evaporated. I can't actually remember what the sex was like—it was just normal, which is wonderful, but it wasn't particularly notable. It was, however, the best thing we could have done and it did us both so much good, we decided if all else failed, we at least deserved a daily bonk! I can well imagine that if Catherine hadn't explained the trap that she fell into, given me the license to invest in myself, my husband and my marriage, I could still be in isolation now." Instead? "The sex is better than ever now because we both know it saved us. After all, despite all the traumas and the losses and the wrongness of it all, we are still here which, if we go back to the survival theme, is what our aim was."

For any other couple who might face such a tragedy in their life, Lucy says this: "Understand the healing power of sex and intimacy. When you are feeling desperate, afraid, lonely, empty, bereft, of course you won't feel horny. But if, rather like jumping into an icy-cold swimming pool, you brace yourself and go for it, you will come out the other side feeling a little more human, a little less afraid, a little more thawed. And each time you do it, it gets easier and the benefits accumulate. So you're healing yourself and your husband and investing in your marriage which, when everything else is called into question, as it was when Thomas died and Harriet was ill, is the most important asset you have."

THE HITCHED CHICK'S GUIDE TO
Losing Lust—and Finding It!

When baby makes your sex drive dive . . .

Working mother Patti, who's married to Tim, says, "Since we had Charlie a year ago, our attitude to sex hasn't changed, but our time has changed. We definitely have sex less now. I could easily get into bed at nine o'clock and pass out by nine-thirty. I was talking to a friend about having a second child. I asked her, 'Do you think you're pregnant now?' and she said, 'How could I be? We never have sex!'"

It's a familiar tale. The arrival of a baby, or babies in thirty-six-year-old Dorotta's case, can get in the way of desire, drive and doing it for not just weeks, but *months*! "Oh, please . . ." she says. "After the twins were born, I was sore, exhausted, emotional and stressed. I didn't know what had hit me. Neither did Colin. I don't think either of us slept for four months. I look back now and think, How the hell did we get through that? We'd always wanted kids, but having them almost broke us up. It wasn't until my parents came over from Poland to stay with us for three weeks and Colin and I were able to get away to a hotel for a weekend, that we were able to say, 'Hello, I remember you.' We had sex twice that weekend and then nothing again for a month. It's taken us two years to get back to any kind of normality."

Episiotomies, C-sections, leaky sore breasts, wildly fluctuating hormones, exhaustion, not to mention baggy tummies, stretch marks, varicose veins . . . the list goes on. Hardly surprising few women feel like having sex straight after giving birth. The majority do retrieve their desire for sex—for some, within days, for others, within a few months—but, they admit, sex often feels different. "Your body changes," says Emily, thirty-three, who gave birth to James just over a year ago. "I used to prefer being on top because I had an orgasm more easily in that position. Now I prefer *him* on top because it's easier for me to orgasm." Then she adds, "Also, I'm totally obsessed with my breasts—I think they're yucky with breast-feeding so maybe I don't like being on top anymore because I feel so exposed."

Post-baby sex salvager? From myself and other Hitched Chicks who are also mothers:

- An entire new wardrobe to reward, celebrate and sexify yourself.
- A dozen sets of new lingerie, comprising underwire bras to boost breasts, which now closely resemble spaniel's ears, control-panel panties to camouflage Mommy tummy and sexy silky slips which feel gorgeous and conceal skin blemishes until they naturally fade away.

✦ A kindly baby-sitter with whom you trust to leave your precious babe for at least two hours (preferably four) on a regular basis so you and hubby can escape and reconnect.

✦ A baby monitor you can plug in so you know she's/he's as right as rain when you snatch a couple of minutes to have a quick session in the kitchen.

✦ A collection of new shoes and handbags. Just because . . .

When work gets in the way of lust . . .

"Garry is a nurse," says Amy, thirty-two, "so he works shifts, which means often we're not in bed at the same time or he's tired when I'm raring to go. It can really ruin your sex life."

"*Both* of us work shifts," says Anne, thirty-seven, an ER nurse, married to Michael, a firefighter for the New York City Fire Department. "It isn't unusual for us not to see each other for four days. When we do see each other, getting back in sync can be difficult."

Says Stacey, thirty, "Ben's under so much pressure at work these days, his sexual appetite has changed massively. He's been through a lot of change in his job, not all of it welcome, so he worries a great deal about it. He's under so much stress, he sees sex as just another thing someone's telling him to do."

Mindy, thirty-five, sympathizes with Stacey and Ben's predicament. "My work schedule is out of control. There's never a downtime anymore. It's hard not to feel sex is just another thing I *have* to do."

"If I'm pissed off at work and hate my job," says Dian, thirty-two, married to Ollie, "those feelings come home with me. My company's been through a restructuring recently and I hate it. Ollie works for the same company, although at a different location, and he's having a hard time too. So sex? No."

As we discussed earlier in the chapter, lack of opportunity for sex doesn't deter us as much as we might suppose. People who really want sex—and we know the vast majority of Hitched Chicks *really* want sex—can always manage to find the time for lust, not just despite their busy schedules, but *because* of them. No, the stress and exhaustion of juggling work with family for women and lack of satisfaction at work for men, are the biggest sex-busters of all.

Work-blues prescription: Um . . . new job? If not, ask for a meeting with your boss, but keep complaints to a minimum. Best tactic: compile a list of ways you could make your job more satisfying for yourself. If you're struggling with juggling work and family, do not be afraid to ask for help. Assuming your husband's doing his half of the domestics and you're still short on time, consider sending out the laundry, increasing your cleaner's hours, recruiting a new babysitter, supplementing a cleaner with an au pair, too. Scheduling noncancelable "play dates" with your husband, away from the home, during which you talk about everything *except* work (where you'll spend your vacation, what to do on your next wedding anniversary to make it extra special, five activities you want to do together in the next year), will help remind you both that pleasure, not work, is what makes your marriage special.

When depression overrides desire . . .

Over one in twenty Americans have a depressive disorder every year. Women are almost twice as likely as men to suffer from depression throughout their lives, and it can wreak havoc on their desire. "I was very depressed after I had the baby," says Rosie, thirty-three, recalling a very bleak period two years ago. "Paulo and I had little to no sex then."

Lynn, forty, says she's still severely depressed about the death of her mother, three years ago. "People think depression is just a mind thing," she says. "But it affects everything, including your energy levels and your sex drive. For me, I feel nothing."

And Una, thirty-seven, says, "I've been having help with depression for two years now. Losing my job wasn't the cause, but it was the catalyst. Slowly, I can feel my sex drive coming back, but we didn't have sex for a long time."

Although married women (along with women in poverty, adolescents and unmarried men) are the highest risk categories, I have, during the course of my research, been shocked at how frequently depression and a subsequent dive in sex drive among husbands has cropped up in conversation. "Robbie was made redundant seven months ago," says Carla, thirty-five. "And from that day, he lost his sex drive. When he first lost his job, we'd have sex about twice a week. Now we're just not having sex at all. He's totally depressed and nothing I do or say is helping him. I tell him there's no such thing as a job for life anymore, but he's not used to not working. I know a lot of men in this situation and they're handling it real bad. There are a lot of depressed men out there."

Niki, thirty-five, agrees: "For whatever reason, there's a lot of men out of work right now and their women are supporting them. It never seems to be the other way around these days." Has she noticed a negative effect on her sex life with Ron since he lost his job a year ago? "Yeah, it's been a bad year. It was waning anyway, and it's almost a year now since we had sex."

Given that I'm writing this book in the middle of a severe recession unique in that it isn't only a more dispensable female workforce that's suddenly out of employment, but full-time working men whose identities and self-esteem have always been inextricably linked to their jobs, this rise in male depression should not surprise anyone. Luckily, a greater awareness among the medical profession concerning the unique ways depression manifests itself in men—drug use, alcoholism, irritable or violent behavior and withdrawing from loved ones or "disconnection"—means better treatment is more readily available. But better medication is not the only solution to increased depression and decreased libido. Says Terrence Real, M.S.W., author of *I Don't Want to Talk About It* (Scribner, 1997) and co-director of the Gender Research Project at the Family Institute of Cambridge, Massachusetts, "Reconnection is key. Depressed women are more likely to talk about their problem and reach out for help. The ideal of male stoicism and the ensuing isolation lie at the root of male depression. Intimacy is its most lasting solution."

When medication means low "mojo" . . .

On the way to elevating mood, antidepressants have a very depressing side effect: up to half of users suffer loss of libido, erection impairment, decreased vaginal lubrication, difficulty reaching orgasm or loss of pleasure from orgasm. "A lot of people are on antidepressants," says Connie, thirty-nine. "Although I'm not majorly depressed, I've been on Paxil and it just takes the edge off. But I don't get horny anymore, which is sad."

Says Una, thirty-seven, "A combination of therapy and Zoloft worked wonders for the depression. But I'm hoping to come off the Zoloft soon, as I know it's stopping me getting my sex life back on track and I miss what I used to have!"

And Stacey, thirty, says, "Ben started to get panic attacks and is now taking medication, but it's really slowed him down. It's gotten a little better, but when he first went on the drug, he couldn't come or anything. It was really frustrating."

If you think antidepressants could be responsible for ruining your sex life, don't be shy about it: Ask your doctor now about lowering the dose of medication you take or switching to another drug, such as Wellbutrin, the antidepressant which, experts say, is least likely to cause sex problems.

When sex stops, it could be sexual dysfunction . . .

What the *hell* is sexual dysfunction? Certainly sounds sinister, but, in short, it's the persistent or recurrent inability or lack of desire to perform sexually or even engage in sexual activity. Why should you know about it? Because it *is* hell for couples if one spouse falls victim.

In women, sexual dysfunction falls into four main categories: low libido or aversion to sex; difficulty becoming aroused; inability to have an orgasm; pain during intercourse. A study in the *Journal of the American Medical Association* reports that as many as four in ten women experience some form of female sexual dysfunction (FSD) to some degree. In men, the condition is mostly associated with erectile dysfunction (ED), which means he can't get an erection, can't have sex and can't come. Some studies estimate that ten to twenty million American men have some degree of ED.

The causes of sexual dysfunction are vast and varied. If you are able to experience neither arousal nor ecstasy, the root of your sexual dysfunction could range from bad sex (you're not stimulated enough) to hostility (never underestimate the effect of anger or resentment) to hormones (yes, the Pill can cause it, and so can any drug that affects your hormonal balance) to vaginismus (involuntary vaginal contractions which make penetration painful, even impossible). If your husband is unable to get in the mood or follow through, his sexual dysfunction could be a symptom of many things. At one end of the scale, he may be anxious, over-doing alcohol (maybe the double whammy of both) or hostile (see, repressing feelings benefits no one); at the other end of the scale, his hormones may be off-kilter (low testosterone levels).

Is there a cure for sexual dysfunction, you're wondering. Yes, of course. But it generally requires either medication (in the event of hormonal imbalances, for example) or psychotherapy . . . or both.

The Thrills and Spills of Baby-Making Sex

I have two gorgeous children and I'm happy to say neither was an accident. It wouldn't have altered the way I feel about them, of course. It just means I got to experience the sheer, animalistic pleasure which comes with throwing away condoms, dispensing with pills, and flinging myself into an event which wouldn't simply result in pleasure, but another person. I mean, *for God's sake*. Now, as anyone who knows me will tell you, I am in no way an Earth Mother type. I positively retch at the thought of hummus and the only crystals you'll find me wearing are those stitched into the shape of a crown on the back of my Victoria's Secret G-string. Not that I have anything against Earth Mothers, but the point is, my experience of sex with the purpose of procreation was that it was the very best sex of all. I felt utterly liberated, wild and abandoned.

I remember wandering around a supermarket shortly after we had decided to try for a baby. We came to a stop by the baby powders. Martin and I looked at each other and I whispered, "Just think, if we went home right now and had sex, we might be buying some of this stuff in nine months time." We didn't even finish our shopping, just made a dash for the exit, jumped in the car, sped home, flung the door open and made love right there on the floor. Frenzied and abandoned, yes. Like animals? Ha ha, I guess so. But also extrawonderful was the closeness and intimacy we experienced afterward, as we cuddled together on the carpet, giggling and wondering whether the baby we may have just created would have Martin's nostrils or my freckles (as it turned out, she developed both).

Many Hitched Chicks with children agree. "Oh yeah, there's nothing like the first time you have sex after you've just decided you're going to have a baby," says Shauneice, thirty-six. "We couldn't wait to get started. Then we had sex all the time. I wouldn't actually be thinking, Oh, we might be making a baby, while we were actually having sex, but I know it *was* different, and definitely better for both of us."

Gabrielle, thirty-two, says, "Before we were trying to have a baby, if one of us was tired or not that interested, it fell to the other to get their motor running with sexy talk or fantasies. But because we were suddenly sharing the goal of making a baby, sex seemed so much simpler. We were making love because we could and wanted to and, only very occasionally, because we had to. Also, because we tended to make love so much more around the time I was ovulating, it would only take about five minutes for me to get excited, which was great as it meant we could have quickies and longer sessions and neither of us felt cheated. Although I didn't come every time, we made an effort to make sure I did as we'd read that it helped the sperm reach the egg. Baby-making sex does give sex an added twist. You realize that when you put your bodies together, you have the ability to make life."

Says Patti, thirty-four, "There's something kind of naughty about having sex without any protection, even if it's with your husband! So we had lots of it!" Mel, thirty-seven, agrees: "Knowing that it doesn't matter if you get pregnant—in fact, knowing that you might *be* pregnant after you have sex—made me horny. Plus, it made us even more affectionate toward each other while we were having sex. I just wanted to kiss Richard more, like tongues down the throat. I wanted to *really* get close to him. It made me so much more passionate. I remember once, Richard even saying to me, 'Wow! I've never seen you like this before.' He was right. There's just something primeval about it."

Carmen, thirty-seven, agrees. "I noticed that Michael was much more attentive during sex. He became very gentle and protective. So he'd kiss me and stroke me all over like I was some kind of prize animal. He took his time more than usual. It just seemed like every time we had sex, it was a very special event."

Without doubt, little compares to the first three or four months of sex after you've made the decision to have a baby. The precoital anticipation of what—*who?*—may result from the next five to fifty minutes, and the postcoital excitement that maybe, just *maybe*, you'll now be pregnant. However, women have admitted that after those first few months of BMS, excitement and anticipation can be replaced with anxiety, even fear.

I certainly recall those feelings. I became pregnant almost immediately with my first child. But it took four months longer to conceive my second. We didn't appear to be having sex any differently. We were no less or more stressed. Nor were either of us consuming more caffeine, alcohol or carbohydrates. Granted, we were older (me thirty-two, him twenty-eight) but only by three years. It didn't seem possible that our fertility could have reduced or disappeared in that time. And yet . . .

Says Patti, "I figured I'd be pregnant in a month or so. When that didn't happen, I started to worry. I mean, I'd spent the past fifteen years trying *not* to get pregnant and, now that I was dying to, I thought I couldn't. It was all my friends and I talked about. We all knew each other's cycles and how long we'd been trying. But every month I got my period, I just wanted to cry, and I did cry at least three times. So sex started to take on a whole new business-like meaning. It was work. In the end, my best friend told me to buy an ovulation predictor kit, so I'd tell Tim I needed an appointment tonight and he'd tell me to check with his girl—it was our little joke, but it *was* unromantic. Anyway, it worked the first month and now, of course, I tell everyone they *must* buy the ClearPlan Easy test when they're trying to conceive."

Gabrielle says, "I must confess, after seven months of trying to get pregnant I started asking girlfriends what worked for them. One recommended putting my legs up afterward, which I did. And I bought a book which was all about maximizing conceiving and tips on how to stop miscarriages. Murray had no interest in this book whatsoever. I think he knew if he began to believe he had a problem, his dick's feeling would be hurt and it would stop rising to the occasion!"

"You take it for granted that as soon as you stop taking the Pill, you're going to get pregnant," says Shauneice. "When it doesn't happen in the first month, you're disappointed, but you just think, Great! The sex is great, let's just carry on. But when it doesn't happen after three months, you start feeling nervous. In fact, four months after we started trying to get pregnant, I went to see my doctor. He said, 'How often are you having sex?' I said, 'We're having sex every day!' He said, 'Well, there's your problem.' I didn't know the more you have sex, the weaker a man's sperm is. Then we started having sex every three days. Two months later, I was pregnant!"

Patti, Gabrielle and Shauneice will never know whether the ovulation kit, waving their legs in the air or reducing the frequency of sex was the solution. The more we know, the more we realize that making babies requires a perfectly timed cocktail of female and male elements ranging from the physical to the emotional. Even the *meta*physical. (Gabrielle confides she saw an acupuncturist who told her she didn't "have enough *chi*" to conceive.) And although we've always known that the older we are, the more difficult it is to conceive and deliver a healthy baby, the arrival of Sylvia Ann Hewlett's controversial book, entitled *Creating a Life: Professional Women and the Quest for Children*, has tapped into this generation of women's most nagging fear: that once she has achieved her career ambitions and found the man with whom she can have an equitable relationship, the final piece of her perfect-life jigsaw puzzle may evade her.

Although an increasing number of married women are choosing

to remain childless (the number of women on both sides of the Atlantic without children is now twice as high as it was twenty years ago), the majority do want children. However, the average age to have a child in the U.S., U.K. and Australia hovers between twenty-eight and twenty-nine, the age at which fertility first starts to drop (it decreases significantly again, say experts, after the age of thirty-five). As a result, says Gabrielle, "When to start trying to get pregnant is a loaded topic for women right now. I was thirty-one when we started and that felt a little early. I would have been happy to put it off until I was thirty-three. But I decided that I needed to find out sooner rather than later if there was a problem so that if we needed to get fertility treatments or adopt, we'd have time."

Whether age-related or otherwise, the discovery that you may not be able to get pregnant as easily as shelling peas can have a profoundly negative effect on lust levels and your sex life. Says Connie, thirty-nine, who's been trying to get pregnant for over two years, "It just becomes work and it shouldn't be that way."

It's the basis of a difficult moment in my conversation with thirty-year-old Mary. She admits, "The worst sex I ever had was baby-making sex. We tried for so long and because my periods are so all over the place, I can't figure out whether I'm ovulating. So I'd take a random guess and we'd have sex every day for the whole week around it and it sucked. You get to the stage where you never want to have sex again." Finally, the stress became too much. "I started harassing the doctor because I couldn't handle it. Now I know we can have sex for fun, but we can't have sex for kids unless we are willing to put down ten thousand dollars for IVF. It affected sex for me emotionally. It's part of your definition of being a woman. The one great thing you can do as a woman is have kids. When you can't, it's a hard realization. So although I didn't turn away from Tom—I still wanted to have sex with him—it's the depression which will make you feel like you don't want to have sex. But I worked through it with a therapist. Now I really enjoy sex and it's great not to have to use condoms. So we have sex for fun and it's great."

Says Jo, thirty-three, "I think the quest for children can really takes the sexiness out of sex. We tried for a year to have children and the sex was fun. I'd shout to Aaron, 'I think I'm ovulating, honey!' and we'd have great sex. But it became mechanical. And every time I got my period, it would be heartbreaking. I'd make up a metaphor that my womb was crying and Aaron would talk about shooting blanks." In fact, Aaron's low sperm count, they have discovered, lies at the root of their inability to conceive. "When we found out we couldn't have babies, it was like, 'Wooah!' I became very depressed and went to therapy. After a year of therapy, our sex life is better. We've gotten through the heartache of knowing we won't get pregnant by ourselves, ever, but we can adopt so we have a different kind of control over when we'll have children. So over the past eight months, sex has improved because I feel, once again, its purpose has shifted and it's all about pleasure again."

3.

Dollars and Sense

My financial independence is really important to me and the main difference between me and my mother. She never had her own money. She just
had the household money, nothing of her own. She always had to rely on
my dad earning money, she always had to budget and make ends meet.
That was what a good wife did. To hell with that!

—Gabrielle, thirty-two

The Hitched Chick
is very much a Material Girl, but her obsession with money is not
Madonna-driven. The anthem many of us danced to in our teens may
have put lyrics to a heightened desire for money, but the first lady of
eighties pop maintained, even then, the best way to get loaded was to
acquire a man with a weighty wallet.

If music is a barometer of our times, Destiny's Child's megahit
nails it. They declare: *The clothes I'm wearing, I've bought it/'Cause
I depend on me!* These sentiments resonate loudly with modern
women who have learned from the plights of financially dependent
women, many of our mothers; women who were smart, beautiful and
wise, who couldn't make even the simplest financial decisions. And
we've seen how that dependency manifested itself in low self-esteem,

lack of confidence, unhappiness, depression. We watched, in despair and disbelief, as our mothers asked permission—*permission*—to buy clothes, shoes, maybe a car to drive us to school. We watched in agonizing embarrassment for her as she attempted to justify the expenditure. And many of us witnessed our mothers trapped in cruel, loveless marriages simply because she didn't even have the personal funds to buy a bus ticket out of them, never mind to support a meager existence until another source of security came along.

But increasingly, the female financial revolution of the past forty years can also be attributed to our mothers as positive role models. Some did contribute to the financial well-being of the family and proved the rewards extended beyond material ones. Others, finding themselves divorced or widowed, had no choice but to fend for themselves and their young families. In doing so, they instilled in their children—girls *and* boys—that money didn't simply represent food on the table; it represented self-sufficiency, choice and opportunity: choice to spend freely or frugally, opportunity to dictate their own future and opportunity to marry next time around (if that's what they chose) for the right reasons, not simply for a roof over their heads.

No wonder we grew up believing financial dependency was an all-around disaster. Today, money is not something we need to marry for. We want money (our own money) in our purses before we even decide whether we want to marry. We want money to be able to travel, entertain, socialize and furnish our lives according to our own standards. We want it to enable us to play and participate fully in the world. We do not regard ourselves as bystanders, we're active, influential and meaningful members of society whose actions make a difference and opinions matter. But we can only do all this when we have money. The more of our own money we control, the more we are equipped to live large and be true to ourselves (and our long-fought-for identities). And the vast majority of us know we can only acquire it through our own merit, wit, cunning and smarts. Should a wealthy husband come along, it's an added bonus, of course (come on, we've all fantasized about marrying a rich guy to ease the financial pressure), but even then, we wouldn't relinquish our personal funds. Are you kidding? The price for doing so exceeds even the grandest collection of Prada handbags.

Says Joan Richmond of *American Demographics*, "Those women whose connection to finance is limited to clipping coupons and paying the milkman are becoming as scarce as, well, milkmen themselves." Today, women regard money as a symbol of independence, freedom, success and control. It's this thought alone that propels increasing numbers of us through school and into college. Our graduation diploma is one piece of paper that *really* means something. A predictor of financial success and independence, a college degree for both women and men will, on average, add approximately $2.8 million to our lifetime earnings. That's a shedload of matching designer shoes and handbags, for sure, but it also buys us cars, technology, health care, a comfortable if not luxurious place to live. And, yes ma'am, whether we decide to marry or remain single, that $2.8 million, most importantly, buys us a shedload more freedom and choice.

Now, some of my financial research makes depressing reading. Women in the U.S. still only earn seventy-two cents for every dollar earned by men (source: *Investors Business Daily*). U.K. figures are similar, revealing that the average full-time male employee earns 23,412 pounds compared with 16,481 pounds for the average full-time female employee (source: U.K. Office for National Statistics). Let's get on our high horses about this, certainly. Better still, dismount and talk to a lawyer if you know equal work does not translate to equal pay in your workplace. But the financial news as it relates to women is not terminally depressing.

Ker-ching! Women collectively now earn over $1 trillion annually (SOURCE: U.S. CENSUS BUREAU), which makes them an undeniable influence on the economy's health.

Ker-ching! One-third of married women are now outearning their husbands.

Ker-ching! Women's earning potential is definitely on the increase, from being around 61 percent of men's hourly rate in 1970 to 83 percent today. This figure increases to 95 percent for women under thirty and it's predicted that women will finally achieve pay equality in 2030 (SOURCE: ABBEY NATIONAL).

Ker-ching! Seventy-seven percent of women feel more comfortable investing than they did five years ago (SOURCE: TODAY/ OPPENHEIMER FUNDS).

Ker-ching! Women are excelling over men in investing. A National Association of Investors Corporation ten-year study shows all-female investment clubs outpaced all-male investment clubs by racking up 23.8 percent average compound lifetime returns compared to 19.2 percent for male clubs.

Ker-ching! Sixty-three percent of women are involved in their family's investment decisions (SOURCE: TODAY/OPPENHEIMER FUNDS).

Ker-ching! Over 50 percent of women know how mutual funds work, compared with just 38 percent ten years ago (SOURCE: TODAY/OPPENHEIMER FUNDS).

Despite all the brouhaha over the rebirth of spirituality and anti-materialism, despite our complaints about the infamous time famine, despite the firmly held belief that money does not buy happiness, Hitched Chicks, mainly Gen Xers, still desire dollars over anything else. When Youth Intelligence asked 1,125 women aged between twenty-five and thirty-five if they would rather have more time or more money, 76 percent said, "Give me the money!" (79 percent of men also opted for money over time). Since we know how much money we have fundamentally affects our behavior and, rightly or wrongly, our attitudes toward ourselves and other people, what level of impact is our desire for money, and increasing piles of it, having on marriage? Answer: a lot.

Cash Cows

W hen I met Steve, it was obvious from the start I was much more successful financially," says Linda, thirty-four, who is a senior executive for a multimedia giant. "I remember our third date. I wanted to celebrate a huge pay increase so I ordered a bottle of champagne and when the waiter pulled out the cork, I yelled, 'Here's to the next hundred grand!' Steve couldn't believe it. He was pleased for me, but it backfired. It was clear he'd had no idea how much I was earning and capable of earning. He said, 'Where does that leave us?' I said, 'What do you mean?' He said he didn't feel comfortable knowing I earned more than him. It ruined the night. I told my friend, Jill, about it afterward and she reminded me that the same had happened to her. So, for a while, I tried to be sensitive to Steve's insecurities. I'd try to compensate and make him feel better by buying him things. That backfired, too. He'd say, 'Oh thanks, but I feel bad. I can't afford to buy you anything this month.' It was awful. Finally, I told him that if he wanted to be with me, he'd better get over himself. I mean, it was getting to the point where I wouldn't tell him I'd bought something, which was just what my mother used to do, but for different reasons. No, I wasn't going to behave like that. *Me?* So I told him just because he was struggling, I couldn't be expected to do the whole sackcloth and ashes thing. It was ridiculous. But men haven't had to cope with this situation in the past. It was always understood men earned more than women. It's not necessarily that way today."

A man can no longer assume he is out-earning his date and that he will continue to do so if and when she decides to marry him. True, the likelihood still is that he *will* earn more than her since women still gravitate toward service industries or creative environments: vocational workplaces in which salary is often grossly disproportionate to effort. But as increasing numbers of women graduate, enter (and improve) traditionally male workplaces, make noise where previous generations of women may have remained silent, break through the so-called glass ceilings, resume their full-time careers after childbirth (if they have children at all), men have had a loud wake-up call in the moolah department. And some are surprisingly grumpy about it.

"You would think," says Linda's friend, Jill, thirty-five, a banker, "they'd be pleased they didn't have to pay for everything. But a lot of men feel emasculated by a woman who earns more. I don't wear expensive clothes—I never have—so before I met Lloyd, I'd go out to bars and I'd just wear jeans and a little top, so they'd have no idea I owned my own apartment and had my own car. Later on, when I'd take them back to my place, you could see them thinking, Shit! Some of them immediately thought I *had* to be a trust-fund kid or that my apartment actually belonged to my parents. When I told them, 'No, I bought it myself,' some of them were pretty weird about it. One guy just sat on the sofa, put his head in hands and then drank my entire bottle of Jack Daniel's. It was as if he thought he was a loser because this woman had her own place and he didn't. He *was* a loser—but not because he couldn't afford his own apartment. Another guy asked me if I'd slept with my boss! He said it was a joke, but I got rid of him pretty quickly. Some guys were impressed. I think they were relieved I wouldn't be expecting them to pay for everything. In fact, a couple were like, 'Woo-*hoo*, she'll pay for *every*thing,' to which I said, 'No, no, no, I wo-*hon't*.' Lloyd was one of the few guys I dated who didn't have a problem with how much I earned. He does his own thing. He's confident about who he is. He's very much of the attitude that we just both bring in as much money as we can."

Even if she doesn't earn as much as a man, the symbolism of money infiltrates how the modern woman dates, who she dates, who she will end up marrying and the role she plays in their financial future. Says Tina, thirty, "I don't think I ever earned more than any of the guys I dated. And I certainly earn nowhere near as much as my husband. But I always made sure I paid for something. Maybe not on a first date, although I'd always offer to go halves. But, for instance, after the first date with Billy, which he paid for, I always made sure we split the check. It may not have been straight down the middle, but I'd offer to buy the drinks. Or I'd say, 'How about we leave here and I buy us ice cream on the way home?' I just didn't want him to think I was sponging off him. But it was more than that. It's about self-respect. I'm not this pathetic, little woman who needs to be provided for. And I didn't want to feel that I owed him anything. Like sex. Because I was paying my way on dates, I felt I had every right to decide where we'd eat and what we'd do."

Says Skylla, twenty-nine, "Carl works on Wall Street. I'm a furniture designer. You do the math. But I was taking care of myself long before I met him. Okay, I wasn't living in a penthouse, but I earned enough to have a great life. I partied, I went out with friends. If I wanted to be extravagant, I'd figure a way somehow, whether that meant eating ramen noodles every day for a week to save money or walking everywhere instead of taking the bus. So Carl knows I'm not with him for his money. In fact, his high salary wasn't exactly a turnoff, but it did concern me. You hear about men who expect all their own way just because they're earning the most money. That wasn't for me."

Far greater than her mother ever had, a single woman's disposable income today is only matched by her desire to spend it. In a 2001 Oppenheimer Funds survey, three out of four single Generation X women said it was important to look successful. The survey also revealed 47 percent have credit card debt and 54 percent say they're more likely to acquire thirty pairs of shoes before saving $30,000 in retirement assets. "Young Women Show Signs of Carrie Bradshaw Syndrome" screams the release. "Why? Because we love shoes?" says Lola, thirty. "Perhaps they'd prefer us barefoot and pregnant . . . ?" We snigger. Oh, those stereotypes . . .

Don't get me wrong. We're not dismissing the seriousness of debt. God knows, for many twenty-something singles (male and female) today, debt stress from college and credit card overuse is very common indeed. A 2002 *Cosmopolitan* article reveals the average woman enters the workplace with a ton of stress, thanks to her $16,000 worth of debt, owing as much as she'll earn in the first year of work. Being in and getting out of debt, however, is a recognized rite of passage for today's Hitched Chick. And she takes it seriously.

Says Tina, thirty, "Who wasn't in debt when they left college? And when you first start work, you go crazy. You buy everything and you charge it. But if you're smart, you realize you can't go on spending like that. Someone has to pay it back and that someone is you. Your parents won't bail you out. I never even told my parents. I don't think I had a decent night's sleep until the whole lot was paid off. It took me three years, but I did it and I was so proud of myself."

Tina's typical. The Oppenheimer Funds survey reveals two-thirds of single Gen X women—sixty-five percent—rate paying off their credit card debt as a high personal priority, *ahead* of finding a spouse, having an active social life or possessing nice clothes or a car. And the lessons single girls learn as they do so will last into their marriage and beyond.

The perils of credit card debt, however, are not the only financial lessons women learn before they marry. In fact, long before they tie the knot, they are far more literate than their mothers ever were (and maybe still are) about money matters, such as savings, investments and retirement funds. In failing to face up to their future well-being, they are aware they may share the fate of their grandmothers, if not their mothers. And that is no happy prospect since 75 percent of all elderly Americans in poverty are women (source: Social Security Administration). And the median pension benefit income for a woman is just $3,000—approximately two and a half times less than a man's (source: Women's Institute for a Secure Retirement). Says Dr. Marci Rossell, Oppenheimer Funds' corporate economist, "Women enter adult life single and many, by choice or circumstance, end up that way. Whether they intend to marry or not, most single Gen X women understand that they are responsible for their finances."

April, forty-three, takes full responsibility for her finances and always has. "I saw one set of grandparents who lived lavishly and spent all their money and my grandmother ended up having to be supported by everyone, while my other grandmother saved her money and invested wisely and ended up with a great lifestyle. I'm not cheap or a miser or a hoarder, but since the day I worked, I always put money away in savings."

Says Linda, "The trouble is, retirement funds just aren't sexy. You can't actually *see* where your money's going so, of course, it's more fun to buy a gorgeous pair of shoes you can wear that night. But I don't want to rely on anyone to see me through old age. That's what my grandmother did. She was devastated when her husband died, but I think as much of it was fear. It turned out he left her well looked after, but it could have gone either way. I'm leaving nothing to chance."

Nor are the 83 percent of single women who do have retirement dollars (source: Oppenheimer Funds). But there's another movement which demonstrates women's increasing money savvy before they marry. The National Association of Realtors say single women are becoming homeowners at a faster rate than single men. Fifty-seven percent of single women own their own homes.

Take thirty-two-year-old Dian. She sold her single girl Miami apartment for $23,000 more than she bought it for when she married her fiancé, Ollie. He, on the other hand, had only $7,000 in savings, despite the fact that he was three years older and had lived on and off with his parents until he married Dian. "My profit made a huge difference in what we could afford next. And because I came into my marriage with more money, I had the final say on which apartment we bought together."

April owned her own apartment before marrying Doug, "even though" she says, "he was earning a lot more money than I was." Same with Suzannah, thirty-nine, who says, "It wasn't big, but it was mine. And I sold it for a profit." Thirty-year-old Stacey did, too. "I had a roommate to help pay the bills, but otherwise, it was all mine. Then Ben moved in and I sold it. But I made a huge profit, which we used to buy our house." I bought my first place with a girlfriend. It turned out to be a great decision since we had great fun and it was a lucrative move, too.

Certainly, there's no guarantee that home ownership will make us money (although recent stockmarket shenanigans make property buying seem low-risk/high-return in comparison), but the benefits are multiple. Owning a home is no longer reserved for marrieds. Not knowing whether we ever will—or want to—marry means we're in the habit of taking financial security into our own hands. So we're not only used to, but exceedingly comfortable and proficient with, monetary matters long before lover boy enters stage left.

THE HITCHED CHICK'S GUIDE TO
Never-Too-Late Nuptial Agreements

The subject of pre-nuptial agreements is as sticky as a termite trap. Although we all see the merit in it, few women I spoke to decided to opt for a pre-nup. They either didn't get around to it, it was seen to be something only celebrities do, or as Emily, thirty-three, says, "It does assume things are going to go wrong." Ellis, forty-three, agrees: "I believe it is possible to manifest your fears, so I have conflicting beliefs about it."

However, for the handful of Hitched Chicks who did briefly push romance aside, they admit they're pleased they did. "Especially since I decided to give up work until the kids are older," says Paulette, thirty-eight. "The pre-nuptial agreement makes me realize I'm not staying in the marriage because I'm dependent on Simon. I'll go back to work one day, definitely, but until then, it gives me extra stability."

Says Joyce, thirty-four, "Mario wasn't thrilled about it, but my grandfather left me a large sum of money when he died. If we ever did divorce, it wouldn't be right for half of that money to go to Mario." Chloe, thirty, agrees. "I'm an only child, so I will get everything my parents worked for. Why should my husband get a portion of that just because of a mistake I made? And if you decide later you want to draw up a will, he might say, "Why do you want a will?' I think my mother wishes she had a pre-nup. She'd be screwed big time if she ever got divorced."

Now that women enter marriage already successful and solvent, experts claim pre-nuptial agreements make a lot of sense. It's best to draw up a pre-nup two or three months before you tie the knot. But it's never too late. Say you inherit a large sum of money, sell a business

When a Pre-nup Should Be a Priority

If you have children from a previous relationship. Say, for example, you have young children and some assets when you marry. If you die, even if you both verbally agreed those assets would go into a trust fund for your kids, you can't be sure they will. Unless you have a legal document stating otherwise, there's a strong likelihood most of your individual and shared assets would go to your husband. The rest would be hammered out in probate, which could be a long and nasty procedure. What about a will? Hmm, it won't cut the mustard in the event of a divorce.

You own—all or part of—a business. Women are now starting new companies at twice the rate of men (source: *Working Woman*). If you don't want to lose your business in a divorce settlement or you want your kids to retain sole ownership of it in the event of your death, seek legal counsel.

You enter marriage with a lot of money ($100,000 plus). It doesn't matter who brought what to the marriage, without a pre-nuptial agreement, everything will be split fifty/fifty.

You're on a fast career path and likely to earn a large salary.

You're anxious about inheriting a large debt. A pre-nup will protect you from liability if a partner is heavily in debt or a compulsive gambler.

You're paying for your partner to have further education.

You have a sudden windfall. Lottery winnings, large inheritances, sensational returns on individually owned stocks . . . if you don't want *them* to be split if *you* do, take steps to find a matrimonial lawyer.

Pre-nup note to self: Ivana Trump's pre-nuptial agreement, written at the time of her marriage to Donald, was revised three times in the duration. When they divorced, the Big D's lawyers called it everything from fraudulent to unconscionable, but the agreement proved mightier and more powerful than all his legal counsel put together. Awarded to Ivana: $10 million, a forty-five-room Connecticut mansion, an apartment in New York and use of the 118-room Mar-a-Lago mansion in Florida one month a year. *Sigh.*

or—who knows—win the lottery, a *post*-nuptial agreement is just as valid as a pre-nup. But you must seek good legal advice. It can be expensive (anywhere from a few hundred to a few thousand), but peace of mind is priceless. True, discussing with your beloved can flatten a romantic evening faster than a cheap bottle of bubbly. However, this legal document (and it *is* legal if you both hire your own lawyers so there's no conflict of interest) could be critical in deciding what happens to your individual and collective incomes and assets after a death, divorce or separation.

What's Yours Is Ours, What's Mine Is My Own

Says Patti, thirty-four, "I can't stand the idea that when my American Express bill comes in, Tim is going to look at it. I don't want him to know what I'm buying or to be judgmental. I don't want him questioning why I bought shoes or saying, 'My God, I had no idea how much that personal trainer cost.' I figure that if I can afford to pay for it and it's my hard-earned money, then he has no business asking how I'm spending it. Tim doesn't think that way as much as I do. In fact, were it up to him, we would probably just have one joint account that we would both use. But I am very possessive about my money."

Patti's no princess. She's a regular Hitched Chick who works and has a child. Like Suzannah, thirty-nine, who says, "I have my own separate account, but his account is our joint account." And also like Joely, twenty-six, who says, "We were going to have a joint bank account and our own personal accounts. Be he wouldn't have his own account. He said, 'No, that's stupid.' But I said, 'I need to have my own account. I need my paycheck to go into an account that only has my name on it.'"

Says Emily, thirty-three, "We have so many accounts. I have my checking account, I have my savings account, we have a joint checking account and we have a joint savings account and then Mark has his personal checking account. But he actually wants our money to become mingled and I'm the one who says, 'It's important to me to have money that remains my own money.' I don't ever want to be financially dependent on him, and there's a teeny part in the back of my mind that says, 'This could all go horribly wrong at some point and, if so, you'd better protect yourself.' He's more of an optimist. Also, there could come a time when I work less so I never want to ask him for money. If I want to go and buy clothes at Barneys, I want it to feel like it's coming out of my money, not his."

Stacey knows that feeling, too. "Even though my mother always worked," she says, "I'd go shopping with my mum when I was younger and she'd make me hold her bags when we went in through the front door. And she'd whisper, 'Look after the bags. Pretend these things are yours!' It was ridiculous. Ben doesn't have any say in what I spend my money on. If he asked, I wouldn't have a fight with him about it. I'd just say, 'Why do you ask? It's my money, the bills are being paid, so what's the problem?' My mother would always be embarrassed by what she'd spent. Even if she'd bought a new duvet cover for their bed, she felt guilty. I keep my own accounts. And I have a savings account, but Ben doesn't. I like to have money for emergencies as well as luxuries. We do have a joint account, but it's purely to transfer money to."

Modern wives do not want to be their mothers in matters of money. "My mother," says Linda, thirty-four, "didn't feel she was worthy of having money, never mind spending money. Even though she stayed at home and did a hard day's work, she felt as though she had no value. I'm the opposite. I earn a lot, but I believe my value is far greater than what I earn. Steve wouldn't question what I spend on myself, but if he did, I'd take it that he was questioning my worth."

(Has Linda been watching too many L'Oréal advertisements? I ask. You know the ones where a variety of celebs give the final punch line: "Because I'm worth it"? Linda laughs and says, "Oh yeah! It's true. I *am* worth it. I'm worth *more!*")

Emily, thirty-three, doesn't want to be her mother either. "My father became an alcoholic. He didn't want to be involved with us and never accepted any financial responsibility for us. She figured she would live this textbook life, but in reality, she was left raising two kids. All the responsibility fell to her when he left and she never had the money she wanted to have. I was twenty-one when she died and it turned out her financial situation was far worse than I thought. It scared me and made me think I never want to have to worry about money that much again."

Joely, twenty-six, doesn't want to be like her mother's friends who, she says, "got screwed. That was why my mother got her own bank account. I need to know that if, for whatever reason, I needed to leave Ali, I could and I wouldn't have to deal with him. Women get married to men they think are wonderful, then they do something their husbands don't agree with and lose all their money. Their husbands cut off their credit cards. Women are not going to talk a bank guy into cutting off their husband's money, but a guy will. It's just a fact of life. If I walk into a bank and say I need to freeze my husband off this account, they're going to say, 'No, it's a joint account.' But if a man wants him to do it, he'd probably be able to get it done because he'd make friends with the bank teller or he'd start flirting. His male personality would carry him through. And I think men have this sense of entitlement that comes out in confidence and exuberance, which enables them to talk their way into things in the way that women just aren't programmed to do."

Seeing the effect of their mothers' (or friends' mothers') lack of financial power and having worked hard to acquire their own, women today regard money as a shining symbol of success and independence. Says Ruth, thirty-eight, "My self-esteem is very much connected to money." She, like the majority, will not relinquish it lightly.

Gabrielle recalls making the decision to have a joint account. "Although we still have our separate accounts, when we moved to America, we decided to put most of our money into one. I found it really challenging, but what happened was that I ended up looking after the finances, so I still use my personal account, and as long as we have enough money to spend on the necessary things and save, there are no questions asked. I just don't want to have to ask his permission to buy something, whether it's for my business, to travel on my own, to lend money to my parents or to buy something frivolous. A digital camera was the last thing I bought. I spoke to Murray about it and he said, 'But we've got seven cameras.' I said, 'Look, I just really want it' and he said, 'But why?' I thought, I do not want to have this conversation. I want the camera because I want it and regardless of the fact that you don't want me to want it, I'm going to buy it. It's kind of like 'fuck-you money,' I'm not going to have a conversation about it."

It's an intensely sensitive subject. After all, we represent the first generation for whom a financially independent woman is the rule, rather than the exception. And having few female role models to ask for advice—as Ellis, forty-three, says, "You can't go to your mom because your mom wouldn't have a clue"—they are focusing *not* on what they *should* do with their money, but on what they *shouldn't*. And what they shouldn't, they say, is compromise access and control.

Which is why although many are happy to pool a fraction of their earnings for bill paying, savings and investments—so long as, mind you, their sweetie is, too—they keep the rest under a lock to which they alone hold the key.

Three Is the Magic Number

"Dez had a much more romantic view of marriage than I did," says Tyler, thirty-one. "Even though his parents divorced and his mother told me she got screwed, Dez just couldn't see why I'd want my own account. He'd say, 'What are you trying to hide?' or 'Do you not trust me?' Finally, he stopped pushing me because he was getting nowhere. Now we have three accounts—my account, his account and our joint account."

The three-account—yours, his and ours—marriage is the solution to the Hitched Chick's money sensitivity. Here's why it works:

+ It fulfills your need for privacy and control. "I hate being checked up on," says Linda. "Steve isn't my dad, he's my husband."
+ Both parties agree to contribute to and share control of a joint household account on a pro rata basis (i.e., if you earn half as much as your husband, you contribute half as much as he does and vice versa), so expenses such as mortgage, rent, electricity/gas/cable bills are covered fairly.
+ It allows you to play out your own money personality without judgment or recourse once the joint household account is stocked.
+ You can continue to build and maintain your own personal credit history.

"I don't want Dez to know how much his birthday present cost," says Tyler, who hated that her parents just gave each other money. Says Julia, thirty-one, "I agree. It does, in a way, keep things more romantic and gives you a sense that you can buy each other treats."

The Clash over $ IDs

Melanie, thirty, married to Danny, says, "Of course we fight over money. He's not cheap, but there are times when everything's about money. He's all about the future. Saving. He'll say, 'We gotta save.' I'm like, 'What are you gonna do? Are you gonna *die* with your fucking money?' He says, 'No, I'm gonna die and leave it all to you.' So that's when I go, 'Okay, *save, save!*'"

When Melanie tells me this, I practically wet my pants. Hilarious, huh? But, seriously, alongside sex, in-laws and how to bring up the kids, money is one of the main sources of matrimonial conflict. A U.S. Association of Bridal Consultants survey revealed 67 percent of newlyweds say the most serious conflict in their first year of marriage is over money. It's backed up by Relate, the leading U.K. organization of relationship counselors, who claim fights over finances split up more couples than all sex conflicts combined. Since women now have a lot more of their own money worth fighting for, they're less likely to surrender. More than ever, they're exerting their "money personalities" and entering the ring intending to fight to the death . . . or divorce.

Whether we're into rock music or soul, whether we love the city or country, whether we're liberal or conservative, our money identities are just as defined. For sure, some of it's genetic, but it's as much nurture as nature and our family influences will greatly determine our attitude to money. According to Olivia Mellan, a leading psychotherapist who specializes in counseling couples about money conflicts, there are five distinct money personalities: the spender, the hoarder, the avoider, the worrier and the controller. And guess what? Just as the outgoing side of you is drawn toward the quiet reserve of your husband, opposite money personalities attract, too. At the best of times, you'll complement each other, but there's a strong chance you'll also clash. And since money is such a loaded subject, when you do, boy are there fireworks. Big boxes of them.

However, understanding your dominant money personality (because it's possible to be a combination of two) and how it can merge happily with his, says Mellan, is the key to resolving differences. Here are the five distinctive types:

The Spender: You love to shop. In fact, you worship at the altar of shopping. And even when you know money's tight, spending is your release, your get-happy-quick fix. When single, somehow you managed to get by. Now married, your lack of financial responsibility causes ructions.

The Hoarder: The polar opposite of the Spender, you're happiest poring over your bank statements, assessing your assets, tallying up your interest. The thought of depleting your reserves manifests itself in anxiety. While in sole control, you're fine. When it comes to sharing—and possibly losing—you're no fun.

The Avoider: You refuse to face up to your financial situation. You have no clue whether you're rolling in it or wiped out. How could you? You don't keep records and bank statements remain unopened. It's your defense mechanism against anxiety. It's also a way of absolving yourself from responsibility.

The Worrier: Spending stresses you, it has a debilitating effect on your ability to make sound financial decisions. Even if your cash reserves are well stocked, you worry you don't have enough. Often derived from childhood and when single, only you bore the painful brunt of your constant anxiety. Now married, the negative effect on health and happiness is shared.

The Controller: If you've ever said, 'Since I'm paying, I'll choose,' this is you. Money gives you confidence, security and a sense of superiority. It scaffolds your self-esteem. Unfortunately, your attitude can also erode the self-esteem and happiness of your spouse.

Merging money IDs is one of our greatest challenges when we marry. Says Jo, thirty-three, "Money has been a *huuuge* issue for us. My opinion was, 'Live every day as if it was your last.' Aaron's parents lost everything, so he worries about money constantly. I would spend money as soon as I got it, he would stuff his under the mattress. One day, he sat me down and he said, 'I can't afford you. I can't keep up with you.' I was shocked. Now we're really working hard at finding a path together. Tentatively, we started walking toward one another and we're finally at that point where we have a common goal, but we have very different ways of getting there."

Says April, forty-three, "Doug is a spendaholic. He needs instant gratification. If he sees it, he wants to buy it. He obsesses over things and has to have them. The cost means nothing to him. Then he'll spend forever trying to get me to agree to his purchase, saying you only have one life. But he spends like there's no tomorrow and I can't stand being in debt or owing anybody."

Alexandra, twenty-nine, and her husband Stewart, twenty-eight, have the opposite money ID combo. "I want to replace our furniture and spend my money on psychotherapy, which is very important to me. He doesn't want me to. His whole attitude is very WASPy. He's very uncomfortable about spending money. He isn't comfortable buying me a present, even if it's jewelry."

Says Dee, twenty-nine, "I'm the controller. Evan likes to buy gadgets and he buys many more of them than I think he should have, so we butt heads. But even though he earns more than I do, he asks my permission before he spends. In a way, my being a controller takes away the responsibility from him."

Different couples, different money ID combinations, but same goal (eternal bliss). Is there any chance they can achieve it? Coming up, how to mend and blend the most common money ID couplings . . .

The Spender versus the Controller

It was love at first sight. The Spender adored the take-charge attitude of the Controller; the Controller fell head over heels with the carefree frivolity of the Spender. A match made in heaven? For a while, until the controlling partner feels threatened by their other half's spending and starts to impose limits. At which point, their spending spouse freewheels out of spite or sheer stubbornness.

$olution: Since the Controller has most to lose—control!—s/he must take the initiative, by asking the spender to record what they spend and face up to the consequences of their slapdash habit. It's the Spender's role to take the power out of money by suggesting to the Controller that affection be demonstrated with symbols of love that are low on price, big on value. (An orgasm, perhaps? Just a thought . . .)

The Avoider versus the Worrier

How cozy. One of you loathes thinking about money; the other does nothing but. *Huzzaah*! And what could be more attractive to a Worrier than an Avoider? Aw, they think, I wish I could be so relaxed. They don't even look at the bank statements! Within months, the Worrier is worrying so much (for the two of you), implosion is just around the corner.

$olution: If the Avoider takes responsibility for even one of the money matters (say, all the deposits), the Worrier will have less to worry about and, fingers crossed, know it's fine to forget about finances some of the time. And once the Worrier can make the Avoider confront finances with, say, a once-a-week discussion, the Avoider will realize financial responsibility is not something to be feared, but to be proud of.

The Hoarder versus the Spender

"You're so giving," gushes the Hoarder. "You're so good," says the Spender. But this mutual admiration society can turn sour before the ink's even dried on your marriage certificate. The Hoarder starts to feel insecure, the Spender starts squirreling away their purchases. Result? Anxiety, guilt, remorse, irritability . . . pop!

$olution: Since a Spender will be spending like crazy at the first sign of trouble, telling them to stop is not going to work. However, a spending plan will. Agree between you a responsible monthly amount. For the Hoarder who hates spending money, the Spender must attempt to take his or her fear out of spending. Not all gifts need to be expensive, you know?

To Have and To Hold
the Purse Strings

Merging money personalities is a priority, but my research (and that of others) knocks squarely on the head the myth of the silly, squandering wife who couldn't control a checkbook even if it was clasped tightly to her Kelly bag. For as well as making a substantial contribution to the money coming in, more often than not, it's today's wife who is the financial controller. She is the one deciding the terms on which money goes out. And, as John Fetto, research editor for *American Demographics*, says, "Their influence isn't confined to the aisles of Shop 'n' Save."

Although only 21 percent of Americans are married women, consumer spending data from Mediamark Research Inc. reveals that they represent a larger share of the population doing the spending in big ticket environments, environments which are typically regarded as male. For instance, 34 percent of all adults who spend $100 or more on cameras in a twelve-month period are married women. They also account for 35 percent of all adults who spend more than $500 on home improvements, 44 percent of all adults who spend more than $5,000 on domestic vacation and 35 percent of all adults who spent more than $6,000 on a foreign vacation. What's more, women influence at least 70 percent of all home-buying decisions, which is why builders and architects who value their future are now tailor-making homes with women's requirements in mind. (Apparently they're demanding low-maintenance perennial gardens, laundry rooms on the second floor so their kids can do their own washing and—get this—more Jacuzzis and—made-for-stand-up sex?—steam showers.)

But the reason they're holding the purse strings extends beyond today's wife's increased income levels and feelings of entitlement. Having spent, on average, a decade earning and spending her own money, making mistakes and resolving them, seeking solvency and starting savings plans, she's acquired a fiercely independent and responsible attitude toward finance. The appearance of that first wrinkle will not have her leaping into the arms of the nearest potential husband. Instead, she will seek out the smartest financial advisor who will remind her that people age eighty-five and over are the fastest growing sector of the economy and women make up the majority of that age group.

When a woman gets married, she's more likely than her husband to leave a freewheeling attitude about finance behind. And when talk turns to the more serious matter of saving and investment, she will not simply be an equal partner; more than likely, she will emerge as the dominant one, says Ginita Wall of the Women's Institute for Financial Education (WIFE), "with a more holistic approach to finance. So she'll look at all aspects of their financial life." In other words, how to save, how to spend, how to have fun with money. Women are more likely to consider how to make money work for them, rather than allowing money to control their lives.

Says Sabina, forty, "I pay the bills. I maintain the checking and savings accounts. I make all the deposits and withdrawals. I make sure the bills are paid on time. It was my decision. In the beginning of the marriage, my husband was doing some of the bills, but he did them incorrectly. He'd write a check and not record it or he wouldn't record it in the right place. Then I might find a bill in the drawer and realize he hadn't paid it so we'd incur extra charges. He also had a credit card I was unaware of and he was only paying the minimum fee so he would have to pay interest. So I told him I was going to be the financial caretaker. Then I had peace of mind because I knew it would be done properly. But I also make better decisions. I tend to have a more considered opinion and he tends to jump into decisions a bit quickly for my liking. It's important to explore the options."

Amy, thirty-two, agrees. "I'm better at dealing with money than Garry," she says. "He's very much of the attitude that you earn it, you spend it very quickly. So he'd get his money one day and it would be spent three days later, and then he'd wing it. I'm much more cautious about making money last. He's the dreamer and I'm the one who weighs up the financial implications and says whether we can afford to make the dreams happen or whether we have to wait. He relies on that. He feels free to keep coming up with ideas. No matter how zany they are, he knows it's a safe environment in which to do that. But I have the power of veto."

Dee does, too. She says, "I hold the purse strings. I'm more responsible with money. I tend to look at the big picture, so I'm in charge of the money and investing. I'm a big researcher. I feel like the father." Says Kath, thirty-three, "I am the decision maker. I control all the money, like he's a child with an allowance. He tips out all his money to me and I give him cash on a daily basis, like I'm the father." April, forty-three, says, "I have to take more control over our money. I don't want to be the person to say no, but someone has to. I'm a saver, he's a spender, so I must be 'the guy' in the relationship."

Hear that? Stereotypes are certainly hard to shake off. After all, it was only ten years ago that two-thirds of women didn't know how a mutual fund worked. And just a decade ago, only half of married women were involved with their family's investment decisions (source: Oppenheimer Funds). It's a very different picture in 2002. Now 50 percent of women know how mutual funds work. Eighty-three percent are involved in saving and investing. Many more women than men become interested in investing due to a life event, such as the birth of a child. What's more, they're more successful at it. (In a University of California study of thirty-five thousand investors, women outperformed men by an annual average of 1.4 percent.)

Emily's a typical example. She says, "I take care of the investments. I'll usually do the reconnaissance and find out what our options are and present Mark with 'This is what I think we should do'—and make sure he agrees!"

Lynne, thirty, is classic, too. The third most important man in her life . . . actually make that the *fourth* most important man in her life after Jonathon, her father and her slinky Siamese, Dude, is her financial advisor. Although financial advisors used to be the exclusive domain of the rich (those with assets over $150,000) and elderly, increasing numbers of women today are plugging into their services. In fact, women are more likely to use financial advisors than men, by a good 10 percent (source: *Money* magazine and Oppenheimer Funds Women and Investing survey).

Yes, women are less likely to be financial risk-takers than men (32 percent of women label themselves conservative investors compared with 22 percent of men. Source: National Association of Investors). But financial experts today say women are *responsible* risk takers who are less likely to act on a hot tip and take more time (40 percent more time than men) to investigate before they invest (source: Conde Nast). Plus, once they decide on their investment strategy, they're less likely than men to run like headless chickens. Instead, they stick with their choices, thereby paying less in brokerage (source: University of California Davis).

This success has dramatically changed the landscape of financial service. Ten years ago, you'd be hard-pressed to find a financial institution that catered to women; now it's tough to find one that doesn't. But, according to the women I talked to, there's a long way to go. Financial services are still male-oriented, focus on women's supposed shortcomings and send deeply patronizing messages to potential female customers. I mean, I like a good body lotion as much as the next person, but I cringed at the Capital One Bank credit card promotion that attempted to woo women applicants with ten dollars worth of beauty products and the chance to produce plastic bearing pictures of puppies. I opted for a bank that took the time to talk with me about their premium savings plans, investment opportunities and offered a bank card bearing great big twenty-dollar bills.

Says Rob Densen from Oppenheimer Funds, whose 1992 and 2002 survey I have quoted extensively and shamelessly, "Women are no longer a gender, they're individuals." Hmmm . . . but individuals who remain back of the mind, nevertheless.

Take Amy, thirty-two, married for ten years. She says, "Until this year, Garry didn't have a bank account. He paid for everything in cash. It's only recently he bought into my way of dealing with money so I decided to add his name to my account, which I've had since I was eighteen. Although the bank was happy to add his name, they wanted me to change my name from Morgan to his name, Nesbitt. I wouldn't. I would never change my name. I'm Amy Morgan. Then they were going to put Garry on as Mr. Morgan. So I had to say, 'Look, can we just start again? I want Mr. Garry Nesbitt to be added to Ms. Amy Morgan's account.' I tried not to lose my temper and just take the broken record approach. Finally, they got it. But when they sent out the new checkbooks, his name came *before* mine. I was furious. *And* he receives our assessments before me. I mean, not only do I earn more than he does, it was *my* account. I *let* him join *my* account. Financial institutions still automatically assume the husband controls the finances. It makes me furious."

I wish I could write about Amy's experience as an isolated incident. But two days later, I'm talking to Linda and she tells me a similar tale. "I ended up storming into the bank one day. I'd been called four times by different people who couldn't get it into their heads that I wanted my name on the checkbook, the name I was born with, and I also wanted my name to come first. I'm sure they thought I was this raging feminist. I'm not. I'm just someone who wants what's fair and right. And I want what I want."

Anabelle's the same. "I want to be called 'Ms.' and I know that grates with a lot of people, it even grates with me. I'm very aware that when you describe yourself as Ms., you give a certain impression to strangers, but I'm quite insistent about it." So after insisting over and over she wanted Ms. Anabelle Brooks and Mr. Peter Pomerantz on their new bank card, they finally agreed. "But when we got our new bank card," says Anabelle, "they had put Mr. Peter Pomerantz and Mrs. Anabelle Brooks. I could have left it, but I just rang up and asked them to send me a new card because I said this sounds like I'm married to my dad! I absolutely hated it."

Dian recalls an infuriating meeting with a financial planner who practically ignored her. "Ollie, my husband, doesn't have a clue about investments. I know more, but I'm not an expert. What made me really crazy was that I'd done some research before our meeting. I wanted to be able to ask intelligent questions and know whether I was being bullshitted. But although I was the one asking the questions, this guy directed everything toward Ollie. He barely looked at me."

Is it any wonder 54 percent of American women believe financial institutions still treat women with less respect than men (source: Oppenheimer Funds)? Their ideal client may be nonconfrontational, reluctant to be assertive, accepting of tradition; someone who gets a lump sum and asks not to be bothered with the details and makes no demands on their time or procedures. But, says feisty Ginita Wall (WIFE.org), "That's the old style of women with money. There aren't enough airhead heiresses out there to satisfy them. It's hard to sell to women because they demand more information and they're more cautious. What I hear from brokers is 'Women ask too many damn questions.'" Damn right.

THE HITCHED CHICK'S GUIDE TO
Finding a Financial Advisor

Says Dian, "After my awful experience with a financial advisor I almost gave up. But I was interested in investing and basic savings accounts don't offer a significant return. Eventually, I asked my firm's lawyer, who put me in touch with his guy." Personal recommendations are always advisable, but they may not suit *your* needs. Here's how to find one that does:

+ *Know* that financial advisors can mean different things depending on who's using it. Brokers, accountants, insurance agents all call themselves financial advisors.

+ *Ask* yourself why you want help: is it for broad, everyday financial advice or for a single purpose, such as retirement or a college fund for your kids? A financial advisor is someone you could turn to for advice on a whole range of short-term and long-term investments.

+ *Seek* personal recommendations. Alternatively, check out the Financial Planning Association—www.fpanet.org—or the National Association of Financial Advisors—www.napfa.org.

+ *Book* a meeting with at least three advisors to gauge your comfort level with each. Says Ginita Wall, "Don't be afraid to ask about their other clients. It's best to choose an advisor who has clients like you."

+ *Brush up* on the basic lingo—mutual funds, hedge funds, portfolio, small/medium/large risk, capitalization, blue chip.

✦ *Note* the following: Do they ask you detailed questions about your financial situation and expectations? (They should.) Do they clearly explain the risks associated with each investment option? (They should.) Do they work on a fixed fee-based or commission-based system? (Answer: Hmm, tricky one, but a fee-based system, especially if you want to invest $100,000 or less, is your best option, says Ginita Wall, and it guards against conflict of interest.) What is the cost of their services? (Answer should be between 1.5 percent to 2.5 percent of the total value of your assets.)

✦ *Request* a financial plan with an investment policy agreement; a monthly statement, summarizing all transactions and current positions; quarterly and annual reports outlining realized and unrealized gains or losses, and fees/commissions; clear and full explanations of any transactions and fees. Keep all correspondence in a file.

✦ *Walk* away if: the advisor makes extravagant promises, such as double-digit returns; tries a hard-sell approach; bases advice on less than ten years of investment returns; claims fund or insurance companies are paying their bills/commissions; discourages you from checking their background; pushes you to make a quick decision; leaves you with a bad gut feeling.

✦ *Double-check* your advisor's credentials. A licensed professional will be registered with the National Association of Securities Dealers. Go to their website—www.nasdr.com—and look into your prospective advisor's Disclosure Events file, which will contain records of dubious dealings.

Here Comes the
Br . . . eadwinner

Sexual predators, boardroom ball-busters, financial controllers . . . all titles which have traditionally been associated with men. Add another to the list: sole breadwinner. Now it's a title and role increasingly applicable to women. Although American polls estimate the number of stay-at-home dads hovers around the two million mark (that's quadrupled since 1986), no absolute figures exist on numbers of childless husbands who stay at home while their wives work. However, a 2002 U.K. survey, entitled "Farewell then Macho Man, New Man, Lad and New Lad," claimed one in ten men have a partner who is the main or only breadwinner. In fact, two-thirds of the surveyed twenty-four- to thirty-five-year-old men said their goal in life was to achieve "a stress-free existence" (ha!) and 42 percent said earning a lower wage than their partner made no difference to whether they felt like a "real man." Hmm . . . I'll talk more about that later when we come to the prickly subject of power. But, significantly, nearly half of women questioned said they were willing to keep their partners in the manner to which they had become accustomed, with one in five enjoying the fact that their financial status gave them freedom to have more say on what they spent their cash on.

However, my research reveals that for many Hitched Chicks, being the main breadwinner is a double-edged sword. While many do indeed accept the responsibility of sole provider, they dislike the extra pressure it puts on them in a world where jobs-for-life cease to exist, and they demand reciprocity. The majority of breadwinning wives say "keeping their men" is not out of choice. "I have financial freedom anyway," says Lynne. "That's just how it is today. But I haven't worked hard through college and in my career just to let Jonathon coast when he wants to. I want to see the fruits of my labor in terms of high standard of living, lots of travel and foreign vacations. We own our apartment, thanks mainly to me, but I don't want to live here forever. I want a bigger and better place in the future. Keeping my husband is not a status symbol."

Says thirty-nine-year-old Connie, "When we first got married, Keith was working and making a good salary. I enjoyed that. It felt like we were a team. Now he's not bringing in any money, I'm the one funding our marriage. And he doesn't have the motivation to go and get a job. Every single idea I bring up, there's a reason why it's not good enough. He doesn't want to do something below him. Even though I don't think I'd ever *not* work, I am disappointed that I've ended up having to take care of him."

Ellis, forty-three, feels the same. "Although I would never give up work and be supported, I found his Boss suit and amazing job with all its perks an attractive quality," she says referring to her first encounter with Jonah four years ago. "So I fell in love with a guy with a posh job and a posh suit and now he's an art student. It wasn't in the program."

As much as we love our husbands, and we will step up to the breadwinning responsibility when necessary, we are not willing to sacrifice all our money for them. Says Ellis, "When Jonah decided to go to art college, we talked about having a joint account. And I just thought, No, I'm not getting all muddled up in that, because I'm really clear that although I would support him if he runs out of money, I don't want to. And I don't want him to think, Oh, Ellis can bail me out, she can rescue me. I don't want to rescue him and I don't think it's a particularly good dynamic. You become a mother figure and I don't want to be taken for granted."

Being taken for granted is what breadwinning wives most resist. "If we had a child," says Lynne, "I'd be happy for Jonathon not to go out to work. But until such a time, I want him out there, finding a job, earning some money so I don't feel like I'm the only one putting in the effort."

Says Eve, thirty-four, whose husband has been out of work for seven months, "David and I have had a tough time with this one. He said to me not long ago, 'You have a problem with the fact that your father was the breadwinner and your mother stayed at home. Isn't this reversal what women wanted? Isn't *this* what feminists fought for?' I almost hit him! I said my father didn't want my mother to work. He wanted her to stay at home and cook him dinner and iron his shirts. She didn't really have any choice. Plus, she wasn't qualified for anything. I have a problem with the fact that my mother didn't have a dime she could call her own. *That's* my problem. I said to him, 'You have a choice.' As for him ironing my shirts, you must be kidding. He does a bit more of the cooking, but he doesn't iron."

Does Eve feel taken for granted? "I don't think he's taking me for granted—yet," she says. "I won't allow myself to be taken for granted. But I could see how it could end up that way. My mother never took my father for granted because she lived in fear he would leave and she'd be destitute. But men aren't programmed to think that way. They have a much greater sense of entitlement than women and certainly our mothers ever had. I mean, I'm sure it hasn't entered David's head that I might leave him if he doesn't get a job soon. I probably won't, but if I did, he'd know with his ability he could always find some sort of decent-paying work. And that's my point!"

I agree wholeheartedly with Eve. While our fathers were forging their careers, our mothers were pulling more than their weight around the house. And they continued to do so if they worked outside the home, too. There was no question about loafing around the house. And as we know, most felt too guilty about spending their husbands' money on basics, never mind frittering it away on themselves. Had they done so, their husbands would have felt perfectly entitled to leave their "bad" wives. And those "bad" wives would generally have ended up on welfare, being under-qualified, under-experienced and under-resourced for child care to get a half-meaningful job.

If the hitched chick is chief breadwinner while her husband stays home to look after the children, the taken-for-granted theme subsides. Most fathers step up to their child-rearing responsibilities with gusto, which also requires keeping the house hygienic and stocking the fridge (even if it is full of pizzas). In fact, a 2000 survey by *Christianity Today International/Marrriage Partnership* magazine reveals 43 percent of women are extremely satisfied with their stay-at-home dad situation; 51 percent of men are, too. The survey also reveals that the second-biggest reason couples took the decision to reverse these traditional roles was because the wives made more money. Not wanting to put their children into day care was the number-one reason.

Says Pat, thirty-eight, a lawyer, "It became abundantly clear that my capacity to earn big money was greater than Mike's. And I was much more ambitious. I actually like my job. But we had a rocky settling-in period when he first started to look after our son, and we spent time figuring out the finances. Now I put a set amount into his account for him to spend on whatever he wants, and, plus, there's always the joint account, and I keep my own. There are times when Mike will do something that I don't agree with or, as he says, doesn't match my standards. But on the whole, it works well. I feel we're both doing our best. And that's important when you're a team."

She's right. It's the issue of lack of reciprocity that causes the conflict in nontraditional hitched couples' homes. Says Niki, thirty-five, "Ron has been unemployed for a year. He used to earn more than me, but we always split everything fifty-fifty. Now I pay for everything. He doesn't mind being unemployed, but I *do* mind his being unemployed. But it's not so much about the money, it's more that he isn't even trying to reciprocate. There seems to be a lot of women out there right now, for whatever reason, supporting men. And at the very least, you hope you're gonna get dinner when you come home or see some effort made. I still come home and empty the cat litter even though he's been at home all day. Because the financial burden has changed, I believe the balance of the relationship should also change."

Lynne says, "After three months, I told Jonathon that he shouldn't assume I'm going to subsidize him forever. He has to get a job at some point, even if it means working in McDonald's. Until he does, I told him he should think of me like a bank. Yes, there's money there, but it has to be paid back later. I won't go so far as to ask for interest—although I've been tempted—but I am not a money tree. My support needs to be reciprocated one day. But so long as I know he's out there every day looking for work, making the effort, I'm okay about it for now."

It's a conversation Niki wishes she'd had sooner with Ron. "When he was first unemployed, he started going to school. The first semester was paid for by our tax return, which was half my money, but I said, 'You take it.' And then he had unemployment for a few months so that paid for the next semester. And the most recent semester was paid for by this year's taxes. He's supposed to go for a summer semester, but the only way he can do that now is for me to actually borrow out of my retirement fund and I wasn't going to do that. I was done. So he had to drop out of school. Now *he* has to come up with some way to pay for it."

Niki believes she has sacrificed enough since she does not see any desire from her husband to reciprocate. She says, "At this point, we can't go on vacations, we can't go to the movies. I mean, I need a new pair of shoes and I shouldn't have to think about it *this* hard. I wasn't going out as much and now I'm not going out at all. No more manicures, no more haircuts. I'm eating noodles for lunch and he didn't notice any change in his own life until the time he has to drop out of school. He's a lovely guy, but I am not going to give up my life's security or retirement money for him. I suddenly thought, What the hell am I getting for it? Now I'm going to take the bigger half of the apple, because I earned it."

When effort and responsibility are reciprocated, says Ellis, your relationship can be the stuff of which marriage manuals are made. "At first, we both felt a bit resentful. I was resentful of Jonah because he wasn't working and had decided to become a student. And I was pissed off I might have to support us both when his redundancy payment runs out. Then one day he said *he* was resentful because he was doing everything in the house since we got rid of the cleaner when he lost his job. It's true, he was doing all the shopping and the cleaning and all the cooking. So I said, 'Let's negotiate this.' I know if I were doing it all, I would resent it. So I gave him some money, a couple of hundred. Because what he was getting was loads of domestic responsibility and what I was getting was no time to do anything, but loads of money, it seemed a way of equaling it out. You have to be open to saying, 'Okay, let me do something for you since you're doing something for me.' " As they say in tennis when advantage is shared: Love all.

Hitched Chick's Dirty Little Money Secret

I love my husband," says Maria, thirty-four, who prefers I keep her real name firmly under wraps. "And I know he loves me, but the economy and love don't go together. I don't like it, but that's how it is. I came into my marriage with more money than Alex. My parents are fairly wealthy, but they worked hard for their money and often they will give me money. But do I tell Alex? No. You always need to have a 'black fund'; it's your final bit of security if the marriage falls apart."

Call it black fund, call it personal protection money, call it a dream fund, call it private nest egg, call it what you want . . . many women I spoke to confessed they had one.

And their husbands have no idea. (Even if they don't have a private stash, a study by the U.K. financial institution Abbey National revealed women are increasingly secretive about how much they earn. One in ten men said they had no idea how much their partner earned, compared to just one in twenty women who claimed to be kept in the dark.)

Although the idea of pre-nuptial and post-nuptial agreements seem sound enough, they lose their charm when the lawyers get involved (which, of course, they must to make it legally watertight). What's more, the cost of putting a pre-nup in place can run into thousands which, for many wives, is more than the assets they want to protect.

Says Maria, "I don't have millions. Nowhere near that. But I started to think seriously about my money after the first year of our marriage. Alex's parents are not wealthy and they expect their kids to help them out. I was willing to help them at first, but then they started to play with me. One minute they're saying they won't take my money. The next minute, they're moaning because they don't have any money and they're trying to make me feel bad. Then they're wanting us to buy a bigger place so they can come and live with us. It's like they resent my money and don't want any of it, then they resent me and can't see why I won't buy a bigger apartment so they can live with us. It's caused a lot of problems between me and Alex."

Increasing arguments and a desire to protect her parents' generous financial gifts started to cause concerns. "I'm their only child," says Maria. "They want to give me money even though I work. But when they give me money, Alex feels guilty he isn't helping his parents more, and then we fight. So now I've stopped telling him when they give me money. I put it away in my black fund. It's there if we ever really need a large sum. But really, it's there in case anything happens to us. I never declare it, no one knows about it. If we did get divorced, it would never come into it. He couldn't touch it and his family couldn't either. That's very, very important to me."

Gemma, thirty, has her own little nest egg. During our interview, I ask her how she feels having given up work to take care of her four-year-old son. She loves it, she says, but admits not having her own money makes her feel vulnerable. "I don't have money I can truly call my own," she sighs, ". . . well, not strictly legitimately." Gemma tells me, "I married Peter at twenty-four, almost as soon as we left college. And we started a family immediately. Money isn't an issue as Peter earns a good salary at the law firm where he works. Like most couples, we have our ups and downs, and we went through a really rocky patch three years ago. During a particularly nasty fight, Peter told me to leave, but that he'd see to it I wouldn't get a cent. He later apologized—he couldn't believe he'd said such a thing—and we've been fine for the past year. But since that moment, I realized how vulnerable I was, and, between you and I, I now stash away money into a private account. Just fifty dollars here and seventy dollars there. Not much at a time, but it mounts up. It isn't enough to live on for long if I ever did leave Peter, but it would be enough for the short term, until I got a job," Gemma says, and then laughs. "Or until I took him to the cleaners in a divorce settlement!"

Gemma's strategy may be misguided even in the unfortunate event of a divorce. After all, from the moment they legally separate, Peter would be required to support his wife and child until a settlement was agreed. However, the stark facts are that, even today, the average woman's standard of living drops as much as 45 percent in the year following divorce while a man's rises 15 percent (source: Long Island University). So misguided, maybe. But Gemma's anxiety has valid grounds.

Says Moira, thirty-three, a beauty technician whose husband is an alcoholic, "I don't tell Jimmy how much I make in tips. We have a joint account, although I control it. But sometimes I wonder what would happen if we split up. He's unemployed right now and if we divorced, I might have to support him. I put my tips—about one hundred dollars a week—in an account in my mother's name. If it was ever discovered, I'd just say I'd given her money as a gift. But it's my safety net. I feel better knowing it's there when I'm feeling depressed."

Sally, thirty-one, feels neither vulnerable nor depressed. But, she says, "I've always, *always* had a little stash. Even at college. I might have a bit of birthday money, leftover foreign currency or if I return something to a store, I might put the refund into the account. Once it's in there, it's never touched. I've been really short for cash at times, but I've never been *that* desperate. In fact, because I've never touched it, it makes me even more determined to leave it that way and cut corners in other areas. I don't keep the account for any sinister reasons. But it's just something I keep to myself and when I remember it, I get a nice, warm feeling knowing it's there in case of a disaster. I'm not thinking about divorce. I don't *think* he would divorce me, but I guess you can never really know."

Says Maria, "You can never *really* know. And at the end of the story, it's *always* about money."

THE HITCHED CHICK'S GUIDE TO
Money Management

You never know what will happen to your marriage. In the event it does fall apart (or God help us, your husband dies), you'll need to be super-savvy and have your personal and financial details at your fingertips. In the event it doesn't, well, it never hurts to know exactly what you have—and where. Here's what to have locked in a secure drawer:

- All your bank account numbers—personal and joint checking and savings accounts
- Social Security numbers
- Insurance policies—life, house, car and health
- Credit card numbers and emergency telephone numbers for lost or stolen cards, plus a year's worth of statements
- Bank statements, spanning five years
- Investment/mutual fund/brokerage numbers and account statements
- All tax return forms and W2 forms for the past seven years
- Lawyers' details—telephone, address, fax and e-mail
- Mortgage statements/lease agreements
- Utility bills (gas, electricity, telephone, cable, etc.)
- Loan statements and agreements
- Retirement account statements
- Copy of your will (keep the original with your lawyer)

And if you haven't done so already:

- Get actively involved in your financial decision making and visit your financial advisor together.
- Bank together and separately.
- Have some assets in your name, both jointly, like your house, and individually, such as savings and investments.
- Set aside an emergency fund—preferably the equivalent of six months' of household expenses.
- Keep a credit card in your own name. Use it, but clear the bill every month.
- Balance your investment strategies—experts call it diversification, otherwise known as not putting all your eggs in one basket.
- Assess your insurance coverage. If you're both working and have no kids, you don't need life insurance. But always ensure you have adequate home, health, car and disability insurance.
- Write a will each. *Now.*

4.

Infidelity

I have this friend who became my Fuck Buddy. We'd been talking and I said, "It's been so long since I had sex, how long has it been for you?" and it turned out he wasn't getting any either. So we negotiated it. I made it clear I wasn't leaving my husband for him, but then it became complicated. I stopped it because he started seeing us as having a real relationship and I couldn't reciprocate.

—*Patsy, thirty-four*

An unfaithful man is one thing, an unfaithful woman is quite something else. Even today. When a man has an affair, no one is *that* surprised. Not really. It doesn't matter who he is—the president, the mayor, the CEO, the bank manager, the schoolteacher, hell, even the rabbi—it's how men are. We may not like it, but, hey, he's a man. He can't control his biological urge to spread his seed and create replicas of himself. He's irresistibly drawn to beautiful women. It's beyond his genetic capacity to deny himself. He's a cad, a charmer, a player, a naughty boy.

In many ways, he's to be admired. After all, it takes *stamina* to satisfy two women at once. It requires *cunning* to outmaneuver obligation. He must be *wealthy* to woo another woman and console a tetchy wife with treats. And are women not always being told we should compartmentalize, detach, not feel so damn guilty about everything? It's a man's ability to do so that provides him with an effective coping mechanism when he cheats. These *positive* male characteristics also earn respect, skyrocket careers, win wars.

When a woman has an affair, it rocks the very foundations of society. It doesn't just threaten the status quo, it destroys it completely. She's rejecting her husband. Hot damn. She's compromising her children's well-being and security. Bad mama. She's putting her desires first. Selfish slut. She's turning her back on all those female virtues— loyalty, conscience, dependability, sensitivity, patience, commitment, caring—which society relies on during times of despair. So long as half the population continues to uphold and demonstrate these values, we can just about cope with anything. Death, destruction, you name it. It's a huge responsibility, of course. And we self-righteously shoulder it. Little wonder a woman who unburdens herself and, even for just one hasty moment, rejects or forgets her responsibilities is condemned. She hasn't just betrayed her husband, her children and her friends (who will be furious with her because she's committed the double sin of infidelity *and* nondisclosure). She's also betrayed womankind. When a woman has an affair, what *is* the world coming to?

Some use anthropological theories to justify our attitudes. According to those who have studied the animal kingdom, males who are less discriminating and more promiscuous are more successful in passing on their genes than those who are highly selective and less promiscuous. For females, however, their sexual selection theory goes that those who are most concerned with securing a single mate fit to take care of a family are more likely to reproduce successfully.

Some evolutionary psychologists suggest another profound difference which may explain our historic acceptance of the cheating male stereotype. Upon learning of her impregnation, a female knows she has been successful in propagating her genetic material. However, her male partner can't be so sure. The precise moment of fertilization can't be determined. And until the recent arrival of paternity testing, the source of the sperm couldn't be either. So what's a male to do? Best he attempts to impregnate lots of females to increase his chances of success.

But hang on a sec. That might have been justification when we were trotting through rain forests, attempting to produce multiple offspring in the event of starvation when we could either eat them, send them off scavenging for food (five will be more successful than one) or rely on them to assure the survival of the species should we snuff it. But if we continue to use animal studies to justify human behavior, should we not all be within our rights to defecate where we like (or perhaps just along the boundaries of our property)? We would, after all, be marking our territory just like animals. Or let's all sniff each other's bottoms in public to determine family background. What's wrong with that? After all, that's what animals do, right?

A woman isn't even supposed to fart among friends, never mind stick her nose up a stranger's ass, which is precisely where these scientific theories should be laid to rest. Unless, that is, we're willing to give as much credence to a 2001 study by the University of California, which suggests it's also physiologically advantageous for *females* to sleep around. Biologists have discovered that female prairie dogs, sand lizards and field crickets mate with many males, and the promiscuous females in such species often produce larger and healthier litters than those who mate with fewer males.

See, whatever our behavior, we can use carefully selected biological studies to substantiate it. But, says Professor of Animal Ecology Tim Clutton-Brock of Cambridge University, England, "Many exceptions have been found to challenge the idea of the coy female and ardent male. It doesn't destroy the principle, but it does mean we have to be careful about how we generalize about sexual behavior." *Hall-oo* to that.

Monogomy?
Schmonogamy!

So what *has* the world come to? What the world has come to is a place where nothing should be presumed. Not even female virtue. A woman cannot be relied upon to stay at home and keep quiet about her unhappiness. You cannot depend on her to sacrifice her intelligence, her needs or sexual desires. Society cannot expect a woman to conduct herself according to an outdated stereotype. What we can expect, however, is that a woman's behavior today will be very different from her behavior yesterday. *That* you can presume.

Our increasing exposure to the world results in increasing opportunities and confidence to experiment with all its dimensions. The more diverse our experiences, the less we are able to categorize, and the more we're knocked, the less sensitive we become to suffering. And our increasing survival capacity means we're more likely to take risks.

Says Carmen, thirty-seven, "We lived in the country and my mother stayed home. She was very protected from the outside world. Some days, she didn't speak to another soul. She seemed happy enough, I think. But if she wasn't, there wasn't much she could do about it. She didn't have her own money. She didn't meet anyone. Even if she'd wanted to have an affair, she wouldn't have met anyone to have an affair with. So I just don't think it ever crossed her mind. It's different for me. Every day, I'm exposed to temptation. On my way to work, I'm being tempted to buy something I shouldn't, I'm being tempted to change the TV channel I usually watch, I'm being tempted to swap my car. Sometimes I'm being tempted to swap my husband."

Says Jill, thirty-five, "From the day my mother got married, my mother hardly spoke to another man, except my brother and maybe the postman and the guy at the store. Women just didn't meet men in the way they do now. They rarely went out to work. If they did, they'd probably work with other women. Their boss was probably a man, but he would have five hundred women to choose from. And women certainly didn't have male friends. But me, I work with lots of guys. A lot of them are assholes, but some of them are really great guys, they're my friends, too. I love my husband, but I often wonder, What if? I wonder what he's like in bed. I mean, if I knew Lloyd would never find out, I think I would be tempted to give it a try. My mother would be appalled at the idea. She's quite self-conscious with men. But I don't care. I'm comfortable with men. And when they see that, you can tell what they're thinking. And sometimes, they're right."

Says Lola, thirty, "You know, all these guys bitch about the shackles and their ball and chain. And I'm like, 'Hel-*lo-o*, the same applies to me! When a hot man walks down the street, you think I don't want to *jump* him?'"

Perhaps today's wives are more naive than they should be about their parents' fidelity. I'm thinking of the hit movie *The Ice Storm*, based on Rick Moody's award-winning book set in the 1970s, which portrayed parents as well as children floundering in the backwash of the sexual revolution. We may not like to think of our mothers having sex—especially having sex with someone other than our father—but even when Alfred Kinsey conducted his famous relationship studies in the 1940s and fifties, he concluded that one half of men and a quarter of women had extramarital affairs.

So believing that female infidelity is a new phenomenon is not accurate. However, our greater acceptance of it and increasing opportunities are, which may explain the recent studies that reveal about half of *all* married people—men *and* women alike—are unfaithful. In a 2001 survey by the U.K. magazine *She*, one in sex . . . er, six married women said she'd be unfaithful if she could guarantee her partner would never find out. Ten percent admitted to having an affair as they were filling in the *She* questionnaire.

The advent of HIV and AIDS may have made monogamy the smart (and stylish) sexual choice of the eighties, but its dictatorship was short-lived. Condom manufacturers rose to the occasion and proved it was still possible, if we desired, to sleep with multiple partners. By the early nineties, everyone with half a brain was carrying and using rubbers. Since heterosexual women had more to fear given that their chances of contracting the virus are higher than heterosexual men (vaginal walls being easily chafed or torn, providing a sensitive entry point for infection), they were the ones ditching the Pill and taking on the condom-using and buying responsibility. But not just singles, marrieds, too. And they had tons to choose from.

Suddenly, there was an explosion of flavored, ribbed and colored condoms. There were even musical condoms which, at the point of ejaculation, burst into a squeaky rendition of the Beatles' classic, *Love Me Do*. Cheeky, saucy, highly hilarious! Sex was fun again. And so were affairs. Some of them, anyway. At the very least, they didn't have to kill you. And in making the effort to prevent the spread of a deadly virus, there was an added bonus with condom-ease: indiscretions were less likely to be discovered via the sudden appearance of genital herpes, for instance, or warts.

If Hitched Chick wasn't married then, she was cutting her teeth in the sexual playground. We've already discussed she's likely to have had far more than a handful of lovers—counting them off will involve toes as well as fingers—and generally enjoyed, even relished, the experience. However, she'll also have emerged with the view that the one-man-for-every-woman theory is shortsighted . . .

Says Dee, twenty-nine, "It's a Hollywood fable."

Agrees Alexandra, twenty-eight, "You're not fated to be with just one person. There are several people who you can create a wonderful

life with. I feel like there could be any number of soul mates.'"
(Alexandra's assessment is reinforced by the *She* survey, which
reveals that one in four married women have met Mr. Right *since* they
got married, with women over thirty-one more likely to feel this way.)

Linda, thirty-four, says, "Like many of my friends, I had long
relationships with quite a few guys before I met my husband. I didn't
marry them not because there was anything wrong with them, but the
timing was all wrong. But my mother didn't have that experience.
She was married by the time she was twenty-four. My father was her
first real boyfriend. So my mother didn't get to see that while there
are a lot of guys you wouldn't ever want to be with, there are also a lot
you could have a very nice life with. That affects you and your view
of marriage. You realize that if you're not getting what you need from
your husband, it's not the end of the line. There are plenty more men
out there who *will* give you what you need. And I don't mean just
after divorce. An affair is always possible."

"Listen," says Shauneice, thirty-six, "I've come really close to
cheating. It wouldn't surprise me if Chester had, too. You have to
know it's a possibility. After all, we're only human. Being with the
same person twenty-four/seven is hard. There are times you just
can't stand to be next to that person. Marriage is not about living
happily ever after. You hope it will be, but you don't really believe
that. I think everyone has different limits. What may make me have
an affair wouldn't necessarily make someone else have an affair. I
don't care who you are, you can never say never."

Sam, thirty-six, says, "I worry, like anyone else does, that I will
eventually want to go and have sex with someone else, just for variety's sake. Not because I don't love Ray, but just for another body,
another being. I don't believe there's anyone in the world who hasn't
worried about the same thing. When we were getting married, I
remember all these things flashed through my mind. That I was going
to be spending the rest of my life with this one person scared the shit

out of me. It still scares the crap out of me. And because I'm a naturally flirtatious person, generally I can just talk to a guy about a game of pool and I can tell he's attracted to me. And I start thinking, Oh my. . . . So I can't sit here and say I'm never going to have sex with another person, because I might. I don't know. I'm not out there hunting, but it does go through my mind."

The view of the one-man woman is a fantasy, say Hitched Chicks. A fantasy of men. And the one-woman man? "The same applies," says Linda. "Except," she adds, "I think women have a much more realistic view about men. You know there's a chance a man will cheat on you. So many men do. But men are more complacent. They think, Oh, she'll never cheat on me. They're more arrogant, too. And when they look to their parents as role models, his father's more likely to have cheated than his mother. I think a lot of men expect their wives to be like their mothers, which we're very definitely not."

Do our expectations of monogamy change dramatically once children come along? Once there's more at stake? When our kids' wellbeing in all areas often takes priority over our own? The modern wife is conflicted.

Says Shauneice, thirty-six, "When you've just had a baby, you can't ever imagine doing anything to jeopardize your child's happiness. I felt very close to Chester then. Like we were bonded even more through the baby. I could not imagine ever cheating on him. But having a child brings its own stresses. After the first couple of months, you're exhausted. You start to fight more. The novelty's worn off and now it's down to the hard reality of responsibility. Even though you love your child more than absolutely anything, you're not as swept up in the fairy tale of it all. I would always think twice before having an affair. Maybe I'd think three times about it now that I have a child. But I still can't say I never, ever would."

Says Rae, forty-one, "Strangely, I came closer to having an affair after I'd had the baby. I think having a child makes you feel old and when you start to feel old, you think of ways to make yourself feel young again. You become vulnerable in ways you weren't before."

Amy, thirty-two, agrees. "You become very vulnerable to compliments from other men after you've had a baby and aren't feeling as attractive."

Rosie, thirty-three, says, "I became depressed. I think a lot of my depression stemmed from the fact that having a baby does not suddenly make your life wonderful. It's extremely hard work. There were days when I wanted to walk out of the door and never come back. I fantasized about being free. For me, an affair was a symbol of freedom. I didn't even think about the baby because the baby was part of the problem."

Says Dorotta, thirty-six, "If I've ever been tempted, the twins are my conscience. I think of them and I know I couldn't do it to them. Colin would get over it, I'm sure. But hurting the twins is something I couldn't live with."

Dorotta has reason to hold herself in check now that she has children. A 2001 survey conducted by the U.K.'s leading marital guidance organization, Relate, and *Candis* magazine revealed that those who had had affairs or observed them in others noted a range of negative effects on children, ranging from becoming withdrawn or aggressive to developing eating disorders.

Certainly, some women whose parents had affairs remain haunted by them. Says Rachel, twenty-eight, "My parents had lots of affairs. An affair—one or two—is fine, but there were *a lot*. I wish I didn't know about it, but my parents have no boundaries. And my mother told me they did it to get each other back, so they'd say, 'I don't care, I'm going to do it, too.' And that's not right. It just plain hurts. I think sometimes affairs happen and I'm willing to accept the possibility of them in my relationship, although I don't believe in them."

Lena, thirty, says, "My father had a mid-life crisis and met someone else. It's a very ugly story. I think he knew he was making a mistake, but he got tied up with someone who wouldn't let it go. It could have just been a fling, but she took action to make sure he couldn't go back to my mother. The other woman became pregnant, of course. It was so ugly. Ultimately, he married the other woman. My father broke my mother's heart and broke mine. I always felt very abandoned."

Says Leslie, thirty-four, "My father had an affair and I saw what it did to my mother. I remember the night she found out. I was eleven. She woke me up and sat on the edge of my bed, crying. It was awful. Terrible. I still remember to this day how it made me feel, like nothing was certain anymore. I was so angry with my father that he could do it to her and do it to me, too. He stopped seeing the other woman shortly afterward and my parents are really happy now—I think. But it really made me take off the rose-colored glasses and realize it can happen to anyone. Now I'm married, I know *how* it can happen. Yes," she sighs, "I *have* had an affair."

Affairs of the Heart?

There's a common myth about affairs: women seek out emotional attachments while men seek sexual thrills. The truth is, men and women generally have affairs for the same reason: because they crave intimacy. If a woman feels neglected, abandoned, disconnected, she will be vulnerable to a man who makes her feel valued and heard. Once valued and heard, she'll want to have sex with him. If a man feels neglected, abandoned or disconnected, chances are he will seek the physical reassurance of sex with another woman and *then* he'll feel valued and heard.

Take Trish, thirty-two. She says, "Jason worked incredibly long hours, sometimes on weekends, too. Often he'd arrive at home when

I was in bed. I tried staying up, but there was no point because he was too tired to talk when he got home. It got to the stage where I was living like a single woman. In the end, I stopped planning nights out together because he'd always call and say he was stuck at work, so I started going out alone with my girlfriends. They were pleased to have me back in the gang and I looked forward to our girls' nights out. It was on one of these nights I met Len. We were in a bar and he offered to buy me a drink. It sounds corny, but that's how it happened. But he was sweet and made me feel sexy. You know? He wasn't creepy at all. And I remember saying to him, 'You're not married, are you?' It's ironic because I was obsessed that he was a married man and yet *I* was the one married!"

Trish's affair came to a slow boil. "I didn't see him alone for ages. In fact, I didn't see him again for about three weeks after we'd first met," says Trish. "Even then, I kept my distance. I certainly wasn't looking to have an affair. But two months later, I said I'd meet him for lunch. I didn't know whether I'd turn up, but when I went to work, I made sure I looked good in case I decided to. In fact, I was really late for lunch. One minute, I was heading out the door, the next minute, I was back in my cubicle telling myself I was playing with fire. But in the end, I wanted to see whether he turned up, so my curiosity got the better of me. The thing is, if Len had been pushy, I would have left immediately. But he wasn't pushy at all. During the lunch I told him how much I loved Jason and he said Jason was a lucky guy. But during our second lunch, I really opened up to him. In fact, I had hardly seen Jason for two weeks. We were like ships in the night. And I told Len how lonely I felt. The next week, we went to the movies and that was it. We were like a couple of teenagers in the back row. Then we fooled around in his car. Later, we went back to his apartment and we had sex. It was wonderful because he was so attentive. I felt needed and sexy again. But guilt always got in the way. I felt so guilty about Jason, but I couldn't help myself. I think we had sex four or five times after that. Len became a drug. Everyone needs somebody to make them feel special and Len made me feel very special."

To this day, Jason has no idea about Trish's affair. Once his work schedule became less time-consuming, Trish says, "He started to want to spend time with me and the bottom line was, I really wanted to be with Jason, although the attention he started giving me took a while to get used to. He'd say, 'What's wrong, Trish?' And I'd say, 'You can't expect me to fall into your arms. I haven't seen you for months!' Len wasn't exactly okay about me breaking off with him either. I never gave him my home number, but he'd call me at work, sometimes twice in one day. Finally, I told him to stop calling. It was too difficult for me to cope with him and Jason. And for a while, I was very upset. It made it harder when Len said, 'I promise you will never hear from me again. But just know that I will always be here for you. If you ever change your mind . . . ' That was hard. It still is, but I really love Jason. And to make our marriage work, I have to concentrate on him and me now."

Had Jason discovered Trish's infidelity, conventional wisdom goes that he may not have worried about her emotional affection for Len, but would have hit the roof once he knew they were having sex. This wisdom goes back to those animal studies again: that a male's instinctive drive is to protect his chances of impregnating his partner. This theory is all well and good, but despite the fact that married women are more lust-driven than we've ever given them credit for, most women also need an emotional connection before they consider having sex. It's this emotional connection *plus* sex (which, during an affair, is often explosive and orgasmic, but more of this later) that poses the most threat to a marriage.

Women know this. And applying this perception to their husband's potential to cheat, wives claim they'd feel less threatened if their partners' affairs were based purely on sex than if love and emotions were involved. A stereotypical attitude to stereotypical behavior? Maybe. Stereotypes certainly seem to kick in when we *suspect* our partners of cheating. According to a report in the American Psychological Association's *Journal of Personality and Social Psychology*, men and women fall into distinct gender patterns of relationship protection. Psychologists David M. Buss, Ph.D., and Todd K. Shackleford, Ph.D., asked 214 people to describe the tactics they used to keep their mate. Men revealed they were more likely to leverage their social status and financial success. They were also likely to make promises to change. Women, on the other hand, were more likely to work on their appearance to keep their mate interested. However, smart women acknowledge that stereotypes are full of contradictions since they are contradicting stereotypes themselves by having affairs.

The *Janus Report on Sexual Behavior* states, "We found in our interviews that, regardless of their actual experience with extramarital affairs, interest in them runs high on the part of both men and women. Frequently, our respondents reported that the only impediment to an affair was the lack of appropriate circumstance or a lack of time. Old standards and demands for performance within marriage have changed; greater flexibility in lifestyle and more explicit expression of individual sexual values are now much more widely acceptable."

Some women I spoke with purposefully sought no-strings-attached affair sex. Knowing they were more than capable of looking after themselves financially and emotionally, they were not looking for deep, meaningful unions in the event their marriage fell apart. Some of them said that precisely because they already had "deep and meaningful" in their marriage, it was the last thing they wanted from an affair. What many say, even if they haven't had an affair, is they crave the rush they experienced at the start of their relationship with their husband. They desire passion, spontaneous sex, the thrill of the unexpected. As Leslie says, "the *not* knowing."

"I don't want anything more from Vic than sex," says Leslie. "When I met him, I was so frustrated with my husband who's kind, generous and we get on well out of the bedroom. But my sex drive was always higher than his, even at the start of our marriage. But as time went by, I started to feel like my husband was just having sex to please me. That's commendable, but it isn't fun. But at the same time, I just can't imagine my life without my husband. He's my best friend more than anything. And I was starting to hurt him. I was becoming spiteful just because we weren't having sex. I was picking on him and making him miserable because I was miserable. I just felt so frigging unattractive. I mean, if you can't get your husband to have sex with you, you feel like there's something wrong with you. Then Vic came along and I felt attractive again. He isn't someone I'd want to marry. God, no! But he is gorgeous and he makes me feel good. I don't think he'd want to marry me either. But that suits me fine. Once either of us stops experiencing pleasure and it becomes work, that's it. It's over. We have an agreement."

It's the same with Patsy, thirty-four. She says, "At the beginning of our marriage, Christian would always instigate sex. But he started to just not be available. I would ask for sex and he'd say, 'No, no, I'm too tired. No, I'm too busy. No, I'm too stressed.' I remember suggesting he should get his testosterone checked, but he wouldn't talk about it. I'd say, 'Look, let's talk about this. I feel like I have joined the convent and I'm having a hard time making peace with that.' But he just kept saying, 'I don't know, I don't know.' It was making me very upset every time I asked. Then he started making jokes. He developed this character, Rabbit Vagina, using his index and middle finger in a V-shape, like legs, and he'd wave them in the air and make this really funny sound whenever he said I'd 'get that look' in my eye." Patsy imitates a high-pitched squeak and we both laugh.

"Yeah, it's hilarious and it was actually a very funny character until I realized it was kind of insulting. Then I'd get upset. I was quietly going crazy, but I was squelching it. So when I spoke to my friend, we talked about having an affair because he wasn't getting any sex either. We said we could pretend we were Italian men, you know we'd have the whole marriage thing over here," says Patsy, pointing left, "and we'd have our little piece on the side over here," she says, pointing right. "So we said, 'Let's pretend we're in Rome!' It was understood I wasn't leaving Christian for him. He was just my fuck buddy. It lasted about a year. We'd see each other for sex about once a month. But the reason I stopped it was because he started to want a relationship."

Says Dawn, thirty-four, whose two brief affairs—one with a coworker at a conference, the other with an ex-boyfriend—ended because she desired nothing more than sex, "Both were short-lived because, in both instances, he wanted more. To me, they were just flings. To them, it was love, or so they said. That's the thing. Men assume if you even have a quick kiss, you want to get married and have their babies. They're wrong. Sometimes a woman just wants to have sex with someone else."

When *Is* Three a Crowd?

We're all familiar with the Benny Hill cliché where the lonely housewife appears in nothing but a nylon negligee and drags the milkman indoors by his collar. "One large full cream, missus?" he asks. "Oooh, don't mind if I do!" An absolute scream and so simple, so long as the neighbors aren't nosing through the net curtains.

Increased opportunities to be unfaithful and a greater ease with sexuality (as well as the prevalence of new devices—such as mobile phones, e-mail and the Internet—with which to conduct relationships) results in a blurring of boundaries and a muddying of definitions. For those who teeter on the edge, it's a challenge to know whether they *are* committing a genuine indiscretion. If discovered, it's easier to declare innocence. For those who sense a betrayal by their spouse, proof is less attainable and more confusing.

For every woman I asked the question "What constitutes an affair?" I received an entirely different answer. For some, most definitely a one-night stand. For others, kissing and holding hands. For others, face-to-face emotional disclosure. And then there are those for whom no physical presence needs to take place at all, the mere meeting of minds in cyberspace is enough to shatter trust.

Says Lena, thirty, "Flirting with an ex-boyfriend or -girlfriend constitutes unfaithful behavior."

Says Gabrielle, thirty-two, "I don't think there has to be sexual contact for it to be an infidelity. If there was someone at Murray's work or someone I hadn't met and he was having lots of sexual fantasies about them, that would be an infidelity."

Argues, Dee, twenty-nine, "But I *have* fantasized about having sex with other people. Doesn't everybody? It's totally harmless."

Says Petra, thirty-seven, "For me, infidelity is sexual or physical contact with another person."

"Kissing, holding hands, anything physical," says Paulette, thirty-eight.

"If Tim had an affair, I think I'd want to vomit," says Patti, thirty-four. "If he had a one-night stand with someone, I don't think I'd want to know, although I would regard that as being unfaithful. But if he was in love with someone else, then I'd want to know."

Says Dawn, thirty-four, "I agree. I had a one-night stand and I didn't think that was having an affair. An affair is more than sex. You really have to worry when love is involved."

Kath, thirty-three, says, "When I think about being unfaithful it's about having a happier relationship with somebody else, as opposed to sex."

Says Shauneice, thirty-six, "It's so hard to define. I think sex is the dividing line, but what if you're talking dirty to someone? What if you've never met them, you don't even know what they look like, but you're having fantasies about them and telling them what you like and what you'd like them to do to you? Isn't that infidelity?"

Rosa, twenty-six, says, "I think that is infidelity. I mean, you wouldn't tell your husband about it, so you have to ask yourself, Why not?"

Laura, twenty-eight, says, "I do have someone on-line I play sort of sexy games with. I don't think I'm cheating on Trey, though. No, I haven't told him because there's no need to. I wouldn't take it any further."

Says Sam, thirty-six, "If you can remember being unfaithful and you think about it afterward, that's having an affair because it must have meant something. But if you can't remember doing it, because you were drunk, then it clearly didn't mean anything at all!"

THE HITCHED CHICK'S GUIDE TO
Modern Affairs

Head spinning? Are you having an affair or a friendship? Guilty or innocent of infidelity? Who can tell anymore? As Lena says, "It's difficult because our generation has friends across the genders. Our mothers' generation didn't have friends who were male. The lines are blurred."

I won't even attempt to tie up the definition of infidelity into a neat little package. However, here are the most common extramarital relationships I came across during my research. Who knew there were so many?

The Almost Affair

He makes your heart race, cheeks flush, knees almost buckle when you see him. He thinks you're smart, cool, witty and sexy, too. The chemistry between you isn't based on a fleeting fancy, but something deeper—a shared past (perhaps you once dated), a mutual interest or project. Maybe you work together. You dream about him, fantasize about him, you even meet up with him, not *secretively*—after all, you're *great* friends—but you don't exactly come clean to your husband about him, either, or your friends because you know in your heart he's more than a buddy, more than a close colleague. You're not having an affair, but you experience the adrenaline rush of excitement when you see him, the buzz from that tantalizing promise of sex. But none of the guilt that goes with a full-blown affair. You're not having sex . . . not yet, at any rate. But you know you're tempted. Oh, God, you're tempted. So how *would* you describe your relationship? Well, you're *almost* having an affair.

Charlotte, thirty-six, identifies with the characteristics of "the almost affair." She says, "I went to school briefly in Spain and I had a boyfriend who I was madly in love with. It fizzled out once I was back home, but when I visited Barcelona again on a sabbatical four years ago, one of the friends I was staying with said, 'Hey, I ran into your old boyfriend last week and told him you were coming. He said we should all meet up.' So we met up and there was an instant connection all over again. I'm having heart palpitations, we're flirting like crazy, laughing like mad things. It was great. The same when we met up the next time. And then he says, 'Look, I have a house in the country and my wife is away. I'd like to see you again before you leave.' I was in total confusion. On the one hand, I'm married to Bruce—*happily* married—and yet I'm so attracted to this guy. There was no way Bruce was ever going to find out if I did go, he just wouldn't, and the thought of meeting this guy was so romantic."

Which is the point about "the almost affair" . . . it's based on gloriously romantic ideals. You know that if you were to cross the line, it might be wonderful, stimulating, passionate, but while it's almost rather than actual, the fantasy can't be shattered by his morning breath, his snoring, his mood swings, his painful hemorrhoids. Nor do you have to agonize over how long it will last, will you be discovered, what you will do when it falls apart? The almost affair has all the romance without the mess of an actual affair. The excitement minus the deceit. The confidence boost without the disillusionment.

Says Charlotte, "I decided to visit him, but I had no idea what I would do when I got there. Anyway, the music comes on and the wine comes out and we're talking and talking and I'm feeling so tempted to take it further. But then he starts telling me about the situation with his wife and I was thinking, No, don't ask, don't tell. Then we started talking about sex and finally, I said that I couldn't do it. I know that although Bruce would never have found out, I couldn't live with myself. It would be a breach of trust."

Charlotte says that she hasn't seen her Spanish tempter since. It was an inevitable ending, of course. Every relationship—almost or actual—needs a conclusion. And once the thrill of the chase of "the almost affair" is over because we recognize the futility of it, the fun is lost. However, albeit minor, Charlotte admits it did leave her with a hangover. She says, "Yes, there's a difference between actual and emotional infidelity, but at the end of the day, even though I knew I wasn't really in love with this guy, I still felt that I was almost cheating because I felt something special for someone else who wasn't my husband."

The One-Night Stand

Dawn, thirty-four, says, "A one-night stand is a purely physical thing. It's just about acting on an opportunity to have sex with someone different. In my case, the guy was cute, I'd had a few drinks, I was away from home, my husband wasn't going to find out . . . I just thought, What the hell?"

The *Janus Report* unearthed some interesting attitudes toward one-night stands. When asked to react to the statement "I find one-night stands to be degrading," there were noticeable differences in response by sex and income level. Men were less likely than women to regard a one-night stand as a degrading experience, although middle-income men (annual salary around $50,000) were significantly less offended by the one-night stand than the lower income (around $20,000) or higher income ($100,000) group. Among women, however, the upper-income women felt least degraded by the one-night stand.

Today's married women have a surprisingly black-and-white approach to the subject. They say that while they wouldn't be thrilled if their husbands had a one-night stand, they don't believe the effect on their marriage would be catastrophic. Likewise, if she had one, she may feel a little guilty, but because it had been purely about sex or physical attraction, her husband shouldn't see it as anything more than a minor indiscretion.

Counselors, however, say one-night stands are often a way to subsidize lack of attention from spouses. If a woman feels unattractive or dissatisfied with her sex life, she may have a one-night stand to prove she is desirable or satiate her sexual needs. It can also be a way of registering real unhappiness with her marriage. When foot stamping, shouting or persistent attempts to discuss an important issue are ignored, the one-night stand is often a take-me-seriously strategy. How to tell: Are you leaving clues? Not covering your tracks as carefully as you might if your fling really meant something to you beyond sex? Are there issues in your marriage which your husband will not address despite pressure from you? If so, this could be a precursor to other affairs. Forcing a partner to communicate and listen to you is essential. Investigate the help of a qualified third party.

The Platonic Pair

No sex takes place, but you can't deny the buzz, the thrill when he strokes your hair or takes your hand. It's the way he listens to you without judgment, the way he always seems to have your best interests at heart, his delight in your success, how he actually notices—and appreciates—what you wear. Although you haven't actually had any sexual contact, there might as well have been. Consider the way you feel after you've been with him: refreshed, elated, joyful, attractive. But you don't feel guilty because your husband knows all about him. *All* about him? Does he know you've often wondered, What would it be like if . . . ?

Says Sylvia, twenty-nine, "There's a guy I met at college called Anthony. Paulo knows about him, of course, but I don't tell Paulo everything we talk about. A couple of times, I haven't even told Paulo I'm seeing Anthony, especially if I only saw him last week. I think he'd wonder why I wanted to see him so often, I think he'd feel threatened. But Anthony is a really close friend. He's been through very difficult times with me—when my brother died of AIDS, he was right there for me. To be honest, I don't think I would have got through that time without him. He has an amazing view on life and the universe. We were never physical, mainly because there just wasn't the opportunity. And Anthony lived in Russia for a year, which was when I met Paulo. But Anthony is an important part of my life. I talk to him about literature and art and travel. He has a different view on most things from Paulo. I don't think either is better than the other, they're just different. But when I'm with Anthony, I am a different person. I feel smarter. Sometimes Paulo rolls his eyes when I make a joke. Maybe he's heard my jokes too many times. But Anthony laughs and that makes me feel great. I do flirt with Anthony, not in a gross way, but I hold his hand and sometimes we cuddle. And I do wonder what would happen if I wasn't married to Paulo. I can't say that hasn't crossed my mind. Sometimes I wish I could take it further with Anthony and be totally in a vacuum. When I think those things, I feel a bit guilty. But it's confusing. Am I having an affair? Maybe I am."

Counselors will say Sylvia *is* cheating, claiming the no-sex aspect is hardly a defense. If there's any element of secrecy, lying or attraction, then they say your friendship has the hallmarks of an affair. That sex is only happening in your head, apparently, means it is a warning sign that you are seeking another attachment. And since you connect on an intellectual level and have a great deal in common only boosts the potency of the relationship.

That may be true, but such narrow attitudes are not in keeping with today's beliefs. The majority do have close male friends in whom they confide and those confidences are not always shared with husbands. The majority also say there's a certain amount of frisson between them. Good, electric frisson, not sinister, tacky frisson. Says Skylla, twenty-nine, "You tend to have friendships with people you find attractive, regardless of whether they're male or female. I do. If I thought someone was ugly or unattractive and boring or just plain stupid, I probably wouldn't want to be friends with them in the first place. If they're men, you can't help but wonder what they're like in bed, especially when they're telling you all the details of their sex life. I wonder all the time. I would never give up my male friends. They have a very different perspective from women. And although it's nice when a girlfriend compliments me on what I'm wearing or my haircut, it's not as nice as when a male friend does the same."

So when *is* there cause for alarm bells? Says Gabrielle, "It's the idea that there's a whole other world, an entirely different part of yourself, that they don't know anything about. *That's* betrayal." Hitched Chicks believe that having flirtations and sexual fantasies are normal and natural. Agrees Julia, "If you say close friendships with men are tantamount to having an affair, we're back in the fifties.

The line for me isn't whether I'd want to have sex with someone I felt a connection with on an emotional or intellectual level—sexual tension is good—but whether I'd *prefer* to have sex with that person rather than sex with my husband."

Says Rae, "Doesn't everyone have platonic affairs? But it's about levels of intimacy and communication. If you know you're being intimate and confiding much more in a male friend than you ever would with your husband, you can't fool yourself. If you're smart, you know where the line is. Ultimately, it comes down to doing to others as you would have done to yourself. If you know you would feel betrayed if your husband did what you're doing, you're having an affair. It's as simple as that."

The Lesbian Lover

Take these two Hitched Chicks' experiences.

One involves Adrienne, thirty-four, who is wracked with guilt. "There was a situation where a girl came on to me. She was a friend and she's had relationships with women. We were both high and she said to me, 'Have you ever kissed a woman?' and I said, 'No' and she just lunged at me. We fooled around and did a bit of groping and a bit of kissing. The next day, I felt ashamed about it. It wasn't going to turn me into a lesbian or anything. I prefer men, I like the smell of men, that whole testosterone thing. But I did feel ashamed about it . . . in fact, I felt more ashamed about that than I did kissing this guy once in the bathroom while my husband was outside playing pool."

Now take Ellen, thirty-two, who says, "I slept with a woman twice. I met her at the gym and we started chatting. Then we went for coffee and we became friends quite quickly. I knew Kim was a lesbian almost from the start, but I didn't have a problem with that or feel like she was coming on to me in any way. I told her I was married and she said she had a partner, too, although they didn't live together. Tuesday's my day off so she asked me for lunch at her apartment and we had a great time, so instead of going home, I called Max and said I was staying at Kim's a bit longer. He was cool, he just said, 'Okay, have a nice time, see you later.' We were going through her music collection and she was making me a CD. We talked about all sorts of things like where we grew up—her aunt lives in the next town from my parents in South Carolina—and where we went to school and how we both ended up in New York. I told her I wanted to go back to school to study design.

"It's strange," says Ellen. "I don't recall exactly how we started kissing. I think she was stroking my arm and she was playing with my hand and then it just went from there. I remember thinking to myself, This is weird. She smelled sweet, not flowery just sweet, and her skin was kind of spongy—she had girls' skin—but I didn't feel guilty or bad about it. It was just cozy and nice. I was very turned on. That time, she just kissed my boobs and fingered me. But then she said, 'Are you okay about this?' and I said, 'I don't know.' I mean, I was okay about it, but I think I was surprised. We didn't go any further that night beyond heavy petting and after I came, we just cuddled. And then she got up to get my CD and I put my jacket on, and went home. I was on the subway and I thought, God, did I just do what I think I did? I didn't tell Max about it, not because I felt it was this big terrible secret, but because I wasn't even sure where to begin or how I felt about it. I saw her again a few days later at the gym and we hugged really tight, but neither of us said anything about what had happened. The day after, she called me at home and asked if I'd like to have lunch again. I kind of knew if I went around to her apartment, the same thing would probably happen."

So why *did* you go? I ask Ellen. "I'm not sure," says Ellen. "Don't forget, I really liked her. I didn't want to hurt her feelings and I also wanted to let her know that I was okay with what we'd done. I mean, I was a willing participant. Actually, the second time, I was the one who started it. There was a part of me that wondered whether I was a lesbian or, at the very least, bi. When she was making the coffee, I stood very close behind her. I didn't know how to approach her, so I just stood really, really close. That time, I did as much of the kissing and touching, but I just couldn't give her oral sex. It had nothing to do with feeling guilty about Max or that this was going too far, I just couldn't do it. No, I couldn't do it. And she didn't push me or ask me why."

Ellen hasn't slept with Kim since. She says, "After the first 'Oooh, this is strange,' I just didn't want to have that kind of relationship with her. I know I'm straight and that's that. Kim and I are still friends. We talked about what happened a couple of and she asked me whether I'd told Max. I said I hadn't. I don't see any reason to. He'd only be freaked out about it . . . or maybe he wouldn't. Maybe he'd be turned on. But I wouldn't want that either. It wasn't like that. Yeah, I want to keep it to myself, but I don't think you could call it an affair and I don't think it's that big of a deal. It was a brief moment, that's all."

Adrienne feels more ashamed of her very brief encounter with another woman than she did over a similar experience with another man. Ellen doesn't feel guilty because an intimacy with a woman, she says, is not the same as being intimate with a man. Experts would call them both "an experimental affair" and caution against brushing them under the carpet, since healthy marriages are built on honesty and trust. That both Adrienne and Ellen were able to compartmentalize their experience as purely sexual experimentation may never threaten their marriage. But as Joely, twenty-six, who has fantasized about sex with another woman, says, "I've never met another woman who I've been physically attracted to. But I think there's got to be one. How could there not be, right? I just feel she's out there somewhere and if I ever met her, that would be the point I would consider an affair. How could you not, really? But I would consider it cheating because I wouldn't just be giving my body. I'd be giving a part of myself. Having an affair based purely on lust I don't think is a big deal, but how could a straight woman have sex with another woman and not give a part of herself? It would just be too overwhelming."

The On-line Lover

Since e-mail and the Internet are relatively new phenomena, not one survey or study could tell me how many women have on-line affairs. However, we do know that big demand generates big supply and, from my own research for this book, there's a big supply of on-line sites to cater to the female cyberadulterer. Offering ways to keep an on-line lover from your spouse to the fundamentals of on-line love etiquette, these sites make cyberaffairs sound so tantalizing, so discreet, so easy and respectable it makes you wonder why the whole world isn't indulging. You can be who you want to be, no worries about being attractive/wealthy/fit/smart/deep enough, you simply share secrets, thoughts and dreams with a faceless entity who validates you every time they sign on.

Says Natasha, thirty-one, "I'm in a chat room asking if anyone has Barenaked Ladies tickets and I find myself flirting with this guy from Florida. I mean, you can imagine it. 'Yeah, I've got Bare Naked Ladies!' . . . ha, ha! It's difficult not to have a really wild conversation. The next day, I get an e-mail from him and we start all over again. Before long, I'm sending and receiving about ten e-mails a day. When the jokes run out, you start asking questions, you give a bit more information and then you start fantasizing. What do they look like? Should we meet? It happens practically overnight—it did with me, in any case. I'd log on before I went to work and when I came home. It was fun, but it wasn't until I told a girlfriend and she said, 'What does Bill say?' and I said, 'He doesn't know' that I started to realize I was thinking *waaay* too much about this guy. I could tell by her reaction she didn't approve and it gave me a real wake-up call. Especially when she said, 'What would you do if you found out Bill was doing the same thing?' That night, I e-mailed the Florida guy and said I didn't think we should continue. 'Course, he just said, 'Why not? We're not doing anything illegal, we're not having sex!' So then I was able to justify it to myself. I was like, 'Uh, okay.' But I just didn't feel that comfortable anymore. My guilty conscience was too much. Bill would wander over to me while I was on the computer and kiss my neck and I'd quickly sign off. He'd say, 'What's so interesting?' and I'd be like, 'Oh nothing! Just browsing . . . ' It didn't feel right. In the end, I stopped the e-mails. I switched e-mail addresses, I blocked his. Sounds dramatic, but it was becoming an addiction."

Sara, thirty-five, also uses the word "addiction" to describe her three-month on-line affair. "We were going through a rough patch, like all couples go through. Except on the whole, you figure them out with your husband. But I met a guy on-line—I wasn't searching—and we started chatting. He got straight to the point. He said, 'Are you married?' and I said, 'I guess you could say I am married,' so I suppose it was evident I wasn't happy back then. It escalated very quickly. I would tell him what my husband had said and done. He'd write back and tell me everything I wanted to hear. He'd say he couldn't understand how anyone could treat me that way. Then he'd say if only he could hold me and make it all go away. I started to believe he was the answer to my problem. In fact, I'd tell him about every little thing Kenny did and suddenly it would become this big issue. It made everything so much worse. It was like an addiction, an escape. I think if Ken hadn't found out, I might have taken the relationship further. As it was, when Kenny did find out, it was awful. He tracked the sites I'd visited and who I'd been talking to. I was forced to tell him. In the end, I wanted to tell him because I wanted to resolve the problems even if it meant splitting up. Ken was deeply hurt. He said, 'Why didn't you talk to *me*?' I said I would have done, but it seemed like we couldn't communicate anymore without fighting. We found a therapist who told us this kind of affair was very common. I felt better knowing that, but I still feel stupid that instead of confronting our problems, I looked for a distraction."

On-line affairs are so common, in fact, that not only are there websites dedicated to those who seek them—one offers a "facility which has been made for married men and women all over the world who want to reignite their passions with an on-line companion while avoiding the complications of a face-to-face affair." There are also websites dedicated to supporting the betrayed spouse and on-line recorders, which, for only forty dollars (infinitely cheaper than any private investigator), can discreetly monitor and record any instant messages should you suspect your spouse of cheating. That they exist at all suggests secrecy and betrayal are major components of an on-line relationship. The combination of the two, in Hitched Chicks' opinion, means an affair, on-line or not, is taking place.

The Star Fucker

When Phillippa, thirty-two, had a fling with a famous soccer player, she didn't regard it as an affair. Not really. "Yes, we had sex, but that was it. It wasn't love or anything. I wasn't about to ask him to leave his wife and I wasn't about to leave Scott either."

Phillippa claims that much as she loved—and still loves—Scott, having sex with the sports star was an opportunity she couldn't turn down. "How could I? I would have kicked myself. I'm sure Scott would get a thrill from it if he knew. You know, secretly. Yeah, he'd be mad as hell at first, but once he'd calmed down, I'm sure he'd think, Huh, how about that? My wife had sex with that guy. That guy wanted sex with *my* wife. You know what men are like."

Scott will never know because Phillippa will never tell him. She says it didn't mean anything to her. In fact, sex with the sports celebrity "wasn't *that* great. But," she says, "it's something I had to do and I get a bit of a buzz when I think about it or see him on TV. I think, I had sex with him!"

Good, harmless, bed-notching fun or a serious threat to your marriage? As far as Phillippa is concerned, sleeping with a celebrity is no threat to her marriage. "I mean, if Scott had the chance to sleep with Gwyneth Paltrow, I'm sure he would. How could he not? I'd feel a bit insecure about it. I'd want to know, what was she like? Did she have a good body? But I don't think for one minute she'd want to run off and marry Scott. It was the same for me. There was no way this was going to be a relationship. He wasn't going to marry me. And anyway, I couldn't cope knowing there were all these women like me who'd sleep with him at the drop of a hat!"

That celebrities are so removed from real life seems to remove the guilt. It's a fantasy writ true, a scene from a movie, you don't actually believe it's going to go any further. Says Phillippa, "I would have run a mile if he'd wanted more!" However, as society's obsession with celebrities continues to mushroom and we begin to believe stars are just like us, they're our friends, isn't the line between Hollywood fantasy and hard reality becoming fudged? What's more, fame is no longer discriminating: the advent of "real people TV" proves even people like us can become stars. And I ask Phillippa, having conquered one celebrity, doesn't she want to add another to her list of star conquests . . . then another, and another? "Let's put it this way, I wouldn't kick George Clooney out of bed. But what are the chances of me meeting George Clooney? Even if I did, what are the chances he'd sleep with me? It's not very likely, is it?"

What makes affairs so compelling is the heady mixture of excitement, desire, pleasure and sheer naughtiness. A celebrity fling is double the dose, which is why Phillippa's affair *should* strike fear. Risk of addiction can be compared to a class-A drug. The reality of your marriage will inevitably fall short of the fantasy of the celebrity, creating disharmony and discontent where there should otherwise be none. Let's face it, which man could *ever* live up to the fantasy of George Clooney? And we haven't even touched on the real marriage wreckers: lying, deceit and betrayal. To say it was "only about sex" can backfire when the betrayed spouse wonders whether the cheating spouse is as dismissive of *their* own sexual relationship.

The Ex Marks the Spot

Lilly, thirty-one, recalls moving back to the town where she and her husband grew up. Having lived in a big city, they were keen to provide a healthier, cozier environment for their baby. But settling in proved challenging for both of them—reestablishing old friendships, finding new jobs, coping with the stresses of a newborn created distance between Lilly and her husband of five years. So when Lilly's old flame reappeared, she was vulnerable to his advances.

Lilly says, "I bumped into him by chance. He couldn't believe I'd had a baby and I was feeling frumpy, so when he complimented me on the way I looked, it was very seductive. He said we should get together for a drink so I organized my mom to take care of the baby and we met. I knew I was playing with fire, but . . ."

Gorgeous, intelligent, successful . . . Lilly's ex was as she remembered him, with bells on. He had his own firm now, he was confident and he was rolling in money. Even better, he was *familiar*. No sticky silences, a shared history, plus, he piled on the attention. Says Lilly, "It was *sooo* flattering. I wanted to see him again, so when he suggested we meet up a second time, I was there. It was just so easy and, for a while, lovely to live out this fantasy where I was just me and not a mom or a wife, just me. So we kissed and played around quite a lot. Then he started piling on the pressure. He'd say things like, 'You should have waited for me, you should have married me, I can get you a divorce, I know people who can get you a divorce.' I said, 'Look, I can't do that, I've got a child, you're not his dad,' and he was saying, 'That's okay, we can make it work.' It was just so seductive.

"It's like being on a diet and having a great big piece of chocolate cake sitting in front of you. You cannot rip your eyes off it. You know it's wrong, you know you shouldn't be doing it, but your mouth is salivating. I mean, this guy was very attractive and although my husband's bright, I know this guy was much more of a match intellectually for me. And, of course, he wanted me so much. I couldn't understand, when I loved my husband and we still had good sex, why he was so attractive. But I know now that my confidence was eroded. I wasn't working, I was feeling ugly, I was lonely. So all this carried on until I found myself a job and, suddenly, I started to feel like I didn't need this guy anymore. So I told him I needed to stop seeing him. I felt that now I was able to like myself and focus on me again, I was able to fall in love with my husband all over again and appreciate my little family."

Many Hitched Chicks talk of the allure of the ex-boyfriend, "the one that got away." They describe the "what-ifs" and sometimes the 'if-onlys.' And it's precisely because they are so familiar—so we know their bad points as well as their good and we continue to find them attractive—that they can drive a dangerous wedge when a marriage is already in a muddle. To run from our husband into the arms of someone who loves us despite knowing our faults is tantalizing in the extreme. Most affairs hit the rocks once the fantasy is shattered and it becomes a proper relationship. This one, however, should have a pretty good chance of survival, right? It may well survive. Some do. But the fact remains that every relationship experiences turmoil and our reserves of ex-boyfriends to distract us from the issues at the heart of our turmoils eventually run out. Studies reveal that if an affair relationship replaces a marriage, it is eventually subject to the same stresses, but twice as likely to crumble. This may explain why 75 percent of those who marry partners with whom they have had an affair go on to divorce. Far more effective insurance is a pledge of communication and commitment to resolve issues, however painful, rather than run from them.

The Get-You-Back Girl

Says Patti, "If I ever found out Tim was having an affair, I think I might do something myself to make me feel better. I think I'd go out and have an affair, just to get even."

Haven't we all felt like that? Competition between wives and their husbands is a common theme today. Who earns more? Whose status is higher? Who does the most (or least) housework? Whose identity takes precedent? Now that women are less likely to be slaves to their marriage, another affair rears its head: the revenge affair.

A revenge affair occurs when one partner is attempting to alleviate the pain of being betrayed. When we are hurting, it's tempting to want to hurt the other even more, to lob back a betrayal like we may a tennis ball to an opponent, or an argument to a stubborn client in a work pitch. It's about winning at all costs. But the victory is often short-lived and rarely satisfying.

Says Alice, thirty-five, "It didn't matter how much John apologized for cheating, I couldn't shake off my anger. No matter how much he tried to make it up to me with gifts and compliments and trips, it was still there, boiling away in the back of my mind. I just knew, even before I met the guy I had the affair with, that I would have to have an affair. And I didn't try very hard to keep it a secret. In fact, I wanted to be found out so John could go through the hurt I went through. Keeping it a secret wasn't enough for me. Knowing I'd had an affair wasn't enough—I had to see John hurt. In fact, I was amazed John didn't find out sooner. But I don't think he wanted to rock the boat, so he may have suspected, I don't know . . ."

During a fight which, Alice says, she instigated to bring her hurt to a head, she told John she'd had a one-night stand. She didn't reveal that it was a miserable experience and she'd felt ashamed—"It was so tacky"—she simply wanted John to know she was just as capable of attracting a lover. But John's reaction was not to burst into tears and express profound pain. "He was silent. It was awful," says Alice. "He didn't want to talk about it. He left that night and stayed with a friend. When he came back the next day to collect some things, I managed to get him to talk. Not much, but he did say that his fling had happened when he was drunk—I know that, he'd been on a bachelor night and he was really sick for three days afterward. So I know he'd been very, very drunk. But he said what really hurt him was that my fling was calculated to hurt him. It's true. I *had* gone out with the sole purpose of hurting him and even I could see it was different."

Although it's been turbulent, Alice and John are still married. As is Lara, thirty-nine, who has been with Geoff for ten years. "I know he had an affair earlier this year," she says. "In fact, I'm sure he's had affairs before, but this one I know for sure. I was traveling a lot for work and he was, too. When we were both at home, I sensed a distance between us so while he was away, I accessed his e-mail. Geoff would have been furious if he'd known as he's an intensely private person, but what the hell . . . I discovered that he'd met someone through his squash club and they'd had various meetings. Although I was very upset, I didn't confront him. Instead, I decided to have an affair. Yes, you could call it a revenge affair, which I think is okay so long as they don't go on for too long. Geoff's affair is over now, mine is, too, and our relationship is even better than before . . . but I don't rule out entirely the possibility that either one of us will have an affair again."

The Fuck Buddy

Remember when we were single, how we had the close male friend with whom we made a pact? It went along these lines: If neither of us has a date on New Year's Eve, we'll spend it together. If neither of us has found a partner by the time we're thirty-five, we'll have a baby together. Now that we're married, we say to him, If neither of us is having sex, why don't we have sex together? No strings. Still friends. What could be better?

Trouble is, we're not single anymore. Oh, for those carefree days. Why does a simple fuck have to be so fucking complicated now? Whether children exist or not, responsibility overshadows sexual desire, no matter how freewheeling we think we are. By now, we have probably confronted our mortality on more than one occasion and realized that most things—even life—draw to a conclusion.

In Patsy's case, her fuck buddy wanted a relationship. He wanted to leave his wife. His relationship with Patsy was more emotionally than physically charged. Patsy, on the other hand, really did only want sex. She says, "Oh, I'm very good at compartmentalizing. It's only like thinking about the people you work with. You know your boss is a complete asshole, but you're still pleasant to them. It's a sick tool, but it's helpful. I knew that the affair would be a big deal to his wife and it would be a big deal to my husband, but I guess it was just a moment of thinking about myself instead of someone else."

All Work and Some Playing Around Makes Jill a Typical Hitched Chick

Karen, thirty-seven, works in the competitive world of magazines where passion and commitment to the job are as vital as talent. She remembers falling in lust with a colleague with whom she worked intimately to secure a lucrative deal. "I thought Gee was hot from the day we teamed up to work on this big pitch. I'd arrange lunch with him on the pretext that our creativity flowed better out of the office. I guess our mutual passion for the job—and each other— was irresistible. One night after work, I suggested we go back to his place, which we did. My husband's firm uses the same car company as mine and as he was traveling home in a car, he heard the controller radio through that I needed a car to pick me up from Gee's place across town. I was *soooo* busted."

It isn't surprising infidelity is on the increase. Work is where most affairs start, and highly charged professional environments which thrive on teamwork, common interests and shared goals are the perfect breeding ground. Better qualified and more career-focused than her mother was, Hitched Chick is dedicated to her job—even after having children—which means she's participating in the inevitable bonding and camaraderie that goes with a high-pressure job. And often taking mutual passions to an intimate conclusion.

The average professional woman spends 52.5 hours per week on the job. On this basis alone, I have always offered jobs to people who I not only personally liked, but who I knew would get along with other members of the team and with whom they would possibly—

hopefully—form close relationships. After all, I'd say, we spend more time with our coworkers than with our husbands and wives.

For a 2002 on-line survey conducted by U.S. *Elle* magazine and MSNBC.com, thirty thousand people clicked and revealed their attitudes toward office affairs. The average female respondent was age thirty-three, the average male thirty-six, the majority held salaried jobs with a bachelor's degree or higher. Over 40 percent confessed to having sex with a coworker. Of those, 42 percent were married or in a relationship at the time of their office affair.

Women at work are complementing their capacity to listen, nurture and multitask with increased assertiveness, pragmatism and compartmentalization. It's an MO which infiltrates every aspect of their lives, from the simplest domestic tasks (if she doesn't have her cleaner or husband do it), to the most complex decisions about love and sex.

As well as arguing that lifetime monogamy may not, after all, be a natural state of being for women or men, infidelity is, well, an occupational hazard for Hitched Chicks if "lack of respect" is what greets them at home. Wait around for hubby to come home? *Pah!* Tolerate boring/bad-mannered/boorish behavior? Not likely. While we know that our colleagues tend to present the best of themselves at work, we are far from oblivious to the superficial appeal. And not beyond playing up our own. In fact, the *Elle*/MSNBC survey's analyst and author, Janet Lever, a sociologist at California State University in Los Angeles, states, "Thirty-four percent of women say they play up their sexuality at work while only twenty percent of men do." What's more, she adds, "We expected more women than men to say they're reluctant to act friendly for fear coworkers might interpret their advances as sexually motivated, but we found the opposite."

How many of those who instigated the affair were women isn't revealed, but you can forget the old cliché of the wistful little secretary being swept off her knees by her male superior. There's every chance Hitched Chick *is* the boss. Even if she isn't, she's as likely to be the hunter as the hunted.

Take Dawn. She had a brief affair with a colleague from her department. "Oh yeah, I went for him. I knew he was attracted to me, but I was the one who took it beyond flirtation in the office. We were at a conference together. I caught his eye during a seminar which was so dull I thought I'd die. When he looked at me, I winked. Later in the bar, I went up to him and said, 'Let's meet after dinner.' To be honest, at that stage, I wasn't thinking about a fling or anything. Most of the people at the conference were in their forties and fifties and dull, dull, dull. So I was just looking to escape the boredom. But when we met, we had such a nice time, then we went for a walk around the city to get some air and it just sort of happened. We were both a bit drunk—actually, we were very drunk—and we started kissing. One thing led to another and we ended up having sex in the park. It was fun, but for me, that's all it was. Unfortunately, he wanted to see me again after the conference and it was a little weird when we'd see each other at work for a while. But we're pretty friendly now. I think he has a girlfriend, which makes it easier."

According to the *Elle*/MSNBC survey, roughly half of those who said they'd had an office affair (married and single) said their romance had not interfered with work. A third reported discomfort in the first two months after the breakup, while 12 percent said at least one of them left the company or asked for a transfer after the breakup. Only 3 percent got fired for their transgression.

However, 9 percent said their fling led to separation or divorce for one member of the couple. It's something Sandy, thirty-one, came close to. "I work for a huge company, with offices spread over the city so Steve and I didn't actually meet *at* work, we met *through* work. We actually got to know each other via e-mail. It started off with a simple procedural question from me to him. He answered my question, then he asked me a question. Before long, we were having this e-mail exchange. We went from nought to one hundred in two weeks. His e-mails were the funniest things I'd ever read. In fact, to start off with, I'd tell my husband, Chris, what Steve had written and we'd laugh about it together. Plus, Steve was married, too, and I'd ask him about his wife. Anyway, I remember one Friday about a month after the first e-mail, I didn't hear from Steve and I was so disappointed, it put me in a bad mood all weekend. He'd been sick and when he came back to work on Monday, he e-mailed me straight away. Oh God, I was in heaven again, so when he said why don't we have lunch, I was like, 'Where? When?'

"When I first met Steve, it wasn't instant lust. I normally go for tall, dark, skinny guys, but Steve was my height, even a bit smaller, and stocky. But we had lunch and, honestly, by the time we were onto the cappuccinos, I was in love. He made me laugh so much. And he was so smart. I just felt like I'd known him forever. Over the next few weeks, we saw each other more and more. Then Chris had to spend overnight away for his job. What was weird was that I told Chris I would miss him. And I genuinely meant it. Just because I adored Steve, it didn't mean I had fallen out of love with Chris. Chris even asked about Steve, for God's sake. It was surreal. Even more surreal, although Steve and I did have sex in my apartment while Chris was away that night, I didn't even think about Chris. It was like the two worlds—me and Steve, me and Chris—were totally unconnected at that time. But, of course, I did start to feel guilty. But even then, I'd meet Steve and say, 'God, I'm feeling guilty about Chris' and then we'd make love. Steve was the same. But, as time went by, some nights we felt so guilty, we couldn't think about sex. We'd just sit opposite each other and try to eat, but would only talk about our partners and how they would feel if they found out about us.

"What ended it was when Steve's mother died suddenly. He was devastated. And I was devastated I couldn't be with him to comfort him. But I didn't know his mother and she had been very close to

Steve's wife and I think that's what finally came between us. I saw him two weeks after his mother died and he was different. I remember getting on the train to go home afterward and I was heartbroken. I cried all the way home. I knew that was the end. I just couldn't imagine living without him. And I couldn't explain to Chris why I felt so bad either. It was absolutely awful. Steve stopped e-mailing me altogether. He called me once at work and I called him a couple of times to see how he was doing, but it was strained and difficult. The last time we spoke—almost a year ago—he said he and his wife were trying for a baby. I don't even know whether he has a baby now. He might for all I know. He works in a different building so I'm unlikely to ever run into him. I look back on that time and I do feel guilty, but generally I just feel really sad. Would I have left Chris? That's a hard question. I love Chris and he's been great. He's put up with my moods, even though he hasn't understood them. But I was so heartbroken over Steve, I never want to put Chris through that. He deserves more."

When I ask Karen about the effect her "busted" affair with her magazine colleague had on her marriage, she says, "Put it this way, it wasn't pleasant. In fact, it was a nightmare. But it brought a lot of issues to the surface which needed addressing." So would she be unfaithful again? "Hmm . . . I'm not sure I would. I mean, you can never say never, but if I did, I'd definitely be more careful."

Why Affair Sex
Is So Addictive

Hitched Chicks agree that the entanglement of emotions is distressing and, more often than not, outweighs the fun of an affair. However, while the simple pursuit of sex is rarely at the heart of infi-

The A to Bed of Affair Sex

"Erotic"—when you can't meet for sex, you talk about it on your cell phone, write about it via e-mail and ensure the fantasies become reality when you meet.

"Exciting"—high on drama and intrigue, adrenaline kicks in.

"Infrequent"—and because it's a rare commodity we anticipate it. The less frequent sex is, the more our desire mounts.

"Intense"—when there's no time to be lazy, the focus is on maximum pleasure in the minimum time.

"Forbidden"—nothing is so desirable as what we know we shouldn't really have.

"Novel"—like any variation from the norm, its freshness delights, challenges and surprises us.

"Passionate"—anticipation and, therefore, mounting desire, makes us hungry and frantic for satisfaction.

"Quick"—which makes us savor every last second.

"Raunchy"—atypical feelings manifest themselves in atypical behavior, which is why many women report trying acts during an affair they wouldn't dream of with their husbands.

"Wild"—animal desires break free when we're not stifled by domestic obligations or surroundings.

delity, a sexual relationship is never far behind. As a frantic expression of longing, the sex we have during an affair is potent and unforgettable even years after the affair has ended.

It would be easy to assume descriptions of affair sex would be loaded with nostalgia, but it hardly comes into it. If anything, a wife's infidelities are often laced with regret . . . regret that she was forced to seek comfort outside her marriage, regret that the affair fizzled out, regret that she had jumped in too quickly, too thoughtlessly, too deep—or maybe not deep enough.

The fact is, affair sex *is* different from any other kind of sex.

While dating sex is joyful and carefree and married sex is reassuring and intimate, affair sex is none of these things. It's unique. Yet the same words and phrases are restated to describe affair sex, the characteristics of which will have a ring of familiarity if you have ever been tempted to just have one more glass of champagne, one more cigarette, just an extra little sniff of something, even a shopping splurge when you're supposed to be saving . . .

Just one or a combination of the above is every reason why affair sex is so uniquely irresistible and addictive. For anyone who has ever been addicted to anything remotely risky—from drugs to alcohol, gambling, shopping or affair sex—quitting can be more difficult than dealing with the consequences of the addiction itself. What we get from our addiction is usually in direct proportion to what is lacking in our lives. The more neglected we feel in marriage, the more we crave the attention of an affair and the more addicted we become to it. Says Dawn, "If my sex life with my husband at that time had been exciting and passionate, I probably wouldn't have been interested in having sex with anyone else." Which is why sprinkling your marriage with some of the addictive elements of affair sex—having frantic sex outdoors, say, or a raunchy hotel rendezvous—is a very smart thing to do.

How an Affair Can Help

I'd be irresponsible to declare an affair a prescription for a crumbling marriage. But it wouldn't be an accurate assessment to say all affairs lead to divorce. (In Youth Intelligence's 2002 Generation X update, 60 percent said they'd give their partners a second chance or seek counseling to work out why the infidelity occurred.) Some affairs actually help marriage by kick-starting flailing sex lives, bringing issues to a head and forcing couples to sit down and talk.

In Karen's case, she didn't feel her husband took her or her work seriously. "His job is better paying and he's a senior vice president, so he thinks my salary is peanuts and that I just shuffle papers. It drove me crazy. When I met Gee, he listened to me and respected my opinion. We were working on a project together where my input was as important as his, so I thought, Hello, I *am* intelligent. I *am* attractive. Fuck you! When Charlie found out, he was so angry. He said I'd disrespected him. I said, 'I disrespected *you*? What about all the times you disrespected *me*? What about you telling our friends, "Karen's job isn't work. All she does is play"? Isn't *that* disrespectful?' There's teasing and then you get tired of it. You start to believe you're not worthy. After Charlie found out about me and Gee, we almost split up. Neither of us really wanted that so we forced ourselves to talk about our marriage, which was difficult since we aren't particularly inward-looking people. But I told him that I wasn't this little fun bunny with no brain. The only way our marriage would work is if he recognized that. Now he asks me about my work and never makes fun of it. *I* can make fun of it, but he can't. We've become much more like equals."

Sometimes an affair can have a stabilizing effect on marriage. (Who knew?) In Lilly's case, yes, she was deeply attracted to her ex-boyfriend, but he was her emotional safety valve, too, when the stresses of moving to a new neighborhood caused her to reconsider her marriage. As her husband attempted to find a new job and together they struggled with the rejections, Lilly was able to let off steam to her lover before returning to her husband, feeling happier, calmer and sexier. Relieving tension temporarily is all well and good, however, only until a lover grows tired of that role and demands a deeper commitment, which is what happened to Lilly. But she does acknowledge that having her brief affair actually stopped her from making a hasty decision to separate from her husband.

An affair can make you appreciate your husband and all the positive aspects of your marriage. Yes, he can be a bad-tempered bastard. (But you can be a bitch at times, too, huh?) Yes, he leaves the toilet seat up. (But, hey, you leave icky Q-tips by the bathroom sink). No, he doesn't bring you flowers anymore—or at least, not as often as when you were dating. And yet . . .

Says Trish, "Even though it was difficult to stop seeing Len, I think I would have grown tired of the secrecy. Also, Len wasn't as smart as Jason, my husband, and toward the end, I'd find myself repeating things to Len that Jason had said to me. Len would look baffled, like he had no clue what I was talking about—y'know, political stuff, the economy, Mike Bloomberg—and it made me realize how attractive Jason's intelligence is. I still feel guilty about having an affair, but in many ways it did help my marriage. I realized that the grass *isn't* greener on the other side. Maybe it is initially. But after the first few weeks when all the passion has died down, you start to *really* get to know them. Then you realize they have the same issues with their family, the same work problems, and you start to see they're a bit fucked-up, too. And then you think, So why am I doing this? Is it really worth leaving my husband for this man?"

To have an affair with the purpose of putting your marriage back on track is just plain foolish. But even the most long-standing affairs can result in improved communication and a stronger bond, as well as better sex, between wives and husbands. Although more than 50 percent of marriages right now may well be existing alongside some form of an affair, only 25 percent of divorces are filed on the grounds of infidelity, which suggests an affair doesn't have to signal the end of your marriage. It *could* well be the start of an even better marriage.

THE HITCHED CHICK'S GUIDE TO
After-the-Affair Repair

When a Hitched Chick cheats, desire for divorce is not her motivation. As we know, affairs happen to women and men for all sorts of reasons—lack of attention, feeling unsupported or disrespected, experimentation, pressure relief, sheer impulse. But once an affair either runs out of steam or is discovered, coming to terms with the emotional fallout can be more exhausting, confusing, painful and stressful than a United Nations summit. Talks will collapse, tempers will be frayed, often it will feel like you're both speaking in entirely different languages, but divorce is not the only option. Whether you have cheated or been cheated on, there's a long way to go before calling it quits. On the agenda:

* ✦ **Understand** what caused the affair. Was it basic animal attraction or was there an underlying reason that you acted on what seemed like impulse? Was it really a shared interest in archaeology that drew you to your lover or a lack of shared goals in your marriage that forced you and your spouse apart?
* ✦ **Devote time** to talking—not just for one hour in a coffee shop, but over and over at home. If you have cheated, it will help you understand the real reasons why, and don't you owe your partner an explanation? If you've been betrayed, you'll feel the need to hash it over, allow explanations to sink in, time to ask lots of questions.
* ✦ **Be 100 percent honest.** This is crunch time, the opportu-

nity to get it all out. However hurtful, painful, silly or childish, soul-bearing is required. You can only move forward when both of you are familiar with every last thought and feeling.

+ **Recognize** relationship trouble is rarely one-sided. Instead of saying, "It's your fault I felt like this," replace it with, "I felt like this when we . . ." Both partners must accept an element of responsibility.

+ **Figure out** all your options. Do you categorically want to split? Could you stay together and review your relationship in one/three/six months? Would counseling help? Could a practical change of work/home/family circumstances contribute to resolution?

+ **Remember** all the reasons you first fell in love with each other. Regardless of who has cheated, both should verbalize those reasons.

+ **Don't imagine** reconciliation will happen overnight. Either one of you may feel relieved the affair is out in the open, and feel ready to move on, but the ripple effect of an affair can be extensive and individuals recover at different paces.

+ **Accept** jealousy and insecurity will be huge issues for a long time. If you have cheated, your husband may feel intensely possessive. (Some women who have had affairs reported sudden pangs of possessiveness toward their husbands, too, sensing the possibility of a revenge affair.) Remember, an affair will crush a partner's self-esteem like nothing else.

+ **Recognize trust** will take time to rebuild. If you have cheated, accept that your partner will be suspicious for the first few agonizing months and may make irrational demands. It is up to you to accommodate those demands, but only make promises you know you can keep. In other words, don't promise to return home by 7:30 P.M. if you know you may be held up by traffic. Instead, you might promise to call when you're leaving work or as your train is pulling into the station. If your spouse has cheated on you, attempt to make only achievable demands. Until trust has been reestablished, pledge to only go to social events together, take up more shared activities, get used to being a couple again and allow yourselves to form in-jokes or silent signals only you two understand.

❖ ***Don't forget*** the healing power of sex. Whether you're the cheater or cheated, having sex with your spouse could well be the last thing on your mind, but re-establishing intimacy goes hand-in-hand with re-building trust. If your spouse has been unfaithful, you may feel torn between feeling angry, hurt and rejected, yet simultaneously crave closeness. You may also want to prove you're every bit as sexually exciting as your spouse's lover. If you're the one who's been unfaithful, just as many conflicting emotions may create sexual barriers—guilt, remorse, shame, anger . . . even grief for the loss of your lover. You may want to reassure with displays of tenderness, yet fear your advances will be unwelcome and rejected. Sexual intimacy, however, doesn't necessarily equate with intercourse. Stroking, cuddling, kissing and hugging are effective and necessary building blocks.

❖ ***Take comfort*** and strength from your own identities. If you have lapsed into thinking life is only worth living for your partner (which may have caused the affair if you started to feel ignored, or may now be how you feel as a result of your partner's affair), reclaim your identity. Personal success, accomplishments and close friends who love you because of *you* will empower and nourish. Once true to and happy with who you are, you will be happy with your life, whoever you choose to share it with.

5.

The Power and
the Glory

The days when women rolled over and took the blows are behind us. We have the power to be anything and have anything we want. Since more women work and travel, we see what's possible, what we can achieve if we exert ourselves and go after what we're entitled to.

—Linda, thirty-four

From Golda Meir to Margaret Thatcher, Sandra Day O'Connor to Oprah Winfrey, Donna Karan to Barbara Walters . . . they have all been role models for female power. These women and others reached their powerful status despite a patriarchal society. Against many odds, they fought the establishment and won, proving that women can wield power to the benefit of all. Part female fantasy, part male nightmare, these women betrayed few signs of their sex's traditional weaknesses, they changed history and proved women *can*.

While the female powerhouse is no longer an anomaly, the days when women felt forced to behave like men, starched their hair into helmets and padded out their shoulders like quarterbacks to overcompensate for their femininity are fading. Thank the Lord. Because if we scorned the demure demeanor of prefeminist women, we felt alienated by the extreme of the feminist almost as much. Brash and bossy, the feminists of the late seventies and eighties without a doubt made us question the allocation of power, but we felt hectored and bullied. We didn't want to hate men. We didn't want privileged status just because we were women. We didn't want to have to bark and bluster and wear silly ties, but neither did we want to have to stop shaving our legs and wearing makeup, suppress our femininity or stop getting married just because it reeked of subjugation. After all, true power is about choice and living life the way we want to live it. It's not being forced into roles which other people—women as well as men—feel are right for us. It's this attitude which characterizes postfeminism.

It all boils down to self-esteem and modern wives are full of it. Reports in the early 1990s stated that boys and girls are equally self-confident until adolescence, at which point girls enter a slump—or "hit the wall"—from which many never fully recover. However, recent studies reveal that notion was grossly hyped. More thorough research conducted by Kristen Kling and colleagues at the University of Wisconsin at Madison in 1999, based on 216 studies involving over 150,000 individuals, reveals the gap between female and male self-esteem is marginal, at just 0.21. (This gap peaked at 0.33 in late adolescence, but tended to subside with age.) In a statement, Kling concluded, "The small size of gender difference suggests that males and females are more similar than they are different when it comes to measures of self-esteem."

Their report vehemently denied dismissing the existence of very real sexist pressures, which, unhappily, are still encountered by girls and women. But Kling and her colleagues pointed out that many girls go on to develop a wide variety of coping mechanisms and strategies which render them far more resilient to sexist attitudes than is commonly assumed. No, they were not closing the book on this issue, but their report stated they believed their findings provide "an important alternative to the prevailing view in the popular media that girls and women are passive victims with poor self-esteem."

Passive victims with poor self-esteem? Don't make me laugh. Yes, many women do still suffer from poor body image and they're less prone to physical assertion, but passive victims? Poor self-esteem? According to Christine Stolba, an advisor to the Independent Women's Forum on economic issues, "It simply doesn't square with the evidence. The apostles of the 'women-as-victims perspective' use selected statistics and anecdotes to illustrate their theory. Although women faced discrimination in the past, the story of their recent success deserves to be told."

This is the story that deserves to be told: the majority of degrees—associate, bachelor's and master's—are awarded to women, as well as 40 percent of doctorates. They're not only represented in greater numbers at college and postgraduate levels, women have also been steadily entering male-dominated programs. In 1999, women represented 44 percent of the freshman class at Yale Medical School. Between 1970 and 1996, the percentage of law degrees awarded to women rose from 5 to 43 percent. The number of women-owned businesses more than doubled between 1987 and 1997 and studies show, should she want to, a woman has as much chance of winning electoral office as a man.

If anyone is being crippled by low self-esteem today, it's men. While women are benefiting from a greater educational focus on sports, science and mathematics (a circular relationship links self-esteem to these activities), emerging from vigorous and esteem-building mentoring programs and taking their greater-than-ever confidence levels beyond school and into the workplace, men are buckling beneath the pressure of the extra competition.

Striving to win in increasingly feminized environments where traditional male patterns of behavior—statistic-driven goals, dictatorship management styles—are proving outdated and ineffectual is wreaking havoc with men's self-esteem. A U.K. report, commissioned by Barclay's Life, reveals women are very positive and optimistic about the power they have over their future, whereas men are having a tough time of it. Faced with a bewildering array of choices from what the report calls the new "supermarket lifestyle," they are unable to pinpoint their identity and role and run the serious risk of being alienated and left behind. Emasculated, confused and bitter, it's men who are the unhappy victims of low self-esteem today, not women.

It's this revelation which caused Alex McKie, author of the Barclay's Life report, to declare that "young men need to redefine themselves, just as women did for themselves in the 1960s." The Hitched Chick's self-esteem and appreciation of her worth and power is certainly ten-fold that of her mother in the 1960s and seventies, when she was at the same life stage. Says Gabrielle, thirty-two, "My mother had affairs and drank too much and did all kinds of weird things, not because she wanted to, but because she had no power over the things she really wanted power over. I think that's what a lot of mothers did, just no one talks about it. They had lots of weird, skeleton-in-the-closet ways of trying to assert their power, but in the end, it was self-destructive."

Witnessing this feeble attempt to gain power, Gabrielle speaks for all women when she says, "Power is important because, without it, you absolutely cannot be happy." Although some would argue it hasn't been dramatic enough, a female power revolution *has* taken place. From barely acknowledging women's entitlement and power (because so many, *too* many, didn't have any), society's preoccupation with it now is hard to ignore. Whether wrapped in a cut-to-thrill suit or swathed in a sweet little slip dress and bed-head hair, women's power today is genuine and attractive. Those so-called weaknesses—empathy, perspective, humor, tolerance—are now smart and attractive, and propel us higher than any dizzying stilettos. And our tenacity, diligence and focus keep us there long after the beer at the boys' clubs has gone flat. Whether we want to excel across the board or onto it, our expectation today is not just that we can, but that we *do*.

In politics, sports, medicine, business, education, nonprofit, marketing, finance, technology, the media, the post-feminist woman is enormously covetable. And her modern-day moxie is giving her the leverage to create work environments that best suit *her* needs.

For an article in the *Houston Chronicle* (1997), Amy Gage revealed the phenomenon is widespread. She quotes Jennifer Franke, twenty-seven, student body president at the J. L. Kellog Graduate School of Management at Northwestern University in Evanston, Illinois, who says, "Women graduates expect a certain level and we'll negotiate until we achieve it. Women are going in with the same training as men and if your performance is better, you're getting compensation for it."

If a woman today is not receiving what she considers to be ample compensation—in terms of finance or flexibility—for her efforts, she will not hesitate to seek an alternative position which fulfills her demands and recognizes and rewards her value. Older generations complain bitterly that their more youthful colleagues don't even consider the necessity of "paying their dues." They claim this generation's sense of entitlement is based on a soufflé of self-confidence and arrogance, and clutch hopefully to the theory that, during recession times, the "last one in, first one out" approach will favor them. Their assumptions are often proved wrong, since downsizing invariably profits those who are most able to multitask, live in (rather than tap in to) the zeitgeist and operate unencumbered by tradition or fear. Rightly or wrongly, these qualities are now as (if not more) important than decades of experience, and are liberally sprinkled over our résumés. Whether we are successful immediately in our endeavors to improve our destiny, the point is, we feel empowered and equipped to do so in the long term.

The Hitched Chick is applying the same principle to her personal life, too. When she takes off her work clothes, she doesn't also hang up her sense of entitlement and power in her closet. It's in her blood, coursing through her veins, fueling her to confront difficult issues with her husband, demanding what's best for her and spurring her on to make changes when she is dissatisfied. Roll over and take the blows? I think not. Meekly defer to his power? Don't even go there. Loaded with the ammunition, confidence and skills to file a case from a pay raise to discrimination, power follows her out of the office and often into her home.

If she doesn't achieve at least a mutually satisfying compromise long term, she knows she has the option of walking away and going it alone. Yes, she knows it will be painful, but not as painful as existing in a marriage in which she feels power*less*. Should she want to embark on a new relationship, she believes there are plenty of men who *will* appreciate her worth and *will* respect her needs.

According to *The Wall Street Journal* (December 2001), two phenomena are conspiring to further increase her value in her personal life: a sharp falloff in birthrates from 1955 to 1973 and the tendency of men to marry a few years their junior. Because birthrates plunged by 40 percent as the Baby Boom went bust, single men born toward the end of the boom (which officially ended in 1964) find themselves fishing in a steadily shrinking pool. Already there is a surplus of eighty thousand single American men in their thirties for every million single women that age. And by 2010, the *Journal* noted, men in their late thirties and early forties will outnumber women five to ten years younger by two to one.

Savvy and self-confident, Hitched Chick is a prized commodity and she can afford to pick and choose her priorities. With a sense of entitlement and power matched only by her desire to flex it, she is not prepared to relinquish it—at any cost. Even if the cost is her relationship with a man she loves.

To Boldy Go . . .

Says Simone, twenty-nine, "There's a beautiful book written by Milan Kundera called *The Book of Laughter and Forgetting*, which says that within the first three months of a relationship there is an untold pact settled between two people as to who is going to be the dominant one. Although women tend to make the shift from 'me' to 'we' more quickly than men do, women of my generation are very firm about not being dominated and, consciously or not, they exert their power very early in their relationship."

My research backs up Simone's argument. The modern woman is exerting her power and entitlement long before she makes her vows. Rather than waiting for the right man to come along and sweep her off her stilettos, she's as much the predator. And when she finds her catch, she won't wait for him to decide when the timing's right. No, she'll fling her handbag over her shoulder, hitch up her skirt, cart him off and make *him* fit into *her* life plan. She's not desperate to get married by any means. We've already discussed the comfort of the single's shelf. But unlike her mother who waited to be asked, once this girl's heart and mind is set on getting hitched, she wants it on her schedule and her terms.

Says Alexandra, twenty-eight, of her relationship with Stewart, twenty-nine, "We fell in love about eleven years ago so we've been together a long time. I had never been interested in marriage, because I felt it was a patriarchal institution that I didn't feel I needed to be a part of. I thought marriage meant that I would be the inherently submissive one, and the whole institution implied that Stewart would acquire me somehow and there was this obedience clause involved with marriage which was untenable. But three years ago, I decided I was ready, that I could confidently marry Stewart and still be me, without any of that. Plus, we both had relationships with each other's families so we were not just in our own little universe. Stewart was still unsure, so we spent about a year talking it over. Then we went to France for a family vacation and we got into an argument over it. Finally, I stamped my foot and said, 'When *are* you going to be ready, because I'm ready *now*.' So he said he was getting there and, at that point, we talked about it for real and just to be official about it, we took a picnic to one of the Hudson River piers to celebrate."

So did Stewart do the asking? Wake up, this is the modern world. "No," says Alexandra, "we asked each other to marry each other. He said, 'Will you marry me?' and I said, 'Yes, will you marry me?' and he said, 'Yes.'"

Says Tyler, thirty-one, "*I* asked Dez to marry me. I'd had lots of boyfriends and never wanted to marry any of them. Dez came along, he was gorgeous, kind, smart and good in bed and I just thought, Yep, I'll have him. He was a bit surprised. But he said yes, straightaway. In fact, he said he'd been waiting for the right moment to ask me. But when I want something, I have no problem asking for it. I knew he was the right man for me, so I wanted to move forward there and then."

Did that set the tone for Tyler's marriage? "Oh yeah," she says. "Dez knows there's little point putting up a fight. He knows if I want to do something, I'll do it anyway whether he agrees or not. He says I drive him crazy—I know I do—but I think he likes bossy, powerful women. If he'd been the kind of guy who believed all that crap about being the master, I never would have married him. He probably wouldn't have married me either. But he doesn't like girly girls, which is just as well. Ha, ha!"

Julia, thirty-one, says of her marriage to Andrew, "The very fact that I was the driving force in our getting together in the first place is indicative of the fact that I have the ability to get what I want. When we met, I already had a boyfriend and he already had a girlfriend, but I was immediately fascinated by Andrew because he was so snotty. Then I got a new job that was closer to him downtown and I e-mailed him and said, 'Why don't we meet for lunch?' He wrote back saying, 'Okay, but I can't tell Deborah because she is so pathologically jealous,' so we met for a secret lunch, then another secret lunch and then we met for secret drinks. I told him how I was trying to break up with my boyfriend and he said he'd been considering breaking up with his girlfriend, so basically I totally undermined this woman in a way that is completely against anything I believe in. I'm not a guy's girl, I'm a girl's girl. But I was totally single-minded. Y'know, I just thought, I have *got* to get him. I wanted it so badly. Then my boyfriend found out about the secret e-mails and called Andrew's girlfriend to say he thought we were having an affair. She called him at work and said, 'Either you stop e-mailing her or we're breaking up' and he said, 'I'm not going to stop e-mailing her.' Then he called me up at work and said, 'You know, Deborah just called and we've broken up.' I said, 'Okay, let's meet up at the Free Times Café,' which I chose for its name and so we met and basically just flew into each other's arms and he never went back again. But when I get some kind of conviction, the power of that conviction pulls Andrew along in my wake. And I think that, yes, I do use that notion of 'Do what I want or forget about it, you can't have me.' "

Sense of entitlement? Feelings of power to determine our destiny? You bet. It's thanks to the media that showed us what we could achieve if only we dared to assert our dreams. It's thanks to modern education, which no longer simply teaches facts, but encourages us to acknowledge our worth by focusing as much on sports, leadership skills and team building. It's thanks also to our parents, especially our mothers, who if they didn't feel powerful enough to make their own aspirations come true, pushed us to make sure ours did. And it's thanks to our own single life journey that made us acknowledge there is no need to settle for second best since there is undoubtedly something better around the corner. Something that *will* satisfy our exceedingly high expectations, *will* prove itself worthy of us, *will* reflect the power and confidence we feel entitled to possess.

Nowhere does it manifest itself more than in our relationships. We won't settle for the first guy who comes along and gives us a second look. If anyone's giving a second look, it's women today. But not just a second look, a third, fourth, fifth and sixth look, too. Is he smart enough for me? Is he handsome enough for me? Is he kind/generous/affluent/fit/witty/traveled/successful enough for me? Does he match my high expectations in bed? Many so-called modern guys declare that women's expectations are *too* high. Rubbish. Those same guys no doubt had fathers who denigrated their wives' ambitions outside the home. Those who say this are simply not recognizing that the world has changed and that power and respect are the rights of everyone.

Like landing a job that satisfies our needs, finding a man who does is only the beginning. If we demand a satisfactory return on our input at work, we expect the same in love. It's a reflection of our value. First stop: the engagement ring. A symbol of love and commitment, of course. A reflection of our own sense of beauty and style, yes. But as important, a statement of entitlement, power and success.

Although her husband, Danny, did the proposing, Melanie's first condition was that he buy her the engagement ring of *her* choice, unlike her mother (and many of our mothers), who got what she was given and was grateful. She says, "I want what I want. I wanted a ring with a one-carat diamond with a half carat on each side. I wanted a ring that equals two carats and I got a ring that equals two carats. This is what I wanted. So when I want something deeply, whether it's materialistic or a hug, no matter how you get it to me, I always get what I want. Danny respects me more for it. I don't think he would have married a pushover because I honestly don't think he would have been happy that way."

Terri, thirty-five, was determined to get what she wanted, too. Whether at work (where she wins million-dollar publishing deals), or at home (where she says, "I have a huge sense of entitlement and can be very bossy"), it's crucial to Terri that everything represents her forceful individuality, even though she admits she isn't perfect. "I didn't want the Tiffany ring. We did go to Tiffany and Chad wanted me to have the Tiffany engagement ring, but I tried a couple on and just felt they weren't me. They made a statement that isn't me, they represented tradition. So I found this very wacky jewelry designer and she made this ring which *I* designed. It's bohemian and doesn't feel like Tiffany. It represents the imperfection of our union. It's lop-sided and irregular, like me."

Says Amanda, twenty-nine, married to Larry, twenty-eight, "I basically bought my own ring. I went with my mom to put down the money. A couple of the ladies in the store felt very sorry for me. They said, 'Is this a gift for yourself?' and I said, 'No, it's my engagement ring.' One of them actually said, 'You're buying it *yourself*?' But I come from an incredibly egalitarian household and I absolutely have the expectation my own marriage will be egalitarian."

Once the ring of her choice is on her finger, and the bespoke vows (minus "obey") taken, it isn't only the new bride's skin that gives off a glow. Her confidence and power positively radiates. And it isn't bluster. I can tell by the way the women I interview talk to their husbands when they call them on their cell phones. Not spitefully, just oozing with self-assurance ("Honey, just to let you know, I'll be back after ten."). When we meet in a restaurant and order dinner, I can see how single-minded ("No, listen to me, I want Pinot Grigio not Pinot Blanc."), spirited ("Why not? I'll try the shark!") and ballsy they are ("I'd like you to cook this for an extra five minutes. I don't like blood."). When I make statements about marriage, they don't simply agree. They challenge, offer anecdotes, quote statistics. They turn my questions inside out, upside down, demanding clarification, suggesting alternative ways of phrasing to get the best and most from the interview. They walk the talk from the moment they start their day to the moment their heads hit their pillows. And when they meet obstacles to fulfillment, they ease them firmly to one side.

Says Julia, "We were at this mountain lodge. We went there with his law firm on a retreat. The bus was leaving at three and I wanted to go rowing on these little rowboats around the lake. Andrew didn't want to go rowing because he was afraid we were going to miss the bus back to the city. But I said, 'No, we have time and if you're not going to go rowing, well, I am,' and I walked down to the dock and I got in a boat and he was just standing there. So eventually he kind of shuffled down and got in the boat with me—he was so sullen and I was like, 'What's wrong? It's so beautiful' and he said, 'My God, Julia, you're so *intractable* and you didn't care that I didn't want to miss the bus.' I said to him, 'You're being ridiculous. You are not going to miss the bus.' The thing is I've always been fearless, but somehow being married makes me more fearless."

Married two years, Alexandra feels the same way. "We were both on vacation from graduate school in January and I wanted to travel, whereas Stewart wanted to do schoolwork," she says. "Although I was disappointed, I decided to go to India anyway. I sent a message out there to some of my friends and one of them just snapped on it immediately. So we spent three weeks in India and it was wonderful. I'm not into being sheltered and protected and this trip reinforced my feelings of power and independence, that I should do what I want to do, even if he doesn't want to."

For Alice, thirty-five, a dream assignment in Europe for two years was a cut-and-dried issue. "There was just no question that I wouldn't do this. I'm very headstrong. I know what I want and this was what I always wanted. My husband did have a choice—he could either stay in America or give up his job and come with me. Either way, I was going. He gave up his job. I can't say those two years were easy. He couldn't speak the language, he found it difficult to make friends, he wasn't earning, while I was working all the time, feeling great about what I was doing, earning a lot of money and having fun. A lot of men say they want to marry strong, powerful women, but when they get married they have a hard time dealing with them. You're not just going to turn into a pushover and say, 'Yes, honey, whatever you want,' just because you're married. It's ingrained into who you are."

Terri agrees. "I'm really headstrong and I do feel entitled to get my own way. I feel entitled to make decisions about myself and my marriage. Partly, it was how I was raised in that I don't want to be like my mother. Sometimes, it's a reaction to feeling I'm going to be stepped on or pushed back in ways that make me feel uncomfortable."

Dee, twenty-nine, identifies with this. "Evan and I had been working so much, I wanted our lifestyle to change. He was very entrenched in his career and I wanted to travel. I said, 'I'm leaving. I'm going to travel around Asia.' He said, 'How could you do that? We're married. I'm not going to see you for six months or a year.' And I told him, 'If you want to come, you can come, but I'm going anyway. If you're interested in coming, we can talk about where you want to go as well, but I'm going here, here and here, and I'm leaving in March.' Yes, I am more stubborn than he is, but that's because I tend to feel more strongly about things. Women used to allow themselves to be walked over because they felt like men should be the ones in charge. I'm not a monster, I just don't believe in that."

Her Way or the Highway?

Power isn't just about striding off toward the horizon, with hubby in tow or him languishing at home. However, many Hitched Chicks recognize that they are so fearful of losing control, relinquishing their power, succumbing to their husband's will so much they lose their voice and self-respect, they run the risk of overcompensating. Little annoyances become enormous conflicts, tiny disagreements mushroom into all-out estrangements.

Sound familiar to you? It does to me, too. Having cut my teeth in publishing, I know how to negotiate a deal to suit all my requirements. I can barge my way through the chilliest of receptions and emerge triumphant. I've been threatened with lawsuits, held my own in televised political debates, confronted prime ministers, had lunch with first ladies and delivered off-the-top-of-my-head speeches to two hundred people. And as for firing out vicious verbal blows to work opponents? I'm certainly no stranger to that. Which is why compromise in other areas of my life is rarely good enough for me now. If I don't win, I think I'm a loser.

I'm not alone. Amy, thirty-two, says, "I am the most powerful one in our relationship. I'm very self-motivated and I'm always the one saying, 'Come on, come on, we need to do this.' I must admit, we've had fights about it. But there are times when Garry will dig in his heels, either because he's hurt or he's right. And when he does, I have to make myself stop and ask myself whether I'm fighting because I really believe I'm right or am I fighting because there's an opponent and I just have to win?"

Says Sabina, forty, "I am a powerful force, but I tend to be over-bearing about wanting things my own way. I have difficulty compro-mising in many situations since I tend to view my side to be the only correct side. Although I make the decisions in our marriage, I know there are always two sides to any situation, so I do try to listen to Matthew and not belittle him."

Maybe it's because female power is a novelty for us that we flash it around like a new Fendi handbag after a hard-won promotion. Sometimes it's appropriate that we do so. No point stuffing it away in the back of the closet. We should display our gains with pride. We're entitled to. Plus, we want to have fun with our new toy, even if it sometimes grates or undermines others.

Says Emily, thirty-three, "I enjoy the drama. I might raise an issue which will turn into an argument, then when it's cleared, I'll say, 'That was a fun argument—done! I didn't really mean that.'"

I've done that, too. Nothing like a good old heated debate at a dinner party. Even if I don't necessarily believe in my argument, I'll defend it to the death. Just because I can. Just for fun. Sometimes it's simply to exercise my brain or to be contrary. I'm not ashamed to say I do it with my husband, too. But whether it's a benign tussle over where we might eat our brunch on a Sunday to a more meaningful exertion of power over how our daughters should be educated, the point is, I march up and shake the hand of conflict, not with sweaty limp palms, but with a firm grasp.

I'm right to do so in many respects. And so are you. If there's one issue relationship experts agree on, it's that habitual avoidance of conflict is the number one predictor of divorce. In consistently walk-ing away from battles—especially those that revolve around values and firmly held beliefs—you run the risk of escalating resentments, crushed self-esteem and layer after layer of unresolved issues.

On the other hand, if you argue over everything, even if some-times it is purely for fun, attempting to exert control all the time, you risk devaluing fighting. How is anyone to know what's truly important to you? Going for the kill *all* of the time may result in you murdering one of the most precious elements in your life. Your marriage.

Hmmm. Just because we don't want to end up like many of our mothers, doesn't mean we should strive to be as domineering, controlling and stubborn as many of our fathers. The key, say experts, is balance. Get your way today, it's his turn tomorrow. If he controls *this* life-changing decision, you'll control *that* one. And power takes on many forms. It isn't simply about making the decisions, it's about participating in them as an equal, which means equal measures of voice, respect, sharing, support and attention.

In recent years, I've come to realize that, as much as it pains me, I am not right all of the time. (I can't resist adding, however, I believe I'm right most of the time. Ha!) There's a lot to be said for compromise. And as the great Larry King quoted recently, "I've never learned anything while I've been talking." How true is that? On the occasions I've zipped up and allowed my husband to get a word in edgeways, I've known that what he's saying is common sense, considered and wise.

It's a lesson Hitched Chicks in the throes of successful marriages have learned, too.

Says Emily, the self-confessed conflict addict, "I constantly raise issues and once we get into an argument, I then say, 'You know what? That really wasn't an issue.' But Mark is way more sensitive than I am, so if we have a disagreement, it will sit with him longer, so I try not to do that too often. But although I tend to be the more difficult one and will find more things to be annoyed about, more things to do, more things that should be a certain way than he will, I have come to trust his way of thinking. I trust his morality so I'll defer to him on certain issues. It's made our relationship a lot better."

Terri agrees. "Chad and I are totally like Mutt and Jeff. I'm six feet tall and he's five feet eight. I have big hair, he has thinning gray hair. He's unflappable, I can be a very big personality and kind of hysterical and spacey. So even if I get mad and I want my own way, I trust him so I try to listen to him. He offers advice, then he steps back. I don't want anyone telling me what to do or fixing things for me. But I have the confidence in myself and the confidence in him that we will arrive at the right decision."

Ruth, thirty-eight, says, "I actually get my own way, too, although I've learned to listen. I tend to be the initiator of everything, but Dennis is very detail-oriented. He'll say, 'Do you have the empirical data to support that?' which annoys the crap out of me, but I'll say, 'Yes, actually I do' and make sure I do."

Says Gabrielle, thirty-two, "I have an awful lot of power and he defers to me a lot of the time. If there's anything at any time that I really wanted, I truly believe I'd get it. I decide what we eat at night, I decide which cable company we use, I decide how we pay the bills, I decide where we live. But there has to be balance. There have been times when Murray hasn't given in to me and, funnily enough, I've actually ended up respecting him more. If he gave in to me any more than he does right now, I'd think of him as really weak."

It's certainly a fine balance. When a husband shows signs of being too domineering, we fear he's turning into our father and we don't respect him. When he shows signs of being too relenting, we fear he's not man enough for us and we don't respect him either. Can we ever fight and resolve conflicts so we both win?

THE HITCHED CHICK'S GUIDE TO
Resolving Power Struggles—So You Both Win!

According to those who spend all their days tearing conflicted couples apart and gluing them back together again, every happy, successful couple has approximately ten areas of disagreement they will never resolve. From opposing political views to how often you have sex, these disagreements will vary in degree of importance to you, but know that even though you are two strong and independent people, it *is* possible to stay together until death, not disagreement, do you part. Here's how:

+ ***Remember you are equals.*** Regardless of who earns more, who works hardest, who's better educated, who has more awards, a whole marriage is made up of two halves which, by definition, means the two of you are equal and have equal rights to happiness and satisfaction. If you fail to recognize this, the marriage is lost before the fight even begins. This is a sensitive subject for Ellis, forty-three, who recalls the startling realization that her first husband, Phil, did not regard her as his equal. She says, "There's this John Updike book about marriage called *Couples*. It's all about marriage and wife-swapping in the 1970s. Phil read it and loved it, but when I read it I just thought, This is dreadful. He asked me why I didn't like it and I said, 'Well, there's this sentence that says every marriage or relationship consists of an aristocrat and a peasant. What a fucking stupid thing to write. I mean, as if . . . ' And Phil said, 'Well ours does . . . ' I said, '*Does* it?' And he said,

'It's obvious. I went to Yale and you went to UCLA.' And I was like, *'What?!?!!'* and we had this great big fight and that told me everything I needed to know about what Phil thought about our relative statuses and, therefore, who had the power." Although individual members of a team may not be paid equally or have the same public profile, for a team to win, each member's position must be valued, respected and their contribution to the team's well-being and success acknowledged.

+ ***Pick your battles.*** Avoiding conflict can have disastrous consequences, but perpetually creating it or launching into each one as ferociously as the next is also a recipe for disaster. Before going into battle, Anabelle, thirty-five, says, "I ask myself, Does it matter *profoundly*? Sometimes it does, in which case, I dig my heels in and don't give up until I'm happy. But if, for instance, Peter has cleaned the kitchen and it's not as good as I want it to be, I ask myself, Does this matter profoundly? It's a great way to determine what's an important argument and what's just downright irritating." Anyway, as Diane, twenty-nine, says, "Life's too short to fight every battle. If you fought every battle, there'd be no time to have fun, right?" Right. Since Anabelle gave me her advice, I've put it in action numerous times. Result? Calmer outlook, better marriage, happier life.

+ ***Strike swiftly.*** If you now know it matters profoundly, don't allow little seeds of anger or resentment to grow into big, raging bushes of fury which become harder to control and calm. Says Ellis, "Sometimes I might get a bit irritated about something. If I don't say it there and then, there comes a point when I'm really fucking irritated about it and I'll shout, 'I'm bloody angry about this, rah, rah, rah . . . !' and I'll go on and on about it and scare him to death so that he goes all quiet and won't talk to me. One of the tricks I've learned is to verbalize my anger earlier. Then it's contained and we can move on quickly without it then spilling over into other areas of the relationship."

+ *Garner your confidence.* Do this to put forward your point of view and to insist your husband listens. According to relationship guru Dr. John Gottman, "Women are already practiced at accepting influence from men, but a husband's ability to be persuaded by his wife is crucial. A true partnership only occurs when you are both able to accept influence." Your opinion counts for a hell of a lot, but don't forget, his does, too. Bolster your confidence, should you need to, with what Ruth calls "empirical data." It will also give your input more credibility. So ask yourself why this matter is of such importance. Why will your opinion benefit you both? Why is this the right course of action? I know when I've ploughed headlong into a conflict either at work or at home and I haven't had the backing of "empirical data" to support my point of view—or enabled me to challenge my opponents confidently—I've had to resort to either flouncing off or stamping my feet. Resolution? No. Simply a big fat zero.

+ *Don't withhold.* I'm not talking about spiteful comments. Those you *should* withhold since they accomplish nothing except hurt feelings. I'm referring to withholding crucial information or emotions. It's tempting to do so, especially since, as Ellis says, "If one of you withholds information or withholds emotions, that person has the power." But this does not constitute fair fighting and destroys the chance of healthy resolution. Ellis continues, "Phil had the power when he had an affair. It gave him a lot of power. I knew we were going through a bad patch, but I felt powerless because I didn't know what was going on. I mean, unless somebody brings all their biscuits to the table and says, 'Here are what my biscuits are,' you don't know which biscuit to choose. Phil didn't bring his biscuits to the table, so when we split up and there were biscuits being hurled around the room and there were crumbs everywhere, there were a whole bunch of biscuits I didn't know we had! I was trying to sort out our marriage from a position of not knowing and he had all the power because he knew what was going on. He was holding all the cards. Similarly, if you withhold your emotion, the other person is always going, 'Give me some emotion, give me some love,' and doing things to please to get love back when it's just not coming. And so those relationships are not equal in power. Information and communication are power and they have to be flowing in both directions."

◆ *If you can't be positive, stay in neutral.* Oh my, it's so easy to blame, isn't it? And to throw crushing blows and vicious comments? But in doing so, we are not being powerful, we're demonstrating a *lapse* in power. I've hurled the most abhorrent abuse to bring an argument to a close, but the victory has been empty. I feel ashamed and my husband is hurting so badly, a high five is the last thing on my mind. These days, I reserve one-liners for times I know they're genuinely witty because they're warm. Dr. John Gottman (adore that guy) says, "In a happy marriage, couples make at least five times as many positive statements to and about each other and their relationship, such as, 'We laugh a lot,' as opposed to negative ones, such as 'We never have fun.'" What's more, you must make it clear that you're on common ground, by stating, "This is *our* problem." He also advises that backing down in marriage, as in the martial art of aikido, you sometimes have to yield to win. Try offering signs of appreciation for your partner. Says Pia, thirty-two, "I often use positive reinforcement. So I'll say, 'It meant so much that you did that and I know you didn't want to do it, but I appreciate you letting me have my own way.'" Experts agree that when fights become too heated and both of you are flexing your power, the best move is to take a break. Allow the temperature to cool. I agree. But I have one other tip to pass on and it's something I learned from my husband, who does this often: in the heat of an argument, I walk up to him and say, "We don't agree on this, but I want you to know that I love you so much." Winning, as you now know, matters to me. As does maintaining my power. But maintaining the love and dignity in my marriage means just as much. Try it.

Power Tools

Flexing power in modern marriage isn't simply about who starts and wins battles. The Hitched Chick's desire to display it emerges in the most unconventional ways, many so subtle they could be regarded as accidental. Or missed altogether. But believe me when I say most moves she makes are with power in mind. At times when it seems like her husband is flexing *his* power, it will not be flexed at the expense of her own. As Melanie, thirty, says, "It's because I'm allowing it. Are you listening?"

Yes, I'm listening. Like I'm listening when Gabrielle says, "I feel it's important that Murray doesn't drive the car all the time. Who drives the car is really important. And how they drive the car. That represents independence and taking control. Our mothers always sat in the passenger seat. But I think who drives is incredibly symbolic."

I'm listening when Anabelle says, "If Pete puts his tea bags in the sink, that's where they stay. I will not transfer a tea bag from the sink. It's a power thing. My dad always left his tea bag in the sink for my mom to scoop out and throw away. I won't do it."

My ears also prick up when Patti, thirty-four, confesses that one of the ways she maintains her power over Tim is, "I tell him when other people have found me cute. It could be the guy in the grocery store. I won't make it into a big deal, but I'll just mention it casually. Or maybe I'll say, 'I went out for dinner with a friend and we ran into this friend of hers from high school and it was the funniest thing. He asked if I was married and when I said yes, he said, 'Oh, that's a shame because I'd really love to take you out some time.' I'd definitely be sure to tell Tim about that."

Patti says her power move is not an attempt to provoke jealousy. We all hate jealousy in our partners since we know it's a way of *their* attempting to control *us*. No, Patti's motivation is to remind Tim of her worth should he happen to forget for one moment that he is privileged to have her company. It's why she also ensures she looks gorgeous when she turns up at the airport to meet him from a work trip with colleagues. "I definitely make sure I don't show up in a big sweatshirt. I'll wear capri pants and a little Abercrombie T-shirt and sneakers. I want those young female assistants to say, 'Oh, did you see what Tim's wife looked like?'" And for Tim to know how lucky he is, too? I ask Patti. "Oh yes, and definitely that," she laughs.

Keeping up her appearance isn't just to exert power over her husband. For many Hitched Chicks, the benefits are internal as well as external. Says Ruth, thirty-eight, "I work out twice a week with a trainer. She comes to my house at nine o'clock in the morning on Saturdays and Wednesdays. It's great. It's made me feel more comfortable about my body and I feel more attractive, too. My husband has said, 'You used to walk down the street and guys would look. But now you walk down the street and guys are *really* looking.' I like the fact that he notices that. But that's not the only reason. It's important for my self-esteem and sense of power and it's about being proud of who you are."

Gabrielle agrees. "I exercise a lot. Like being committed to my own goals, it's something I need to do to maintain my own sense of personal power and feeling power*ful*. And I need it to feel strong and powerful on a physical level, otherwise you start relying on your husband to say, 'No, you're not fat, you're really attractive.' That's a way you start giving away your power. You put on weight, feel really bad about it, don't do anything about it and expect them to make you feel okay about it. I've been there, done that and it doesn't work."

Neither does allowing your brain to become flabby. Expecting hubby to be your sole source of news and intellectual stimulation is a sure way to give away power. It's why so many Hitched Chicks absolutely refuse to quit work even when they have kids. Studies may suggest that the main reason women work is to bolster their standard of living. (It's one reason certainly. And they do have extremely high standards. As Maggie, forty-two, puts it, "I don't want to keep up with the Joneses. I *am* the Joneses!")

However, as important as the economic power they derive from work is, intellectual power is a motivating force, too. Says Amanda, "I don't like it if Larry seems smarter than me. If I ever gave up work, I'd be concerned that the intellectual equilibrium would be sent off-kilter. He's very smart and it's important for me and my self-esteem to be as well-informed and be able to talk as intelligently as he does."

It's something Shauneice, thirty-six, says she was very conscious of when she *was* at home following the birth of her baby. "I made sure I read the papers every day and I'd do the crossword while I was breastfeeding. It was a way of exercising my brain power. It's easy to lose it when all you're thinking about is diapers and feeding schedules."

Says Gabrielle, "I wouldn't like Murray to come home and have to tell me there'd been a train crash somewhere. I pride myself on being able to tell him first. So I do a lot of reading and communicating in order to exercise a certain amount of connected power. I like him to feel that I'm in the know. I'm conscious that intellectual power is important to feel like an equal."

Catherine, thirty-four, says she derives power from "shaking up the status quo." This is how it works: we know that the well-documented male longing for variety can be a very powerful force. Except when it comes to food (when they'll happily eat ribs, chips, hot dogs and pickles every day of the week), variety excites them. Ever noticed how even the pig-ugliest guy in the company of the most beautiful woman still ogles everything with a pulse? On this basis, Catherine will often substitute the expected attributes of dependability and consistency with capricious unpredictability.

Catherine admits, "I don't plan it, but some days I'm sweet, cuddly Cathy. Then other days, I just wake up and decide I'll be a bit distant, aloof and mysterious. This tactic works especially if I think Jeremy is showing signs of taking me for granted. Within hours, he's circling me, nuzzling my neck, asking if everything's okay, telling me how much he loves me. At that point, I could have anything I want. But I only go so far . . . two days of being aloof is enough. Then I become fun-loving, slightly wild and crazy Cathy. Works like a charm!"

It works triumphantly in bed, too, according to Natasha, thirty-one. Anyone can see her husband, Bill, worships at her altar. (He even has Natasha's face on his coffee mugs and mouse pad at work!) Natasha attributes some (though by no means all) of her power over Bill to her elusive and unpredictable behavior in bed. "Sometimes, I feign a little bit of boredom so he might wonder if he's good enough for me. And then there are those nights when he comes to bed, I throw back the sheets and I'm dressed in the full-on red-and-black lace. Bill never knows what to expect from me. It's one way of feeling powerful, but the bonus is, it keeps our sex life from becoming stale."

The Power-Sex Connection

Physical power, intellectual power, economic power . . . Hitched Chick ensures she enjoys them all. Now add to the list sexual power. Because a little-known fact is that women who have careers and enjoy their work are the happiest, most sexually fulfilled and confident women of all.

For sure, work exhausts us. It certainly stresses us, although we know from Chapter 2, the lust chapter, that a by-product of stress can be a sizzling libido. And God knows, there's a lot to be said for the orgasmic rush of paying for something—shoes, jewelry, car, home— from our own salary check. But everyone agrees that the soaring self-esteem and sense of power which comes from stimulating, satisfying work outweighs all the negative aspects of work, and even overshadows the other positives.

See, at work, you're more likely to experience boosts to your self-confidence than from anywhere else. Think about it for a second. For starters, when we work, we can't turn up in egg-stained leggings and a T-shirt that looks like something the cat left in the corner. We have to look polished, respectable, powerful. Focusing on our appearance isn't the sole reserve of the silly or vain. How occupied and satisfied we are with our looks dramatically improves our esteem levels, which in turn can improve our health.

Once we arrive at work, it's not just our polished appearance that generates confidence-building compliments. Our ability and competence is being judged hourly. A great part of the satisfaction of success comes from recognition from others. Feeling valued and recognized boosts the power you have externally, yes, but internally, too. Nothing like meeting a deadline, winning a salary raise and securing a promotion to send self-esteem skyrocketing. Work is truly medicine for the mind, safeguarding our sense of power and protecting against depression, one of the symptoms of which we know to be . . . yes, low libido.

Simply doing housework, even if it *is* in conjunction with raising children (a most worthwhile job by anyone's standards), just doesn't do anything for your level of self-esteem. In fact, the longer a woman is at home, the more housework she does, the more she associates her home with tedium and drudgery. And we know the power of association. When a woman goes out to work, as modern wives tend to do, her associations with the home are positive—it's a wonderful place to relax and play, the two vital components of sex. Hardly surprising that working women have fewer sexual problems than those who are at home all day, vacuuming their hearts out, cleaning their houses and their self-esteem away.

What's more, those qualities and skills that make us successful at work—confidence, focus, assertiveness and our ability to negotiate, prioritize and confront—are rarely left behind in the office. They're whizzing around the sitting room, kitchen and bedroom, too. So used to asking for what we want at work, we can hardly stop ourselves asking for what we want in bed. Just as well. Not knowing how to ask for pleasure is the most common reason people have dissatisfying sex lives.

Lottie, thirty-two, the commercial Realtor we met back in Chapter 2, says, "It's impossible to imagine being the same person making demands at work and not being demanding in bed. Surely asking for a better office or a salary increase is more difficult than asking for oral sex?"

Says Mel, thirty-seven, "I'm sure Richard thinks I'm bossy in bed. I *can* be quite bossy, I know, but I get so used to bossing everyone around at work, it's hard to switch off. But I think you have to be bossy at times. I mean, if I didn't tell Richard to stop sometimes, he'd play with my nipples all night. I like it when he does, but I'm like, 'Hell-o, I do have other bits that need attention as well, you know?' I think Richard likes me telling him what to do. And he *loves* it when I initiate sex."

Who initiates is all about self-esteem. Hitched Chicks say they're most likely to make the first move when they're feeling powerful and confident. Says Lottie, "I always do when I've had a great day at work. In fact, my husband will often say to me when I walk in the door, 'How was your day?' and I look at him as if to say, 'I know what you're thinking . . . '"

Says Gina, thirty-four, "You have to have confidence to instigate sex. What happens if he turns around and says he's not in the mood? If you're feeling insecure about yourself, the rejection can really hurt. If you're confident, you just accept he's not in the mood and either roll over and' go to sleep or sort yourself out. It's no big deal."

Thirty-six-year-old Sam's certainly not short on self-esteem. If her husband doesn't respond to her advances, she says, "I use the Jedi mind trick. I'll start talking to him about his work like I'm really, really interested. That seems to get him all excited. He designs computer software and if I start talking in computer jargon, I swear to God, the old packet gets aroused and I'm like, 'Okay then!' Whatever it takes . . ."

Some husbands can feel intimidated by their wives' confident sexual advances. Or, says Stacey, thirty, "bullied into it." Who'd have thought it? Isn't it the wife who feigns a headache at the first sign of

sex? Not any longer. "Although Ben likes it when I initiate sex," says
Stacey, "I think when he's under stress, he sees it as just another thing
someone's telling him to do." It's the same for Emily, thirty-three.
"Mark thinks I'm trying to tell him to have sex and what I know is that
if you tell him to do something, he just won't do it."

Maybe not. But what I know is that if Hitched Chick doesn't get
what she wants at work—an assistant, support, resources—she'll
attempt every trick in the book to get it. Likewise in bed. She won't
hesitate to talk dirty, perform a striptease, jump on top into her
favorite sex position. But there's one surefire power-sex strategy the
modern Mrs. implements to start the balls rolling.

When all else fails, she gives him a blow job.

Says Amy, "If I'm giving him oral sex, it makes me feel powerful
that I can turn him on and arouse him by what I do. And I like to do
it because that turns me on—a lot. By turning him on, it turns me on
far more than anything else because it's in my head that what I am
doing is making him come." Same for Jess, thirty-four, who says she
feels tremendously powerful "because Bob loves it so much. Plus I
find it a turn-on, too."

Lottie agrees, "I think a lot of women used to think giving a guy
oral sex was degrading. I guess it is if you're sixteen and you're being
pressured into it. I mean, the idea of a guy holding the girl's head
down? *Ugh!* That *is* degrading and if he's doing that, he deserves to
have his balls bitten off. But when you're doing it because you want
to, it isn't degrading at all. How can it be degrading when you're
turning him to jelly? Also, he's entrusting you with his most precious
possession. Oh God, yeah, I feel powerful."

Melanie agrees. "There's nothing like it. Especially when you
really love someone. When I used to do it with other guys, it was just
a job. But with him, I get physically turned on when I go down on
him. He moans and shows me he loves what I'm doing. It's a very

powerful feeling and it gets me going. When he gets excited like that, it turns me on immensely to the point that I'm soaking wet."

If some women don't like giving oral sex, says Joely, twenty-six, it's because they don't know how to do it properly and they're not applying the same amount of focus as they might when they're persuading a work colleague to relinquish some of their power. She has a right to hold this opinion: at college, her friends affectionately called her the Blow Job Queen and she applies the skills which earned her that title to great effect on her happy husband.

THE HITCHED CHICK'S GUIDE TO
the Power Blow Job

With thanks, in particular, to Joely, Jess, Lottie and Sam, who made this section so much fun and yet so damn useful.

+ ***Define your purpose.*** Says Joely, "Are you doing this so he can get off and you can move onto the next step or do you have a gift to give him? It's all about power—remember, you have power when you're giving him a blow job. You're taking him on a journey he won't go on via intercourse, via a magazine or Vaseline. Only you are going to be able to give this to him. And if you have that sense of power and privilege, it makes a huge difference."

+ ***Squish your squeamishness.*** Joely says, "You have to be willing to accept whatever you may find. Many women are put off oral sex because it's stinky. Unless your husband has just stepped out of the bath, he'll be stinky and sweaty, but you really have to learn to believe and understand that smell is sensual." Oh, I'm sorry, but I have to agree with Sam here when she says, "There's nothing that puts me off more than a been-under-the-blankets-for-seven-hours crusty willy. I mean, I wouldn't have Ray go down on me when I haven't had a shower. No, let me go and fluff it up a bit, get some suds going in there and then we can get down to business. It's about respect." But Joely is insistent. A shower can hold up proceedings and sometimes you just don't have the time to wait. *Hmmm . . .* okay, next?

* *Get to grips with the basic technique.* Sam says, "I just hold the base hard and get my laughing gear around it." But Joely says, "Hold his dick firmly with one hand and hold his balls with the other and stroke them very lightly as you move your mouth up and down."

* *Gauge your speed.* Says Lottie, "Many women don't know how fast to go. When I'm moving my mouth up and down, I'm saying to myself, One elephant, two elephant, three elephant, four elephant . . ." (!)

* *Don't use teeth.* "Unless they want teeth," says Joely. "But a lot of women don't realize exactly how sensitive it can be. You have to focus more on lips and tongue. A little teeth sometimes are okay, but a lot of men freak out. Pain is not comfortable. Oral sex is not munching."

* *Touch his sensitive parts.* "That bit between his testicles and his anus. If you can't go there with your tongue, you *have* to go there with your fingers. Massaging. Just stroking it very lightly," Lottie says. "When he's really wet from my saliva, I insert a finger." Into his anus? "Yes," she says, "just gently and when he's almost on the point of coming."

* *Take him as far back as you can.* Says Jess, "It massages the tip if it touches the back of the roof of your mouth."

+ ***Swallow.*** Okay, this is where many women draw the line. But, says Joely, "Shutting your mouth is for junior high school. You can't get grossed out." Jess advises, "It's difficult to do without gagging, but the key is to breathe through your nose and swallow in rhythm so it massages it at the same time. It doesn't always work." Meaning? "I had a stomach bug and it wasn't long after one of my little spells and I was giving Bob a blow job and I was trying to do the whole deep throat thing and I threw up all over him. Ha, ha! Hoo, hoo! He's never let me live that down. It's our own private little joke." While Joely and Jess firmly subscribe to swallowing, Sam and Lottie aren't so rigid. Says Sam, "I'm a gagger." Says Lottie, "Me, too. I don't think there's anything wrong with holding it in your mouth then letting it seep out over him. Men are usually so blissed-out anyway, they don't really care."

Married to a
Son of a Bitch

Whether you have equilibrium or you're the benign dictator at home, nothing, no one, it seems, challenges it more than the other woman in your beloved's life. I'm talking about your husband's mother. Your mother-in-law.

Lucky you if her presence extends only as far as the odd night of baby-sitting, the perfect recipe for pastry and the framed photograph on your fireplace of her bouncing your husband, aged one, on her knee. If so, you do have cause to be smug. Because the mother-in-law, specifically the husband's mother, is attempting to exert so much power, thereby causing so much conflict in modern marriage, the British Psychological Society focused their end of 1999 symposium on her. Reporting on studies conducted by Cambridge University, the BPS states, "The mother-in-law may have long been the butt of many a male comedian's humor, but to the daughter-in-law, her spouse's mother is no joke."

They can say that again. For a shocking number of the Hitched Chicks I interviewed—I'd say 70 percent—mother-in-laws are a major obstacle to marital harmony. The issue of money is certainly up there, as is sex, as a common conflict-source, but His Mother (or HM, rather like Her Majesty, huh?) is desperately jostling for the number one slot.

Dr. Terri Apter, who conducted the Cambridge study, says, "There is a basic conflict between a wife's desire to be equal to her man and a mother's need to put her child first." Fair enough. But if that were the sole reason, wouldn't all mothers—yours as well as his—be as equally intrusive, demanding, controlling and undermining? Are they suggesting mothers of daughters don't love them as much as mothers of sons? Give me a break.

No, the conflict is more complex than a parent's basic desire to look after her offspring. It's about power. Sad, really. See, HM didn't hold much power in her relationship with the other man in her life, her husband. So what better substitute than a son? Here was a male over whom she *could* have power. That is, until you came along and spoiled it all. She was, quite possibly, perfectly amenable when you were her son's girlfriend since, she believed, you probably wouldn't be around long enough to challenge her influence. But from the moment you said "I do," you posed a serious threat to her power. And she doesn't like it one bit.

She won't get it, of course. If your mom-in-law has daughters as well as her son, those daughters will be Hitched Chicks just like you and, whilst respecting her, will probably be intending to carve out lives vastly different from hers. Feeling rejected and intimidated by her own daughter's independence, she will endeavor to seek and maintain power in her son's life. If your mother-in-law doesn't have a daughter, she will not comprehend that any woman could possibly care for a man in the way she can. (She will be right, of course. Your Hitched Chick view is that her caring is suffocating, patronizing, ridiculous and downright unhelpful.)

But that her son is in love with you, not to mention having sex with you (after all, aren't hers the only nipples good enough for him to nibble?), will be a huge slap in the face for her. Considering all she gave to him, all she did for him, everything she invested in him, doesn't her devotion deserve reciprocation? But how can he possibly reciprocate when he's married to someone more powerful than she is? You.

Irrespective of who you are and all your accomplishments, you will not, in her mind, be good enough for her boy. And because of who you are and your accomplishments, the devotion your husband shows to you will be in direct proportion to the despisal *she* has for you.

As I say, it's sad. Sad also because, chances are, HM is actually a very good person. She is, after all, responsible for bringing your beloved into the world and impressing upon him all the values and beliefs which made him so attractive to you in the first place. In many ways, she has been the major influence in his life as she will have brought him up practically single-handedly as your husband's father will have off-loaded most, if not all, child-rearing duties on her. And that your husband displays such bouts of kindness and sensitivity, so many good and decent qualities, and has achieved so much already in his life, will be down to your ma-in-law's tender loving care.

Unfortunately, the majority of Hitched Chicks are unable to yell a big "yaaay for His Mother!" because any affections they might have possessed for her will have been strangled out of them over the months, *years.* Her negative interference, snide comments, public put-downs and all-around devious, undermining, dangerous behavior makes Saddam Hussein look like the tooth fairy.

Now, this may all sound extreme. But, I kid you not, I've been forced to give the subject a lot of thought. Almost every married girl I spoke to had some eyebrow-raising comment to make when I brought up HM. Even if they claimed to get on well with her, they usually added that it was on sufferance or because they rarely saw her, perhaps as a direct result of her living in another country, or because they have endured such big bust-ups the power positions are now firmly defined. For the majority, His Mother is an on-going thorn in their side, whose prickly force has been felt since day one.

Says Madeleine, thirty-nine, married for ten years, "Andy and I rarely fight except about one thing, his mother. She didn't want us to get married from the start. I'm not sure exactly why. Perhaps it was because I came from a different country and that I spoke a different language that threatened her. She has this overwhelming fear of other women who seem smarter than she is. But from the moment we told her we were going to get married, she referred to our wedding as 'the party.' Finally, I had to sit her down and say, 'Look, this is not a party, this is a wedding, and you may not want to accept it, and you don't have to come, but this is a wedding.' She did come, but not until she'd done everything she could possibly think of to hurt me and spite me."

For instance? Says Madeleine, "I said to all of the women attending the wedding, 'I don't care what you wear so long as it's not cream.' So, of course, on the day of the wedding, she shows up in cream. I had been asking her before the wedding if I could see her outfit and she kept saying, 'No, I haven't picked it out yet.' So on the day of the wedding, I'm walking out and I see her in her dress in the *exact* color I had asked her *not* to wear."

Madeleine continues, "Plus, Andy and I had decided to walk

down the aisle together, but she was also walking down the aisle whispering to Andy all the way down, 'You don't have to do this. If you want to walk away, you can. You don't have to do this.' I was really, really angry by the time we got to the vows. She totally ruined my wedding day."

Pia wasn't oblivious to her mother-in-law's negative behavior either. She says, "Straight after the wedding, Michael's mother was talking to my father and asked him if he was sad that he was losing his daughter. And, of course, my father said, 'No, Michael is such a great guy, I feel like I'm gaining a son.' And Michael's mother said to my father, 'Yes, that's exactly how I felt about Fiona,' who is her other daughter-in-law. At that moment, Michael said, '*And* Pia!' But it was such a painful moment because it was her opportunity to say something nice, but she didn't. She's very intelligent, so I couldn't put it down to stupidity. On the contrary, she knows *exactly* what she's doing and saying . . ."

Pia says HM knew what she was doing the following Christmas, too, when she made the family dog seem more important than her new daughter-in-law. She remembers, "That first Christmas, we were driving to their house and Michael said to me, 'I know my mom is already knitting you a stocking, it's her tradition.' So when we arrived, sure enough there were the stockings hanging up. They all had names on them except for one which had a picture on it. So when the time came to hand out the stockings, it turned out that the one with the picture on it was for the dog! It seems so ridiculous to be hurt by such a thing and I'm embarrassed about it, but I was very upset."

According to the study presented to the British Psychological Society, mothers-in-law claim they generally have no idea what they are doing wrong and genuinely want to forge a good relationship with their daughters-in-law. Really? That's certainly a commendable claim. Unfortunately, their actions tend to contradict their words. And, Hitched Chicks say, it's all part of their strategy to undermine the daughter-in-law. Says Madeleine, "Oh yes, she won't come out and tell you to your face she doesn't want you around, she'll come at me from the side, saying things when Andy isn't around and then when he finds out, she'll say, 'What? I didn't do that,' or 'No, of course I didn't mean that.'"

Same for Naiela, thirty, who's married to Pete. She says, "Pete's mother never exactly said she couldn't stand the sight of me. But I'll give you an example of how she showed it. My parents live on the other side of the country and I missed having a family. So I was happy to visit his mother and father every two weeks or so. We'd go to their place in the country on a Sunday and his mother would put out a spread . . . you know, cakes, sandwiches, cookies, meats, the whole thing. Instead of a bowl of salad, though, she'd make individual salads and hand them out. She'd say, 'That's for you, Pete, and this one's for Naiela, and this one's mine and that's for Dad.' We'd been visiting for a few weeks and it dawned on me that my salad was always the one with the very green leaves. You know, the outside of the lettuce, where all the leaves are almost dead and you can see where the bugs have bitten their way through? I didn't say anything the first time, but when it happened again and again, I said to Pete one day, 'Have you noticed how your mother always gives me the dead lettuce leaves?' I mean, it sounded ridiculous and Pete said, 'Don't be an idiot. I'm sure it's not intentional.' But the next time we went, I told him, 'Look at the salads. I bet you she gives me the dead leaves.' Sure enough, that's what happened. Now, bear in mind, I hate confrontation. But I also won't be intimidated. So when I saw the salad—oh, and she never fills my cup, either, so she'd pour extra coffee for Pete and his dad, but she'd just walk straight past me—anyway, when I saw the salad, I looked at Pete and raised my eyebrows. He saw what she'd put on my plate and he just closed his eyes as if to say, 'Oh, no.' So I said—ha! ha!—I said, 'Betty, look I'm not so hungry and I have more than you, why don't you have mine?' and I quickly swapped plates before she could say anything. Oh my God, it was hilarious. But actually, when we drove home that night, I was really upset."

Says Sammi, thirty-seven. "My mother-in-law won't actually say anything nasty to my face, but it's the little things she does—or doesn't do—that can hurt as much. For instance, she doesn't have a single photograph of me on her fridge. She has photos of my husband. She has photos of the kids. She has photos of her and the kids. And she has photos of my husband and her and the kids. But not a single photograph with me in it. I said to her, 'Liz, why don't you have any pictures of me on your fridge?' and she said, 'But Sammi, you don't like having your picture taken.' I said, 'That's just not true. I *love* having my picture taken, especially with the kids.' So then I decided to *give* her a photo. My husband had organized a studio portrait of me and the girls and when I saw them, I was thrilled. So I chose a nice frame and gave her one of the photos of us. She looked at it and said, 'But why isn't Bob in the photo?' For ages, she didn't stand the photograph up. I hunted high and low for it. Finally, I discovered she'd stuck it away at the back of a shelf in the guest bedroom. I just couldn't believe it."

Neither could Bettina, thirty, when she gave her mother-in-law a carefully chosen framed photograph from her wedding album. "I spent weeks searching for the perfect frame. Then I chose the best wedding photograph with the four of us—me, my husband and his mother and father—and gave it to her as a gift. She invited us to her house for Thanksgiving along with lots of other people and I saw she'd replaced the photograph with one that didn't include me. Over dinner, I said to her, 'I notice you've taken out my photograph from the frame.' And she said in a voice which everyone could hear, 'Because, Bettina, your arms just looked so *fat!*' "

Ouch. If you saw Bettina you'd know "fat" is one word which cannot be applied to any of her body parts. Despite her healthy appetite, she's reed-slim, and enviably so. In fact, envy was undoubtedly behind her mother-in-law's spiteful jibe and her reluctance to display her photograph. Pia says, "I know that feeling. It's visual exclusion." What she means is, if HM doesn't acknowledge your existence, she can convince herself you aren't really real. She can fool herself that she's still the only woman in her son's life. "Even," says Sammi, "if you are the mother of his children!"

Says Madeleine, "*Especially* when you have children! The moment we had children, she became so much worse. Up until then, I had been able to limit my interactions with her. But once we had children, it became very hard because I understand the need for children to see their grandparents. But she uses the kids to get her way and get at me. You see, although she doesn't like me at all, she wants us to visit her because she adores Andrew and loves the kids. But nothing is ever enough. If we see her four weekends in a row, why not five? So what she'll say to the kids is, 'Oh, I would love to see you, but you can't come,' so they'll say to me, 'Mom, why can't we go, why can't we go?' It drives me crazy."

All the women I spoke to said they would have loved to forge a good relationship with their husband's mother. Bettina says, "Especially as my mother died when I was in my teens, I had really hoped we could be close." Are daughters-in-law and mothers-in-law rarely destined to get on?

Cambridge University's Dr. Terri Apter is pessimistic. She says, "Complaints seem to center on the unrealistic expectations that the mother-in-law has of her daughter-in-law in terms of traditional wifely roles. These expectations undermine and challenge both the value of the wife's work outside the home and her competence in the home. Daughters-in-law complain that their mothers-in-law ignored or denied their professional status outside the home and often interfered in domestic situations—spoiling their sons and expecting the wife to do the same. Even women who might have feminist values in other spheres seem to expect their daughters-in-law to be there to help their husband with traditional duties."

Amanda, twenty-nine, closely identifies with this. She's an investment banker, but Amanda's mother-in-law talks to her like a kitchen maid. Actually, Amanda believes, her mother-in-law might prefer it if she were. "I like our house to be clean, but I hate house-work. She, on the other hand, is a great housekeeper and the food she cooks is insane. But it's not at all the kind of thing I enjoy or take great pride in. So we have these constant moments where she'll say something and I show some resistance and Larry will say, 'Ma-a-a-a, why are you talking to Amanda? Why aren't you telling *me* about the plants or how to clean a stainless steel pot? I have no idea either!' I mean, when everyone's over for dinner, she expects all the women to help out in the kitchen. But all that gender crap is irrelevant to me."

Says Suzannah, thirty-nine, married to David, "Oh God, yes. When we first got married, his mother tried very hard to get me to be domestic. And she'd make snide remarks that I wasn't maternal or that I wasn't domesticated. She'd say, 'You know, Suzannah, David's looking so very tired. Are you looking after him properly?' I'd say to David, 'Tell your mother to mind her own fucking business.'"

Amanda's mother-in-law said similar things. "Larry and I never cook. I just don't like cooking and neither does he. But that really bothered her. She said she didn't expect Larry to cook, but she did expect me to cook for him."

Suzannah laughs at the idea. "David might be in the kitchen doing the washing up and I'll shout from the living room, 'Can you make me a cup of tea when you've finished?!' and I can hear his mother huffing like a billy goat: '*Herumph! Moooreufgh!*' Or I'll say, 'I'm just going outside for a cigarette, make sure the kids don't get up to anything!' and again she'll be '*Hoooreuuufh!*', snorting away. I love saying to her, 'I'm going to Paris on a writing trip,' or 'Can David bring the kids around to you next Sunday because I'm off to Monte Carlo!' It's a way of establishing boundaries, as if to say, ' . . . and if you have a problem with that, just forget it.' She just doesn't like me working. She's always saying, 'Oh, it would be good if you gave up.' And when I'm coming to the end of a project, she'll say, 'Oh great, that's super!' She's very disapproving and she can't hide it. She'll say, 'David needs help. He needs you to be here for him,' and I'll say, 'No, he doesn't, Ivy, he's perfectly capable of managing by himself. It's none of your business.' "

Playing one daughter-in-law against another is also a common mother-in-law tactic, particularly if one of them shares her physical characteristics or values. After all, when a son chooses a wife who is similar to his mother, what could be more validating for her identity than that? What could be more empowering in the face of a power challenge from the other daughter-in-law?

Says Pia, "I'm not very competitive, but I can see they love the other daughter-in-law. In fact, she looks like my mother-in-law. But in choosing me, I think they feel that Michael has moved away from them and maybe they resent me for it, like I've taken him away."

Sabina, forty, says, "I've seen the way she is with the other son's wife. It's diametrically opposed to how she is with me. I am definitely the *second* daughter-in-law. I think it goes back to the children issue—that I just don't want to have children. I think she thinks, Why does my son have to marry someone who is not maternal? I think she resents me. We just spent the Fourth of July weekend with my husband's family and his mother and sister-in-law spent a lot of time exchanging recipes and thoughts. I was not a part of any of that. In fact, I was seldom included in the conversation at all. I genuinely feel I take a backseat because I don't have children. In fact, my husband's family did have a conversation with him about the children issue and he told them it was a mutual decision. They were very surprised because I'm sure they thought, Oh, it's Sabina's fault."

Sara, thirty-five, says, "I just hate his family get-togethers. I've told Ken now that unless it's a wedding or funeral, I'm not going. Not after the last time when I walked into the kitchen to get myself some lemonade and his mother and the other daughter-in-law were talking. When they saw me, they shut up and his mother leaned over to Caron and said, 'I'll tell you about it later,' as if they were two kids with a big secret. Caron is a two-faced bitch anyway. She pretends to be sweet and innocent and will say, 'Mary, these cookies are *wonderful!* You must tell me how you made them,' and then she'll leave them on the side of her plate. But Ken's mother falls for it. I think she thinks Caron is a kindred spirit, whereas she can't connect with me. We have nothing in common whatsoever and, unlike Caron, I don't even try to pretend."

Ostracizing one daughter-in-law while showering the other with affection, however, can backfire on her horribly when they both refuse to be a part of her bullying, schoolyard games. Says Amy, "My mother-in-law is very manipulative. She has four sons and somebody is always in her bad books. It's a way of psychologically controlling them so that when they are in her good books, they feel really grateful. Very recently, one of Garry's brothers was splitting up with his wife. I was quite friendly with Jill so I called her up and said, 'How are you sorting this out? Do you need a lawyer? I really think you need a lawyer.' What I didn't realize was that Jill's husband, Garry's brother, was listening in on the other line. Next thing I know, Garry comes home from work, the phone is ringing and his mother is on the phone saying to him, 'You must tell Amy she is not allowed to talk to Jill.' So Garry said, 'I can't tell my wife who she can and can't talk to.' So his mother said, 'Well, she shouldn't be fraternizing with the enemy.' It was ridiculous. So then she wouldn't talk to me."

Amy continues, "I was not going to be intimidated by anyone, least of all his mother. But I was boiling inside—after all, she had never made me feel accepted. I've always felt I was only invited to her house on sufferance because I'm the mother of her grandchildren. She'd made it quite clear that whether I live or die does not matter. And now she was expecting me to side with her all of a sudden because the other daughter-in-law had fallen out of favor. Forget it. Anyway, I was so furious, I texted my mother on my cell phone to say, 'Listen to this. Mona phoned Garry to tell him to tell me not to speak to Jill. Cheeky cow!' But I was so flustered because the phone was ringing at the same time and who knows, maybe it was Freudian, but I sent the message to Mona and not my mom! Maybe it was because I was thinking of Mona. I don't know . . . you know how it is? I was just so emotionally charged up. But the minute I sent it, I knew I'd sent it to the wrong person and I was like, 'Fuck!'"

For Hitched Chicks with a mother-in-law from hell, it's not enough that they feel powerful and confident enough to deal with her, they need the positive reinforcement of a supportive husband. Without a strong husband who will stand up to his mother, the divisive tactics *can* tear a marriage apart. However, they are not stupid. They recognize they walk a fine and dangerous tightrope between asking their husband for support and forcing him to choose between the two women with whom he has the strongest of bonds.

Which was why Amy says, "I felt sick. In the end, I decided I had to go straight to Garry and confess. I just had to tell him that I had made this horrible situation even worse, but hope that he would be sympathetic to my side. I was really expecting him to be furious. But he just burst out laughing and said, 'Of all those names on your mobile phone, you had to send that text to my mother. You idiot!' So I said, 'I want you to read the message so that if anyone says I sent a horrible message to your mom, at least you know exactly what I've written.' He kept saying, 'Why did you do it?' but he is also aware that, in behaving as she does, his mother drives everyone away. And he said, 'I don't really care if we don't see my family or not, so don't worry,' which is great."

It's that kind of reinforcement which the majority of women claim is crucial for their feelings of power in their marriage. Says Pia, "I need Michael to at least acknowledge his mother's behavior is intolerable. I know she doesn't understand me, neither does his father, who turns away when I start to speak. I'm sure they both think I'm a spacey artist type. And one of my biggest fears about marriage has always been that I will be stifled and I'll stop feeling that sense of play which is so important to me. It's like that Rick Springfield lyric, 'There's an affair of the heart.' My friend always thought it was 'there's a bear in the park' and I thought that was so great because when there is a bear in the park and you're a kid, you can't play freely, you're scared and you're contained. I don't want there to be a bear in the park in my marriage. I have to feel like I have the freedom to express my feelings about his mother to my husband and not have him dismiss them. But I think if Michael called his mother on her behavior, it would make things worse."

Says Rachel, twenty-eight, "Patrick's mother is very snippy and bossy. She expects me to fit in with her and her family unit, but I never will. I'm not like her. She thinks I don't do enough for her and puts on so much pressure, it's just not fun. I've tried to talk to her about it, but she bites my head off or she'll burst into tears. So I've given up. But if Patrick tries to talk to her, she then complains I won't talk to her. It's a disaster."

And Petra, thirty-seven, says, "My mother-in-law's game playing and interference did put a strain on our marriage. My husband recognized her interference and always put a priority on our relationship, so we ended up in a situation where my mother-in-law and sister-in-law didn't speak to us for some time. It was very confusing and I never quite understood it, but this has resolved itself over the years, mainly, I think, because she realized she was missing out on her grandchildren."

Says Suzannah, "It's difficult knowing what to do so you don't make the situation worse. And I've got a really naughty streak so it's very difficult for me. Also, I respect that David really loves his mom."

Can there ever be a happy coexistence between mothers of sons and their wives? As we've heard, the Hitched Chick, with all her power and confidence and spirit, is unlikely to roll over like a puppy. And I don't advocate that behavior one bit anyway. Nor does the in-law have to be out-lawed entirely for you and your hubby to live happily ever after. This just may help . . .

THE HITCHED CHICK'S GUIDE TO
Mother-in-Law Control

Not one women I spoke to had all the answers to putting her mother-in-law firmly in her place—behind you. But many of them offered great strategies for a certain amount of peacekeeping that won't compromise your power either.

+ ***Try and understand her values and get her to understand yours, too.*** Says Naiela, "It's difficult when you don't actually like the woman, but I've tried to understand that she's very set in her ways. There's no point in attempting to change her, but if I can at least understand her, I feel more in control. So I might say, 'Betty, I'm no cook and I know you love it. What is it that you love about cooking?' I've done this and almost choked in the process, but you can see her all puffed up with pride. It makes me laugh a bit. But it's been interesting to see how she's as into doing all that domestic stuff as I am about my work. She rarely asks me questions about my work, but I'll tell her about it anyway. If I don't, I'm denying who I am and she has to get used to the fact that I am not like her. And Pete will say stuff like, 'Naiela just got a promotion, which means we can afford to move out of our apartment into a better one. Isn't she great?' "

✦ *Be honest.* Says Suzannah, "You cannot hide any aspect of yourself. You have to be completely honest with them, as honest as you are with your husband. If they think you're something you're not, there'll be conflicts down the line." I totally agree with this. After all, they tend to have no hesitation in being honest about their own values. Why should you not be honest about your own? If HM is determined not to like you, at least let her dislike of you be based on truth.

✦ *Don't dole out ultimatums to your husband.* Chances are, he'd choose you, but the big Louis Vuitton suitcases of unhappiness or resentment he'll end up carrying around with him could very well come back to break you. Says Madeleine, "It's difficult not to say, 'It's her or me.' You have to diffuse the situation." How so?

✦ *Talk to her calmly and together.* If your husband can see you're not going out of your way to cause trouble, says Madeleine, "Sit down with her and get it all out. But it's important you don't do that alone. Andy had to be there, too, because she has a tendency to change things and do the he said-she said thing. It's nerve-racking, but it works, although we've had to have more than one of these sit-downs with his mother."

✦ *Reinforce your power.* Says Suzannah, "My mother-in-law will phone and say, 'Now, Suzannah, I know you're very, very busy,' and I'll say, 'Yes, I am, can I call you back?' and then I'll leave it for a few hours." It's not childish or intended to annoy, but says Suzannah, "She has to know you are not always at her disposal." However, Suzannah also adds, it's a good idea to . . .

✦ ***Surprise her.*** "No, she can't come steaming 'round when she wants. But sometimes I'll cook dinner and invite her over, for no reason, just because it's a nice thing to do. This way, it's a pleasant surprise for her and she feels involved in our lives, we're not shutting her out, but it's on *my* terms."

✦ ***Remember all families are difficult.*** Even yours. Says Suzannah, "My family is damn hard work and I expect David to put up with all that entails. So I have to expect to put up with a certain amount of crap, too."

✦ ***Let her know you do care.*** Says Amy, "I'm the one who reminds Garry to phone his mom." Says Naiela, "If it wasn't for me, Pete's mom would never get a birthday card or Mother's Day gift. I made sure Pete told his mother this. I could see she was pretty upset about it, but I noticed that her attitude gradually changed toward me. Last Mother's Day, she actually said, 'I can tell Naiela chose this. Pete would never have known I love lavender.' It was very interesting and very nice for us both."

✦ ***Use humor.*** Our man, Dr. John Gottman, says humor is a wonderful conflict smoother. I agree. It's tricky, but if the tone is *just* right, resentments and annoyances can be diffused while a point is being made. After a sticky start, I'm now able to gently rib my mother-in-law about her single-minded devotion to her son to the exclusion of everyone else. We have a standing joke that when we visit, she doesn't simply feed my husband grapes, she peels and predigests them for him, too! I knew we had made progress when we turned up at her house and she presented me with my own bowl of purples and greens. Just one small, but significant, step for Wifekind.

6.

Secrets and Lies

There are some secrets you should have in marriage. You are a person entitled to have secrets. You are a human being entitled to have secrets. You're not completely open with your mother, you're not completely open with your sister or best friend and that's what makes you who you are. It's good to have some things inside that only you know about.

—Patti, thirty-four

Communication is regarded as the cornerstone of relationships. I can't tell you how many column inches I've written, read and edited encouraging women to open up and spill every thought and feeling in minute detail. For the most part, I stand by them. Don't think for one moment I'm backtracking on bringing important issues out into the open. Sweeping them under the carpet doesn't make them disappear. They just materialize into one big hairball of dissatisfaction which, if it doesn't choke you, will certainly create one hell of a hump.

Being able to express and share our feelings is a symbol of power, something to prize and cherish. A mutually satisfying financial decision, a strong personal identity, a clear understanding of long-term goals and dreams, a sexy sex life . . . all these elements of a happy marriage are often only a sentence away. So you're probably wondering why, for the love of a good conversation, I'm including a chapter that challenges the communicate-at-all-costs theory.

Here's why it's important I do. For a start, if our mothers weren't successful in securing their husbands' hearts via his stomach, they attempted to do so via his ears, believing the more they talked, the more they'd be heard and the better he would become at revealing his innermost thoughts, too. It was a well-intentioned strategy, but it backfired. If they were lucky enough to have a husband who knew how to listen, our mothers often didn't know how to choose their message and get it across. Nagging, whining, moaning . . . all labels associated with traditional female modes of communication. Little wonder "we need to talk" has become the most loathed and feared statement a woman can make. If hubby didn't run screaming for the hills, he spontaneously shut down his aural passages.

As far as men were concerned, women were all talk and no action. The sad truth is, they often were, since many rarely had the power or conviction of a strong identity to reinforce their vocalizations. And because much of the time their wives' heartfelt feelings were meaningless to them, husbands did not become better communicators. If traditional wives didn't know how to edit what they said, traditional husbands didn't know how to edit what they heard and were, therefore, even less able or willing to rectify their encultured inability to communicate.

As Gabrielle, thirty-two, says, "Our parents didn't live in a world where people had communication skills. I don't think my mother knew how to communicate with my father and he didn't know how to communicate back to her. Women now are just so much more emotionally skilled."

Women today have honed their communication skills to such a sophisticated extent, they know exactly how to address any audience, from a cast of hundreds to a one-on-one. So finely crafted is our ability to communicate (and back it up with genuine competence), women are winning in every area. Female high school students are scooping covetable college places from under the noses of male peers. Young female interns are eloquently upstaging their superiors. And the Hitched Chick's ability to verbalize emotional needs supported by data means they're often in full control of how money is spent and invested, how and where they live, when and how they have everything from children to vacations to sex.

Today, women don't feel the need to talk to their husbands about every major and minor issue. Confident with who she is and how to communicate that to the greatest effect, she also has many outlets for her desire to express herself. No need to store up her dreams and demands then spew them out to a partner who doesn't want to participate on the rare occasions he's home. Now that she is an active member in society, she can pick and choose her audience from a vast range of friends and colleagues who will empathize, encourage and provide feedback. And, when necessary, provide a discreet sounding board for closely guarded confessions which, if her man only knew, he'd be sure to sit up and listen to . . .

But, you know, this wife probably wouldn't want him to. After all, we know from the chapter on power that there's something empowering about holding back. In some cases, it can be negative power. (In the case of forty-three-year-old Ellis's first husband, Phil, who withheld the fact that he was having an affair, he was withholding negatively.) But in some cases, editing what we say can be enormously positive.

As far back as the 1960s in *Sex & the Single Girl*, Helen Gurley Brown wrote about the benefits of putting communication temporarily on hold. She advised her single girl readers to lock the phone in the fridge so a) you couldn't hear it ring, so b) you wouldn't be tempted to pick it up and c) so your beau would think you were out having fun without him, thereby creating an attractive, tantalizing air of mystery and elusiveness with the added bonus that, d) if the desire took you to reveal your innermost confidential thoughts you wouldn't have the opportunity . . . and then live to regret it.

But married girls go one step further. Having secrets and keeping silent has surprising benefits: for her emotional and mental health as well as for the harmony of her marriage. In 2001, Mori conducted an exclusive *Reader's Digest* poll among 971 married adults over sixteen throughout the U.K. and discovered that 44 percent of women have kept secrets from their husbands (this compares with 39 percent of men).

Today's wife protects her right to have private thoughts and feelings as passionately as she applies her right to be vocal. Now it isn't she who sits opposite her husband and whines, "Honey, *tell* me what's on your mind." No, she knows exactly how to extract what she needs from him. It's her husband, who, seeing a glint in his wife's eye or a kittenish twitch on her lips, should be kicked out of his complacency and compelled to inquire, "Sweetheart, *what* are you thinking?" Because her answer—in the unlikely event she chose to be 100 percent honest—would surprise, even shock, him.

The Rush of the Crush

A secret crush? Are we out of our minds? Hmm, the word is certainly associated with spotty pre-teens writing love letters to their unattainable objects of desire on pink paper embellished with kitties. But, according to Hitched Chicks, the secret crush plays just as big a part in our adult, married life as it did in our adolescence.

Whether it's a periodic crush on a celebrity or a fleeting crush on the pizza delivery guy who we chat up while our husband orders the Friday night movie, having a crush provides a tremor of excitement to our lives. When the mundanities of marriage verge on boredom, an innocent dalliance with "what if?" brings a little welcome texture, a spark of fire, a way to (momentarily) live out a fantasy that is sexy, spontaneous and perfect, and which has an intrinsic sense of dignified defeat (oh well, fate has dictated this was never meant to be. *Sigh.*).

Thirty-six-year-old Sam's recent crush is classic. "One of the guys at my gym is really hot. Really hot. And he has those hot, dark eyes. I found out from one of the trainers that he's going into the military so he's really focused on his training. But every now and again, I'll look up and he's staring at me with these big, black eyes. He's not the most handsome man in the world, but I'm really intrigued. And I found out his name is Benjamin and I'm like, 'Oh my God,' because I love the name, Benjamin. And he doesn't grunt like a lot of the guys at the gym, he'll have his head down and every now and again, he'll be staring at me. And the way he looks at me really gets me going. I don't want to speak to him or anything because it's just a crush, an intrigue between the two of us. So we look at each other and don't say a word. It's fascinating. I love it."

There's a huge difference between this classic, innocent, fun crush and the kind of delusional crush that leads to dangerous infatuation and stalking, often as a result of feeling hopeless. We don't hope for one second that our crush will materialize into something real for we know if it did, its unsuitability and faults would certainly destroy its beauty. No, far from being a way to fill empty hours at home or a loveless void, the modern wife's crushes are fast and sporting. These little secret mind games she plays with herself are healthy. They don't imply an affair is around the corner. They're simply a way of acknowledging that despite our power and all the responsibilities that go with it, we're still capable of *feeling*: feeling attraction for the outside world; feeling confident enough that, however remote, we could be attractive and intriguing to someone else; feeling fun and mischievous and playful.

Says Mary, thirty, "I share most things with Tom, but marriage is not the end of attraction. You're still going to meet people that attract you, but I'm not going to tell him about that. I don't tell Tom about crushes that I get for a week."

Neither does Ruth, thirty-eight, who says of her brief crushes, "They reassure me I'm not a flat, unpassionate, lustless person. It reaffirms that I can feel that way, that I do have lust in me."

Says Julia, thirty-one, "When I have a small crush, I want to tell Andrew about it so his interest will be piqued. But if it's spoken about it would just seem ridiculous and boring, and maybe it would hurt Andrew's feelings when it was nothing more than a moment. I mean, when I decided Andrew had a crush on Gwyneth Paltrow, I interrogated him for four hours and finally he was like, 'Okay, okay, maybe I find her a little attractive,' so I couldn't even enjoy *The Royal Tenenbaums*! But when you get married, one thing you give up is the rush of the first interest of new romance and part of the appeal of that is the narcissistic chance to represent yourself to another person. It's like a new self-invention and just that act of having someone get to know you with the underlying lust is a thrill. I had a bit of a crush on a guy I had an e-mail friendship with. I originally made contact with him to help with a project I was doing. That's the funny, weird thing about e-mailing because it allows you to do that playful seductive thing where you ask yourself, Do I have the power to draw someone in? Am I sexy and funny? You don't have that thrill anymore when you're married, right? So you try and find other little ways of getting it."

Ruth agrees, "When you get married, your relationship with your husband evolves into a much deeper, satisfying bond, but when you have this quick chemistry between you and another person, it reaffirms that you can still feel this way and be attractive to other men. It's very good for your self-esteem."

Ruth has hit the nail on the head here. According to Karen DeMars, CEO and cofounder of the website e-crush.com, which has been following this phenomenon, crushes can provide a huge boost to self-esteem. Knowing someone is attracted to us provokes a warm glow of confidence and encourages us to maintain self-improvement. Conversely, fleeting fantasies of being noticed by our crush can inspire us to make changes in our appearance and manner if we have become a little complacent of late.

Sara, thirty-five, says, "It's true. Although I love Ken and wouldn't want to be married to anyone else, I still enjoy the flutter of excitement when you meet someone new and there's an attraction. A new guy appeared in our organization and I had a crush on him for the first month. I felt like a silly schoolkid and it was a great, unexpected feeling and I found myself taking extra care over my appearance. If we were in a meeting together, I was aware that I was stepping up to the mark more than I might have done previously. It sounds silly, but I wanted to impress him and I did. I impressed other people, too, and the more positive feedback I got, the more I wanted it, so that two months later I got a promotion. Good, right? Amazing what a crush can do. But when I started to get to know him better, the crush became a friendship. How can you have a crush on someone when you realize they have faults and insecurities, too?"

Rae, forty-one, says, "I have crushes all the time. And I don't think they say anything negative about my marriage. My husband's a perfect match for me in almost every way, which is why most of the guys I have crushes on are totally the opposite. Like our decorator. Frankly, he wasn't very smart and he wasn't at all good-looking, but because he was so different from Louis in that sense, I had a crush on him for about two weeks. If I'd told anyone, they would have thought I'd gone crazy. But I'd get little palpitations when he arrived in the morning. It was fun. But it was over as soon as he finished decorating our house. There was certainly no question that I was ever going to act on it. That's just ridiculous."

Did Rae ever confess her crush to her husband? "God, no," says Rae. "I mean, he'd think I'd lost my mind. Anyway, he might have been weird about this guy being in our house, knowing I had a crush on him. If I'd told him, it would become this big issue, which is not the case at all. It was nothing. It was just a silly little crush." Sara didn't confess her crush either. She says, "If I'd told my husband, it would have been difficult to become friends with this guy when I'd stopped having a crush on him."

Phoebe, forty-three, says, "I am not by nature a secretive person, so I tend not to keep secrets from my husband. If I do, they're more like unnecessary discussions. They're interior, private thoughts. Like I had a crush on one guy who was a photo editor. We were on an assignment together and there was serious flirting going on. He was younger than me and very smart and very cool and I started to wonder whether the crush was verging on cheating because I had all this stuff going on in my head. I told a girlfriend about it and she was like, 'Oh, Phoebe, we all have crushes, it's quite normal,' so I stopped obsessing. But because I worked with him, I saw him almost every day. He had this big office and he kept it dark and he'd play music and there were big comfy chairs. So I would go in on crazy days and say, 'You are the quiet zone. Can I just sit here for a moment?' And then we'd have a chat and then I would leave. But I was starting to find myself in constant need of the quiet zone! And I began to wonder if people noticed I was always going into his office and did they know I had a crush on him, so I began avoiding people I thought knew and . . . oh my God! I was paranoid. So every time I'd go into his office, all I'd ever do was talk about my husband. That way, absolutely nothing could happen and I don't think he ever had any idea what I was thinking. When he quit, I was actually relieved that he did, so I was finally free of thinking about him. To this day, my husband doesn't know."

Silly, fun, naughty . . . but, nevertheless, something to keep to ourselves, huh? Especially if our crush happens to be on our mind when we're in bed.

Thirty-five-year-old Alice recalls confessing to her husband that she was thinking about her crush-of-the-week, Pierce Brosnan, as they made love. "He was weird about it," she says. "For weeks after, he'd say, 'So, how was Pierce?' after we had sex. He stopped eventually. Now I tell him no one turns me on like he does. But, the truth is, he's put on a bit of weight recently and although I still love him, I just sometimes enjoy sex more when I'm thinking about Justin Timberlake, or whoever I happen to have a crush on that week, going down on me."

Says Rae, "I may be over forty, but I don't think of myself as middle-aged. Trouble is, Louis and I can get so bogged down with paying the school fees and whose in-laws are coming for the holidays, it's sometimes difficult to feel sexy and it's difficult to see Louis as this virile sex object. I'm not supposed to mind when he talks about having a crush on Britney Spears with his guy friends. That's what men do. But I know he would feel very insecure if I mentioned I got horny just thinking about the cute guy in the grocery store or Cristian de la Fuente. He wouldn't mind as much if I was hot for Bono or Sean Connery, but they do nothing for me. Too old. They have too much baggage and are probably as exhausted and stressed as my husband."

Says Sabina, forty, "More than once, I've thought about someone else while I was having sex with my husband. And that someone tends to be someone I know. Maybe I'm visiting that person at their house and things start to happen and we end up on the couch. I would never confess to Matthew, but I use this fantasy crush to get me in the mood and bring myself to orgasm faster."

Dee, twenty-nine, says, "Doesn't everybody? It's totally harmless. If you're hoping to have a marriage for the long haul, you have to do whatever you have to do to keep it exciting. It doesn't mean you don't find your husband exciting. I have a couple of times fantasized about sex with someone else while I've been with Evan. It's the naughtiness. It's like putting on a nurse's uniform!"

The Ex-Files

He's the man you loved before you met your husband. More than a friend, not quite a relative, he knows you better than almost anyone else. He was the first man to whom you confessed your wildest dreams, revealed your most intimate self, understood your PMS, supported you during those turbulent family feuds in your teens and twenties, cheered at your graduation and celebrated with a magnum of champagne when you landed your first real job. You dated for a couple of years or more. You may have lived together. Hell, you considered *marrying* the guy.

I'm talking about the ex-boyfriend with whom you remained in touch or reunited with after years apart. (Many women who experienced painful breakups with their exes describe their tentative approaches now the dust has settled, via websites such as Friends Reunited.) Most Hitched Chicks have one, the *special* ex, the one who got away or the one they let go. He lurks on the edge of our lives, reminds us of our pasts and puts our presents into perspective. And, for many, he provides a comfortable, familiar, almost risk-free fallback when our future with our husband seems momentarily uncertain.

We call him from time to time. We may even ask his advice since we trusted and valued him enough to share a chunk of our formative years. This is a man whose impression on us is indelible, having helped shape us into the women we have become. Sometimes we think about him when we know we shouldn't. On our birthdays, at Christmas or Thanksgiving, when we're at work, even when we're in bed. Oh yes. And we meet them, too. Not, mind you, in a highly visible place. No, we choose a little nook out of the way, somewhere we can chat, remember old times, share experiences, offer advice, ponder on the possibility of what might have been . . .

We'd never confess. Not to our mother. She belongs to a different generation, one in which women weren't single for long (remember, even in 1971, almost a third of brides were *teenagers*. Source: OneplusOne). And she belongs to a generation for whom pre-marital sex was still sinful. If she had previous lovers, she wouldn't admit it, less likely remain in touch with them. She'd be shocked and scandalized at the thought. As Joely, twenty-six, says, "If your mother dated a guy, there was a definite understanding that she'd never see him again once she was married."

Nor would we confess to a friend, unless she was very, *very* close and promised on her soul she'd never spill. Once the initial thrill of a shared secret subsides, you know it could be an uncomfortable collusion since she might know and like your husband, too.

And we'd certainly never confess to our husband. God, no. He gets miffed at the mention of your ex's name. Although your husband is confident and successful, he's aware this man still occupies a place in your heart and represents a time in your life when you were younger, freer, wilder. (Happier, too, maybe?) What, your husband wonders, did you do with him that you don't do with me? Your husband believes he should be your everything . . . soul mate, confidant, advisor, lover. Why would you need or want to see your ex? If your husband ever had the courage to ask you this, you would, of course, reassure him that the appeal of your ex had long gone. Your affections are innocent, nostalgic, platonic. He has a girlfriend, for goodness sake. Maybe even a wife. So how could there be anything to worry about? And yet . . .

You love the fact that your ex still enjoys your company. You can call him at work and he'll be sure to speak to you. You don't make life decisions to seek his approval, but you can't help basking in his admiration of your accomplishments. Nor can you resist a smug little smile when he suggests regret that he wasn't "the one." You take a teensy bit longer to get ready to meet him than you might if you were just seeing a friend. You don't want to look too provocative (no, your conscience couldn't handle it), but neither do you want to look like—gasp!—a *wife*. You love your husband dearly. He still turns you on and makes you laugh. But, oh, do you remember when you and your ex . . . ? Why exactly did you not marry him? Strange, but when you see him and talk to him these days, you can hardly remember why. Even if you do remember, maybe the reasons don't seem so important.

Says Carol, thirty-seven, "I keep in touch with my ex-fiancé. He was very successful, very outgoing, but as we got closer to getting married, I really started to see myself having my parents' marriage. He felt like he was the leader, he felt superior to me and I decided that this wasn't what I wanted. I didn't want to be my mother. I felt like I was in this gilded cage, a wonderful, beautiful house with all this money and all this stuff, but I wasn't happy, so five weeks before we were due to get married, I called it off. It was extremely traumatic and stressful for everybody and we didn't speak for a long time. But now we're back to being very good friends and we speak to each other on a regular basis."

I ask Carol why she keeps in touch with a man who, she claims, treated her as an inferior. "It's a very strange relationship," Carol admits. "But we were together six years and I feel like he formed me in many ways. He helped make some of the characteristics I have, so I feel very close to him in that sense. I've known him for so long, I have this need to talk to him. We've never gone longer than four months without speaking so we talk on a fairly regular basis. Thank God for cell phones."

Meaning that Carol never tells her husband, Rick, that she keeps in contact with her ex? "Rick has said he would rather I not speak to him. He's quite a jealous person. He hasn't told me that I can't speak to him, like, 'I forbid you from speaking to him.' If Rick did turn around and say, 'I absolutely forbid you from talking to him,' I'd say, 'You cannot forbid me from doing anything.' But I know if he found out I met him for lunch, he'd be upset. I don't think talking to him on the phone would upset him as much as knowing I'd had lunch with him."

So does Carol lie? She says, "I don't really lie. I just don't tell him where I am. But as for lunch, I just don't tell Rick about it because I know he'd be upset when there really isn't any need for him to be upset."

Rae doesn't exactly lie, either. She says she just doesn't say anything to Louis about meeting her ex. "We bumped into each other— it was a pure coincidence—and I agreed to have a drink with him. I was, *am*, happily married, so I wasn't about to be tempted to have an affair. I had a few cocktails with him and I was totally flirty, but I didn't fool around with him. Then I saw him when I was pregnant and I was, in a weird way, more tempted then because I felt very vulnerable and I thought, Omigod, I'm pregnant. I'm going to have a baby and no one's ever going to find me attractive again. I think I needed to prove that someone found me attractive and he clearly still did. No, I didn't tell my husband. Although this guy is special, there was really nothing in it. I could convince myself that I wasn't cheating so it was okay. But I must admit that if I knew right now my husband was sitting in a hotel bar, having drinks with his ex who was being flirty, no, that would not make me thrilled."

Says Lottie, thirty-two, "I told my husband once that I'd seen my ex and he totally freaked. He was so jealous. He started working up these ideas that I was having an affair. And when he discovered we worked in the same neighborhood, it was awful. It's his own baggage, but I don't want to go there. I have two exes who I'm still very close with. My husband knows about one, but he doesn't know about Anton. He knows Anton's a friend, but he doesn't know he's an ex and I intend to keep it that way, especially as I often have to travel with him for work. Like, one time, my husband found naked photos of me giving a guy a blow job. We'd been drinking Bloody Marys and fooling around with a Polaroid camera. It was basically my head and a huge penis and my husband found them. He couldn't tell who the guy was so he still doesn't know to this day it was Anton. If he's going to get jealous or upset, he doesn't need to know everything. It would be nice to say we have no secrets from each other, but I've also learned that I don't need to tell him every little thing. I don't need to tell him when I see my exes. It makes him upset, so why go there?"

Says Jill, thirty-five, "I was just about to get married and I had a very troubling experience with my ex, whom I'd gotten back in touch with. He basically expressed his undying love for me ten years after we had split up and asked me not to go ahead with my wedding. In some ways it was pathetic, but it was also confusing for me. I definitely experienced temptation. I think I was partly flattered in that he obviously adored me. And he has this ideal of romance which he pursues, which is very different from my husband. My ex is an artist and he taps into my creative, spiritual side. He represented what I was when I was in my teens—I am a very different person now, but I think part of the appeal was that I was longing to be a teenager again. It was really very difficult. We have a very strong connection that cannot be erased."

For some women, their desire to reconnect with their past is so overwhelming they continue to see their exes, even if they dislike them, even if they were badly hurt by them. Jill identifies with this. For despite confessing to this "strong connection" to her ex, she also admits, "I don't like him. It's a connection that is full of contradictions."

For Audrey, thirty-three, it's the combination of familiarity and danger that compels her to meet up with her ex, unbeknownst to her husband, when she occasionally returns to her hometown. She says, "He was a bastard. He was a liar and a cheat, and he brings out the worst in me, but there's just something about him that's hard to resist.

We've had lunch and, both times, I was even tempted to sleep with him. Even before we had our main course, he said, 'Let's go back to my place and have sex.' But I haven't slept with him. I said, 'You know what, that's *not* going to happen,' but knowing he wants to, that I still turn him on, is very seductive."

Carmen, thirty-seven, can still recall the nightmare of her ex. "We were engaged. I was totally in love with this guy, but he totally screwed me up. He cheated on me with another girl and left me for her, then we got back together and then I broke up with him on my terms, which did me the world of good. But I have a little bit of a hangover from him." Carmen often sees her ex in the bars in her town. She says that sometimes she and her husband will hang out for a couple of drinks with him, but she never meets him alone ... except in her dreams, the content of which she keeps a secret.

She says, "Every now and again, he'll crop up in my dreams. I might dream we get back together. But I never tell my husband. I don't want him to think I've still got a thing for my ex because he knows how much this guy meant to me."

Loathe them or like them, exes continue to be a presence in the Hitched Chick's life and although she'll rarely fess up to her husband exactly what form that presence takes, most of the time it simply reinforces that she made the right decision to marry her husband.

Says Carol, "Each time I see my ex, it strengthens my marriage. You can take your husband for granted so I think you almost have to be on the outside and look at your marriage. When you do that you see what you have and think, What I have here is so much better. The more I talk to my ex, the more I realize I never would have been happy married to him and then I thank God I called off my marriage to him. It makes me really appreciate the marriage I have."

Rae agrees, "When I see my ex, much as I'm still very fond of him, I don't want to have an affair. He just gives me a confidence boost and makes me realize that I actually love Louis very much. My ex is married and he's the kind of guy who doesn't need to fool around, but he shares the same feelings of 'Oh, I just need to know you still like me and I still like you, isn't that great? Let's see each other again in a year.' It's nice to know you're still attractive to your ex, even though you're not as cute and perky as you were ten years ago. But I would not rather be married to him than to my husband."

Lilly, thirty-one, agrees, although she did cross the line with her old flame in a moment of conflict with her husband. She admits that while she still finds her ex dangerously attractive, and isn't proud of her deception, the brief affair with him gave her a jolt of appreciation for her husband. However, confesses Lilly, "I must admit, it's quite nice knowing there's always someone else in the background who adores you. He's never got married and says he never will. Maybe he's my safety net, that if anything ever did go wrong and my marriage ended, maybe I could make a life with someone else. If it came to the crunch, I don't know whether I'd make a life with him, but knowing my ex is there makes me feel confident." For now, Lilly's feelings continue to remain an unsolved mystery in her "Ex-Files."

Secret Solo Pleasures

Although Kath, thirty-three, does not keep in contact with her ex, she confesses she has secret sexual fantasies about him. She says, "I have an old boyfriend I was obsessed with. My fantasy is that I bump into him and, of course, I look fantastic, prettier than I am or ever was, and we're at some bar where no one sees us and we fool around a little and go off to a hotel."

Kath says she's most likely to have this fantasy while she's masturbating, another secret activity she keeps from her husband, Noah. She's not alone. The vast majority of women do indulge in secret sexual journeys while they're playing solo and they don't feel ashamed about it. Unlike previous generations of women who subscribed to the literal definition "to self-pollute," associating masturbation with uncontrollable sinful behavior, women today merrily stroke, massage and knead themselves on a regular basis.

A recent Kinsey Institute study revealed women masturbate almost as much as men—almost a 100 percent increase on their initial study of American sexual behavior fifty years ago. What's more, women are beginning to explore and discover their bodies at younger ages. In a 1966 study of college students, 18 percent of those surveyed said they began masturbating by age twelve; fifteen years later, the number jumped to 31 percent. According to the early nineties *Janus Report*, around 20 percent of women were masturbating by the age of ten.

Which means that by the time we reach adulthood we are a dab hand at masturbation, what works for us and what doesn't. What's more, we continue to prize our private pleasure, long after we are married. While masturbation is often associated with single women who indulge to compensate for lack of coitus, married women use "me sex" to *complement* "we sex." Research reveals that wives who masturbate, desire and enjoy sex more than those who don't, which testifies to its power as an effective aphrodisiac.

It has tangible health benefits, too. At the touch of your button, menstrual cramps are alleviated, and it can help fight pesky yeast infections. Best we keep it up, especially since menopause is never more than a nightmare away and masturbation is known to help vaginal dryness in post-menopausal women.

Pleasing ourselves is a popular way of relieving stress, too. A 2001 *Good Housekeeping* (U.K.) survey revealed that one in five women feels stressed at least 50 percent of the time. And two out of three respondents firmly believe women's lives today are more stressful than fifty years ago. Could masturbation now be our most popular solo sport? Free and relatively fast with immediate and obvious results, it certainly seems like it's the best value workout all-around. And especially when combined with mind-bending sex fantasies that, say many, are as vital to the process as privacy and touch technique. It's this delicious mixture of mental and physical activity that, experts concede, is one of the most interesting differences between female and male masturbation. As June Reinisch, Ph.D., director emeritus of the Kinsey Institute at Indiana University, says, "We do quality masturbation. They do quantity."

Seems to me, however, from my research, that we enjoy quality *and* quantity. Hitched Chicks I talked to said they masturbated, on average, a couple of times a week.

Kath says she masturbated even more than that when she was pregnant. "I was beyond horny. Nobody had warned me about that. I felt like I was a guy. I walked around thinking about sex. I'd watch porn or fantasize about a celebrity. George Clooney, the obvious, or Luke Wilson. I like funny guys. They're just so sexy."

Says Petra, thirty-seven, "It depends on how I'm feeling. There are some weeks when I feel more sexual than others. So sometimes I masturbate almost daily, sometimes even twice a day. Other times, I might not masturbate for a week or two."

Emily, thirty-three, says she has regular bursts of masturbation, especially "when we haven't had sex for a while or when I'm stressed. It's like working out, it's a physical release and I feel much better afterward. Or when my husband's traveling and it's late at night and I'm tired, but not tired enough to go to bed."

It's the same for Mary, thirty, who says, "When my husband's away, I'll masturbate once or twice a week, mostly when I'm having trouble sleeping. I'll be trying to sleep and I'll have all these words in my head, all this language from what I've been studying all day, swirling around, and I need to distract myself away from that if I'm going to sleep. Like doing yoga or listening to soothing music, masturbating is a great way to put that stuff aside."

Says Sam, "I masturbate every day. Sometimes when I'm in the shower, I'll get a little bit 'Oooh!' Or some guy might have been working out at the gym and I'll be like, 'He's adorable, I think I'll go and have a wank and think about him.' But lots of things get me going. I masturbate even more in the summer. When I've been in the sun and the heat's been on my body and I've had a little swim in the pool and my body's glistening as it's drying in the heat, that gets me a bit 'Oooh!' And I was talking to a friend the other night. He said, 'Do you get horny when you're hungover?' and I said, 'Actually, I do.' So if I'm hungover, I'll have a wank. And also since my hair's been long, I get checked out more. I'm walking along the street and I'm getting checked out right, left and center and I'm like, 'Oooh! *This* has never happened before' and *that* gets me going."

Unlike her mother, Sam is not backward about coming forward concerning her love of sex—either with her husband or without him. "My mother can't even say the word masturbation," says Sam. "But I don't have a problem talking about it or writing about it. I even wrote about masturbating this one time on my website. We had guests at our summer house on Fire Island and it was one typical weekend. Everyone was on the beach and I'd had enough. I'm fair-skinned and I'd had enough sun for one day, so I went back to the house and I took a shower in the outside shower. It was beautiful, the birds were tweeting, the sun was beaming down on me and I just thought, Why not? It was fabulous."

Sam and Mary aren't thinking of their husbands while they're pleasing themselves. In the main, women don't, and claim that, as much as their husbands say they'd like to watch their wives masturbate, they prefer to keep it a private pursuit. "We sex" and "me sex" are entirely different experiences. One is about intimacy, the other is an assertion of absolute independence during which their own selfish pleasure is everything. Masturbation for women is a wonderful physical release, but we love the opportunity to release our imagination, too, which often means allowing it to cartwheel into the land of the taboo; a land where we are not wives or mothers, colleagues or bosses, but someone without any inhibitions, responsibilities, obligations, even morals. And if our husband thinks he has any role in it, he can think again. His presence, either in the room or in our minds, is an unwelcome intrusion into one of the few private worlds we still possess. As is his desire—be it based on ego or simple curiosity—to know the content of our fantasies. As the terrific Nancy Friday wrote in her notorious book on women's sexual fantasies, *My Secret Garden,* "One thing I've learned about fantasies: they're fun to share, but once shared, half their magic, their ineluctable power, is gone. They are sea pebbles upon which the waters have dried." We believe her, which is why we keep our most satisfying, liberating solo-sex fantasies firmly locked away.

Twenty-six-year-old Joely says, "I have fantasies about everything and anything that doesn't involve my husband. My sexual fantasies tend to revolve around what I read at college, erotica like Anais Nin's *Delta of Venus.*"

Says Alexandra, twenty-eight, "Masturbation and sex with my husband are different things. What I think about when I masturbate is separate from him. Some days, I masturbate in the afternoon when he's out, then we might have sex that same day, so I just feel like they're two different things. When I masturbate, I'll often fantasize about a Hollywood movie star. Movie sex is very powerful, so I'm often thinking about that. Even a terrible movie like *Pearl Harbor*— I hated *Pearl Harbor*—but there's some very romantic kissing. Or books like *Cold Mountain*, which is about the American civil war. It had a very romantic ending and I remember feeling very turned on by the last few pages."

Sam says her favorite fantasy during solo sex is "the old *Mills and Boon* fantasy with the dark stranger whose face you never see. Or the total stranger who you meet in an elevator in Bloomingdale's and he gives you a passionate kiss, then he just leaves you there wanting more. That's what I think about." Ruth, thirty-eight, admits, "Yes, being seduced by a stranger in a public place is my major fantasy, too." Same for Simone, twenty-eight, who describes it as "I meet a stranger and there's that terrific high of overwhelming passion."

Mary says, "It feels too weird to be thinking about my husband during masturbation. I'm thinking about fine art. I think of paintings—all the colors are very stimulating." Jess is also stimulated by the thought of color. She says, "You know those kids' playpens that are full of soft balls? I'm imagining being surrounded by all those little balls."

Joely adds that one of her favorite fantasies during "me sex" is of "other women. It's not necessarily me with other women, it's just women." Connie, thirty-nine, agrees. "Maybe because the female body is more beautiful than the male body and more voluptuous. Fantasizing about women often gets me hornier than thinking of a man."

Melanie, thirty, says, "My secret fantasy is two guys on me. And me doing absolutely nothing but laying there."

Says Tracy, thirty-four, "Me, too. I fantasize about two men on top of me. And the happy rape fantasy—but the fun, fun, fun one, not the hurtful one. The one where I'm saying, 'No, no,' but he's saying, 'Oh yes you are.' Where he's throwing me down and tearing my clothes off."

Lottie says, "I used to worry that I fantasized about being raped while I was jerking off. But I got over that when I talked to my girlfriends who confessed they did, too. Obviously, I don't want it to happen in reality, but I like to imagine that I'm not in control for just one brief moment. Don't you think responsibility can repress you? Like you always have to look in control, otherwise you worry you won't be taken seriously anymore? At least when you're jerking off, it's totally private—you can imagine you're not in control and you're being

taken over by a more dominant force without anyone judging you or
saying afterward, 'So, er, you like being dominated then?'"

THE HITCHED CHICK'S GUIDE TO
Masturbation Max-Out

Look, this isn't intended to teach you how to please yourself. You've
already had a couple of decades of experience so you're an expert
already. But I can't resist passing on some pleasure-boosting tips
from other Married Girls that are too good to keep a secret.

- ✦ *Vary pressure and movement.* Says Shauneice, thirty-six,
  "For years, I just stroked gently and it always worked.
  Then one day, I'm sitting at the kitchen table, planning a
  menu and I start tapping on my crotch. I wasn't even thinking about masturbating, it was purely a subconscious thing
  as I was trying to concentrate. But as I was tapping, I
  started feeling aroused. I slipped my pants down, and
  tapped myself through my briefs, first lightly, then hard,
  then lightly. It was amazing."
- ✦ *Experiment with positions.* Changing how you lie, sit or
  stand can dramatically alter sensations. Lottie, thirty-two,
  says, "I've found it works the best when I sit on the edge of
  the bed or a chair and then lie back." Lottie says this position makes her clitoris pop up and more sensitive to her
  touch. Freya, thirty-five, says she often tucks cushions
  under her stomach and lies on her front, "Especially when
  I'm fantasizing." Rae says, "Standing with my legs slightly
  apart allows me to insert my fingers, which I can't do when

I'm lying down." Fingering yourself is a great way to discover your G-spot, if you haven't already. Use your middle finger, slip about a couple of inches into your vagina and then in a movement as if you were beckoning someone, gently press the wall closest to your stomach. It'll feel spongy (that's why another name for the G-spot is the urethral sponge). Some women say they don't like the sensation, others claim it makes their solo-sex orgasms even better.

♦ ***Indulge all your senses.*** Lottie plays heavy rock ("It's wild and exciting"), while Mary prefers to listen to soft music. Rae uses scented massage oils and Freya lights scented candles. ("My favorite scent is amber," she says.) Sam and Kath watch porn sometimes, while Joely reads erotica.

♦ ***Play with toys.*** In a mypleasure.com poll ("in honor of Independence Day!") among 2,736 customers, 26.5 percent of respondents said their favorite way to masturbate was with a vibrator or dildo. Half of mypleasure's customers are married, and spokeswoman Melissa Brockgreiten tells me, "You'd suspect married women would purchase mostly couples toys, but that's not the case at all. The majority of our married women purchase vaginal vibrators, particularly dual action ones, and they purchase more expensive ones than single women. My theory on this, backed up by reading correspondence with these women, is that women tend to learn the value of their sexuality more after marriage. Not that sexuality isn't important to single women, but generally, married women are a little older, more experienced and more willing to pamper themselves sexually. Married women seem to know and understand more about how being at one with your sexuality is important."

What's more, Melissa says, "The other big one with married women is anything waterproof, which makes sense if you think about it. When you're married, the most private place to masturbate, fantasize or indulge is in the shower or bathtub. I wouldn't have thought of it either until I got an e-mail from a woman talking about it and then looked at the data. Suddenly a light went on!"

Mypleasure's bestselling toys for Hitched Chicks are:

The Rabbit Pearl—you may have heard about this toy with ears designed to flutter against the clitoris, from *Sex and the City*;

The Orion—an all-silicone, dual-action vibrator with gyrating beads;

The Tsunami—this smooth, ice-blue, waterproof vibrator has a gentle curve to caress your G-spot;

. . . and, reiterates Melissa, "anything waterproof."

Further specific recommendations come from Melanie and her friend, Tracy, who says, "I have the Matador, which every woman should have." Melanie bought hers from the Adam & Eve catalogue. She says, "I have a full drawer of toys, but the Matador is the best. The head is like a bull with horns. And at the head is also a little bullet vibrator. I have an orgasm each and every time. You have no idea." Stella, thirty-two, prefers the Butterfly. She says, "It's a vibrator in the shape of a butterfly with a protruding head." Stella adds, "You can wear it under your clothes, too, and it has a hand-held on-off switch and speed control. I've never worn it out of the house—it's pretty loud so I can't imagine you wouldn't draw attention at a restaurant, club or the movies—but I think it could be great fun!"

Just Between Friends

I'm having cocktails in a bar overlooking the park with two of my best friends . . . let's call them Anita and Courtney. Anita is married to Richie and Courtney has been married almost ten years to Jann and, generally speaking, they both have good marriages. We're discussing modern marriage (for a year, I've discussed nothing but). "Do you," I ask them, "have any secret thoughts you'd like to share?" Following a surreptitious glance around the bar, Anita whispers, "Have you ever had the death fantasy . . . ?" Courtney and I gasp loudly—because it's not just us who have, at odd, crazy moments in marriage, given brain space to the darkest, most taboo fantasy of all . . . the death of our husband.

Patsy, thirty-four, confesses she's shared this dark, dark fantasy with very close friends, too. "Yes, the death fantasy. I mean, I have friends who got divorced and you see how hard it is. You hope it's going to be amicable, but it never ends amicably. It may be amicable ten years down the road, but you're going to go through years of hell in the meantime. It may be nobody's fault, but some relationships do wear out." Or, I suggest, there are times when a tough patch seems so tough, you just can't seem to garner the energy or fighting spirit to get it back on track at that moment. Patsy agrees. "Sometimes you start to wonder how you could have everything you have right now, but without the obstacle."

Patsy says she also calls her death fantasy "the go-away fantasy," thoughts she has mostly, she says, "when I'm at home with him and feel as lonely as I did when I lived alone." We can all identify with that, during those periods of unresolved conflict and constant head butting. Says Melanie, "Look, it's never peachy all the time. Whoever told you it was going to be peachy is a fuckin' liar. You're living with another human being who isn't perfect either and eventually you're going to think, Get the fuck out of my face!" Her friend Tracy agrees. "Yes, it's mostly when we're fighting, and after twelve years of hearing the same things, you'd think he'd let go of it. Then I get really mad and think, I don't want to have to answer to you anymore or hear this again."

But the bottom line is: Tracy and Melanie want to be married. Patsy wants to be married. Anita, Courtney and I do, too. And we want to be married to our husbands. We do, we do, we *do*. Truly. Just sometimes, well, we long to be single again. To throw off the shackles of responsibility, to not feel overwhelmed by our spouse's needs, to feel carefree and giddy, to lose control, to only think about our-selves . . . for a while, at any rate. Because, you see, for the very first time in female history, there are almost as many great reasons to be a single woman as there are to be married. And we all would have been genuinely content to remain on our own had we not fallen in lust and love with our husbands.

We know our marriages aren't *that* bad. In fact, they're pretty damn wonderful in the overall scheme of things and if our husbands were to die, we'd be utterly heartbroken and devastated. As Char-lotte, thirty-six, says, "I've had days when I've thought if he would die, then I would die. And then there are times where I just don't want to answer to anyone, you just want your freedom to live your own life, but divorce isn't an option." Death would genuinely be a no-fault, no-guilt way out of the vows we made before our families and friends. It would be considered a "respectable" end to our involvement in an institution which we still sanctify. Says Beverley, thirty-two, "I fantasize about him dying when I'm so mad at him. Then I wouldn't have to deal with him. If he died, then I could just date because I was a widow and it's not my fault, I had no control over it."

Should Patsy, Charlotte, Beverley, Melanie, Courtney and all the other women who shamefully confess to close friends that they indulge in "the death fantasy" once in an insane while feel so bad? This is what I think: no. Well, not unless fantasy becomes possibility and you start dabbling with arsenic cocktails. No, I believe it's better, *healthier* than fantasizing about your own death. Nothing is as dark and destructive as being so unhappy that you want to kill yourself. Now that, as any therapist will verify, is cause for concern. And a cause for a combination of counseling and medication. When you feel so deeply despairing and hopeless that you feel your family and friends, your children, the *world* would be a better place if you weren't in it, that's when you really need to take a long, hard look at your marriage and consider calling it quits. But, says my other friend, Billie, "The death fantasy is no more sinister than when you were a kid and you didn't get your own way and you'd start wishing your parents were dead. You didn't really want them to die, but it was just an empty fantasy that allowed you for a moment to feel rebellious and free."

What keeps us sane during moments of marital craziness (and sometimes murderous thoughts) is our circle of close friends to whom we often reveal more than we do to our husbands. Every married woman says that since close friends often knew us long before we met and married our beloved, their insight and perspective is invaluable. Unlike family members who often have their own agenda or bring sibling issues into the mix, close friends—of which we tend to have two or three—offer advice based on a deep understanding of who we are minus ulterior motives. Much as they might adore our husband and be godparents to our children, their sole and primary concern is our well-being.

Our friends might be single or married and we might meet up with them with our husbands. But it's vital we carve out time to see them alone, to *really* talk, reveal our innermost thoughts, rediscover who we really are. As Joely says, "You go and stay with married friends or they come and visit you, but when husbands are around, you never really talk about stuff that really means something."

Gabrielle, thirty-two, agrees, saying, "When you start socializing only as couples, the questions that need to be asked of friends don't ever get asked."

Says Amanda, twenty-nine, "Larry and I spend a lot of time together with friends. I also make sure I see my girlfriends by myself. And I never talk to them on the phone when Larry's in the room. I'm very private with my friends on the phone."

This is a common scenario. Our instinctive (even primitive) desire and skill to bond with other women about what's really in our heart is so great, we don't hold back. If we discuss our husbands, what we have to say will sometimes be unflattering and, despite the fact that he's the focus of our irritation, we don't often want to hurt him. (If we did, or wanted genuine resolution, we'd say it to his face.) And often we don't seek a solution from our friends, just an opportunity to vent in an empathetic, supportive environment. But female bonding isn't always at the expense of our dearest's reputation as the perfect husband. Unless we're seeking solace from our marital rough patch, he invariably occupies only a fraction of our conversation.

Says Suzannah, thirty-nine, "Being in a gaggle of women where none of them are close friends drives me mad. I can't stand it. But being with really close friends, I really enjoy that. I have lots of friends, but I only have three or four really close friends, people who've known me all along, people who I can express myself to and tell them things I won't say to my husband. They provide empathy, shared experiences, belly laughs, the chance to air views and opinions about things I really care about, issues that I can't talk to David about because when I talk about them, he rolls his eyes. Like if I'm going on and on about pedophiles, he starts rolling his eyeballs, but that issue is really important to me and I love the passion you can have when you talk to girlfriends. If I haven't seen my girlfriends for a while, it's like the feeling I get when I haven't had sex for a while. I feel really isolated, I pull into myself and I feel like I haven't had a laugh. I really feel the need to tune into their lives and what they're going through. I get a bit miserable and a bit down . . . it's really important to me."

Same for Sam, who says that from her five really close girlfriends, "I get support, understanding, commiseration and confidence building. I'll tell them things I don't tell Ray because, well, they're women. We all have issues. We're all watching our weight, we complain we don't have enough sex, we complain we don't have as much money as we'd like, we complain we all have gray hairs. No matter what I've done to Raymond, they'll always say, 'Come on, don't be so hard on yourself.' We've got so much history together. I've known these girls for over fifteen years, longer than I've known Ray. I mean, if Ray hadn't passed the test with the girls, I wouldn't have ended up with him. No way. *That's* how important they are to me."

Says Joely, "When I'm with old friends, I always remember my dreams, the stuff that I always wanted to do, but that you put off. They're so unequivocably supportive of me that I decide to do that stuff right away. I mean, I get unequivocable support from my husband, but it's different. It's like your mom. Of course your husband thinks you're wonderful. That's totally his job. But it's about support and history. So I might tell my husband about a situation I'm having with someone else and I'll say, 'What do you think about this?' and he's always pessimistic, so he always talks about the worst-case scenario. He'll say, 'I don't think you'll ever repair that relationship' and then I'm like, 'Oh *nooo*, you don't *ever* think I'll repair that relationship?' But if I see one of my close friends, one of these people who have always been in my life, they'll say, 'Oh yeah, remember when she did this or that?' Old friends remember stuff that's useful now that I don't even remember."

Being with friends alone reminds us of who we were and still are inside when our freewheeling spirit gets overwhelmed by marital obligations. For a short while at least, we can cavort with being single, wild and uninhibited again. They never judged *then* when we'd get roaring drunk, laugh loudly and inappropriately, dance on tables and curse at cabdrivers. And when we feel the urge to recall or repeat that behavior *now*, they don't judge either. For the moment, we can be silly, abandoned, experimental, 101 percent true to our instincts—not a wife, a mother, a worker or a boss. Just us.

Joely says she told her fiancé that she would only marry him so long as he accepted she would continue to see her friends alone. "That," Joely declares, "was a really big thing. We got engaged in May and I went on vacation with my girlfriend in September. Then he said, 'You're taking your vacation time and you're spending it with your girlfriend?' as if she were a piece of shit. I mean, this is a woman who I've been friends with since I was eighteen years old. Anyway, we went to a Caribbean island and drank the whole week and flirted with guys. . . . Even three days before I got married, I called up my fiancé and said, 'I'm not coming home' and he said, 'Yeah, I assumed you weren't.' This was on a Wednesday night and we were getting married on Saturday. I still do a lot of stuff like that, except now I come home. But I still take vacations alone with friends. I went to Vegas last September with my friends and we drank and partied—it was amazing. And I went to California by myself to stay half the time with a girlfriend and half the time with an old friend who is a guy. My husband said, 'You're staying with a *guy*?' and I said, 'Yeah, I'm going to do this and you can either be pissed off about it while I'm gone or you can be okay about it.' "

Says Lottie, "I really look forward to going out with my girlfriends. I always drink much more than I do than when I'm with my husband. And I'm much more obnoxious. If he could see me, he'd say, 'Who the hell is *that*?' I don't feel like I pretend when I'm with him. I don't feel I need to. But let's just say *different* sides of my personality surface when I'm with my husband and when I'm with my friends. I don't always want to behave in one way so I wouldn't *always* want to behave like I do with my girlfriends. But it's really, really important to me that all the aspects of my personality have an airing."

Lena, thirty, agrees, "I had one of the best weekends ever recently when I visited a friend in Maine alone. I wound up with my friend in a bar, singing at the top of my lungs until four in the morning around a grand piano. Show tunes! My husband would have hated it, but I didn't have to worry about him, what he was feeling. I had such a great time."

Diane, twenty-nine, says, "I don't do that 'Are you okay, honey?' stuff when I'm out with my husband. But if he's got a face on him like a wet weekend when I'm being loud and obnoxious and just having fun, it'll make me so mad, I behave even worse and then we usually have a fight when we get home. So I have to see my friends alone at least once a week. It's great to flirt with other guys, too, and remind yourself that other men find you attractive."

Says Karen, thirty-seven, "My husband hates when I go out drinking. So even though I still go, I'll say I've had two whiskey and Cokes when I've really had five. I don't tell him either when I go out with friends and take cocaine. I don't take that much—just one line."

Like many Hitched Chicks, Karen says that there is an unspoken agreement that whatever happens while she and her friends are together remains a secret. She can be free in the knowledge that the full extent of what she does and says among her closest friends will never be revealed publicly.

Carmen also says there is a code of silence among her closest friends, a small, select group she calls "the Angels," based on the 1970s TV show *Charlie's Angels*. Carmen laughs, "It started when we were at school. There were three of us and we all chose a character and we'd act out these little scenes. Hilarious. We'd come to the end of a plot and one of us would say, 'But what would Charlie say?' And it stuck all through college and years on. Now I say to my husband, 'I'm going out with the Angels,' and he knows not to ask questions. Whatever is said or done when we're together is our business. If we know one of our husbands wouldn't approve, one of us'll say, 'But what would Charlie say?' and we just laugh our asses off. Like I was flirting with a guy, and Nathalie leaned over and said, 'What would Charlie say?' Sometimes, one of my friends might tell me something I'm dying to tell my husband, but I haven't yet shared a secret. I couldn't do it. I would feel too bad."

Carmen admits that she almost broke her Angels' code of silence when one of them confessed she was having an affair. "I couldn't believe it. I knew Delia had a crush on a guy, but when she told me she'd slept with him, I said, 'Are you *crazy?*' She said, 'I know, what would Charlie say?' but I couldn't joke about it. I know her husband too well. He's a great guy—we're all friends. Delia's one of my best friends, but I still felt I was betraying Neil. Much as I wanted to tell my husband, he's become close to Neil, too. They've gone to the Superbowl together. I said to her, 'Listen, I don't want to know the details. I'm here for you, but I can't be an accessory.'"

Carmen says, "Although Delia never told me why she stopped seeing this guy, I know that my reaction was a big factor. I think I was her conscience, probably even more than her husband. I've known her so long and we have so much shared history—there's so much trust there—I had to be honest with her. For God's sake, I was concerned. Yes, for Neil, but mainly for Delia. I was happy to go along with the drama when she had a crush—we all have them—but when it became an affair, my reaction kind of showed her she'd gone too far."

Says Carmen, "Good friends are friends that love you for all your imperfections. They allow you to misbehave and express your wicked side. But really good friends are those who also see the bigger picture and can say, 'You know what? *Now* you're behaving like a frickin' idiot.' It has nothing to do with them being a wife. It's about honesty and respect. I had enough respect for my friend Delia to tell her the truth. And she had enough respect for me to listen to my unbiased opinion and know I was making sense."

Support, empathy, light relief, history . . . our friends embody all these vital aspects combined with a built-in behavior regulator that we respect and trust. They allow us to liberate our "other" side and benefit from its healthy release while monitoring our boundaries so we don't overstep the mark of what's right for us. In spending quality time with close friends, we are able to graze unfamiliar terrain in trusted and safe company, before returning to our husbands happier, saner, sexier than ever.

Sealed with a Kiss

Carmen says that as well as having close friends in whom she can confide, she also keeps a journal. "There are just some things that you don't want to share with anyone . . . your husband, your kids, your mother or your friends. They're my secret thoughts, my secret fears and hopes. I don't write in it every day or even every week, but then I'll go through phases when I write in it every day."

I do this. So does Gina, thirty-four, who says, "After my mother died, I became obsessed with dying. Sometimes I wanted to, I felt so bad. Sometimes I was consumed with fear. The only way I could control my thoughts and express them was through my journal. There comes a point when you can't talk to your friends about it anymore. My husband was very supportive and really gentle, too—I appreciated him so much. But he'd try and give me solutions or answers.

He's very male like that. And sometimes there aren't solutions or answers. I took to writing at length in my journal, describing my darkest thoughts, thoughts I couldn't share because they were often too crazy or bleak."

Sally, thirty-one, says, "It seems like keeping a journal is a very female thing to do, don't you think? I've never met a guy who keeps one or understands the benefit. But I write everything in my journal, and have done so since I was a kid. I look back over past journals and they make me laugh or they'll remind me about dreams and hopes I had that I put on the back burner, stuff that's really important. I caught my husband flicking through my journal a couple of years ago and I just yelled at him, 'What are you *doing*?' I felt like he'd invaded my privacy. I said, 'If I wanted you to read this stuff, I'd send you a letter or say it to your face.' Naturally, he thought I'd been writing awful things about him. I had sometimes, but they were often silly, little things that were too trivial to mention, but drove me nuts nevertheless. My journal is the one place I can express exactly what's on my mind. I don't need to edit myself, I don't need to be tactful or reasonable. I can just write how I feel."

Says Jenny, thirty-six, "I write everything in my journal. I'm no holds barred. Everything from what I've been doing, where I've been, who I've been thinking about, secret crushes, dreams, fantasies, you name it. I went through a period when I had recurring dreams of being chased and raped. At first they were more like nightmares, then I had a similar dream where I was actually enjoying being raped. I was really bothered by it, but I didn't want to tell anyone, I just needed to get it off my chest. If anyone ever read it, they'd be shocked. They'd think, Jenny wrote *this*? Jenny really felt *that*? I've often thought, What if I suddenly got hit by a truck and died? They'd go through my stuff and then they'd come across my journal and it would all be in there, what I really think about everyone—my friends, my family, my boss, my husband. But you can't think about that or the point would be lost. If you start monitoring what you write, you may as well not bother at all."

Keeping a journal is a way of immortalizing ourselves. It's a way of reminding us who we once were and the lessons we learned, recording our triumphs, giving meaning to tragedy and pain. It's also a way of putting ideas and dreams out into the universe. Once we write them down on paper, we take the first step to making them come true. A journal provides a secret checklist for our future.

Says Skylla, twenty-nine, "I'm forever coming up with crazy ideas. I might tell them to my husband, but then he'll ask me why I want to do this or that. Sometimes I can't or don't want to explain why, I just do. Or then he might start telling me all the reasons why it can't be done. The great thing about a journal is that it never answers back. It doesn't judge. It doesn't challenge. It doesn't feel threatened. It just absorbs."

My journals are just about my most precious material possessions. They're crammed with small yet significant moments that, if left unrecorded, would be lost forever. And dreams for the future which, if undocumented, would remain in never-never land. They're packed with lessons I've learned and wish to pass on one day. They're a memoir of a life and period in time which is admittedly tiny in the scope of the universe. But more important than anything else, they're an all-out expression of me (which, despite my marital status, is often unpredictable, contradictory, mischievous, unresolved), and a chronicle of my life in progress. And until only *I* decide otherwise, the secret thrills and spills of its journey will remain a closely guarded secret.

Epilogue

When I first voiced the idea of this book to publishers, friends, colleagues and family, I did so adamant this was neither a pro- nor anti-marriage book, more an at-arm's-length report on matrimony today. Nor was it to be a frivolous little style guide, sprinkled with, as Helen Fielding of *Bridget Jones* fame would say, "smug married" cocktail party tips and trivia for "staying sensational." No, this was to be the definitive, warts-and-all guide to modern marriage, in which the serious, as well as not-so-serious, complexities and challenges would be outlined and explored, and the variety of coping mechanisms we choose (or resort to) would be described in nonjudgmental detail. What's more, the confessions of real, not idealized or cartoon, wives would be laid bare, from which the rest of us could derive comfort, encouragement, inspiration and, okay, a certain amount of voyeuristic titillation.

I have achieved what I set out to do, with one exception. Rather than upholding neutrality, *The Hitched Chick's Guide* naturally evolved into a book that is pro-marriage. Granted, I based this book on interviews only with women who are married. However, my criteria was not that they should be *happily* married. But what I discovered was that irrespective of my insistence that being a single woman today has much more going for it than it ever did, and despite the gloomy divorce statistics, marriage remains a highly covetable status. (Three out of four single women say they want to be married. Source: *She* magazine.) This isn't simply because human beings are biologically programmed to thrive on interaction and intimacy—if it were, cohabitation would be seen as the glorious end, rather than the pragmatic means. It's because marriage genuinely offers something unique and valuable beyond the dress, the ceremony, the party, the endless gifts—and the potential tax concessions.

Yes, conflict arises—most women claim the first five years of marriage (not seven, as is the cliché) are filled with conflict. The birth of a child, the death of a parent, redundancy . . . cornerstone events that we usually first encounter in our thirties combined with all the emotional and practical readjustments of early marriage conspire to shatter our dreams of happily ever after. What's more, now that marriage tends to be comprised of two equals who demand equal say and satisfaction, tussles and disagreements are inevitable.

However, the effect of conflict pales into insignificance beside the rewards of marriage, *modern* marriage. And there are many. Women talked enthusiastically to me about the unique feeling of being a team, a secure and united force against the uncertainties of the modern world. It's a characteristic that hadn't materialized before they married or when they'd cohabited. And its value multiplied after the terrorist attacks of September 11 (which may explain the flurry of proposals and "I do's" in the following months).

Although Hitched Chicks remain fiercely protective of their identities, they also enthuse that, in many wonderful ways, modern marriage heightens their sense of self. It provides a trusted sounding board for ideas; a safe environment for experimentation in every context, from sexual to financial; a cheerleading platform from which to take personal risks and stretch what they are capable of achieving. Rather than holding us back, modern marriage often reinforces our courage and sense of adventure. And since we don't want to be perceived as "the weaker sex" or "the lesser half," it motivates us to *exceed* our potential.

While sex after marriage is invariably less frequent than before marriage, modern wives report it's more intimate and satisfying. Foreplay has more finesse, orgasms are more intense. They feel freer to make demands, more confident to offer suggestions and less likely to crumble if a sexual overture is not reciprocated. Far from withdrawing sexually, some women even say that once married, they made the commitment never to refuse their husbands sex. One reason, as I explained in the chapter on lust, is because we are all knowledgeable about the benefits of sexual intimacy in marriage. However, the other reason they never refuse, they say, is because now that they're married, they feel they *can* refuse. Power certainly manifests itself in a multitude of surprisingly beneficial ways for modern marriage.

Rather than being an outdated, suffocating institution, marriage today appears to offer the majority a flexible environment from which to grow and learn about themselves, about love and the world. If it doesn't, it's not the fault of marriage, but the result of reluctance by one or both spouses to respect individuality. Because we enter into it from a position of strength, rather than vulnerability, we are now afforded the opportunity to create our own rules and make them our own. If we don't, assuming that marriage controls us rather than we control it, we are using it as a scapegoat for our lack of responsibility or effort.

I spoke with a male acquaintance recently about this book. Married three times, he claimed, "Marriage didn't work for me," as if it were a dysfunctional employee, an object like a washing machine which refused to fulfill its mechanical duty. I don't assume this man's attitude is unique—how could I, considering the divorce statistics? However, those with the most successful marriages, I discovered, are those who embark on marriage not with the view that it is a static cure-all commodity, but a fluid and organic and potentially infinite existence during which, periodically, the participants ask themselves, Am *I* working hard enough for my marriage? Am I investing all *I* can to keep it breathing and growing and flourishing?

While researching this book, I was enormously heartened to hear commitment toward asking these difficult questions and courage to act on them. I admit, I was a little surprised, too. Like many, I guess I had fallen prey to the negative brainwashing. The more we hear that couples today don't respect the value of marriage, are not committed to making it work, expect it to fulfill a celluloid fantasy, the more we tend to believe it. But for the most part, I found the opposite to be true.

Infidelities of varying degrees do exist. And many of the day-to-day conflict strategies modern wives use may be unusual and flout conventional practice. And, yes, we are all too aware the ultimate escape clause—no-fault divorce—is a mere phone call away. But our desire to succeed where previous generations have failed motivates us to keep pushing, stretching, refining ourselves and our relationships. There *are* more positive than negative examples of marriage . . . just enough for us to be reassured that, despite its challenges, marriage can be a fun, fulfilling, stimulating, youthful and sexy place to be.

The women I spoke to—from across the world and varying cultures—opened their hearts and revealed their experiences not to fulfill their fifteen minutes worth of fame. Instead, under pseudonyms they disclosed because they believed what they had to say was important and worth documenting. Happy to acknowledge their faults as well as virtues, they were keen to reassure others that acceptance of humanity—not striving for perfection—is critical for modern marriage to work. And they offered gems of tried-and-tested advice, hoping, *willing* it to help, at the very least, one more marriage to succeed.

On that note, as I said at the start of this book, I am far from perfect. And my marriage, while wonderful, is not perfect either—and still isn't. However, since writing *The Hitched Chick's Guide*—and anyone who has written a book, speedily or otherwise, will testify that it's a crazy-making process—my marriage is better than it ever has been.

When I feel a twitch of irritation, I now take Anabelle's advice and ask myself, Does this matter *profoundly*? Now I fight only when it does. From Ellis, I've learned not to withhold information simply to reinforce my feelings of power because resolving *is* so much more satisfying than winning.

Although I've been faced with hand-wringing deadlines and felt overwhelmed by family obligations, I've followed Rachel, Sabina, Paulette and Sally's "selfish" examples by carving out "me time" in the form of piano lessons. My schedule may well be even tighter now, but my ability to cope with it and enjoy it is enhanced, since I feel calmer and more centered.

Instead of exhausted weeknight sex, I've woken up to the joys of morning sex, preferred by Sonja, Suzannah, Alice and so many of the women I interviewed. The rewards are disproportionate to the tiny adjustment in our sex schedule.

To all the Hitched Chicks I interviewed, I want to yell a huge "thank-you" for making this book possible and so much fun to write, but also for talking so freely about your own joyful as well as painful experiences, and donating so enthusiastically those real gems of advice. No, you don't *always* get it right. Like you, your marriages aren't perfect either. You may well sometimes be reckless, sometimes outrageous, sometimes stubborn. But mainly you're strong, determined, fun-loving, courageous, smart, powerful and, above all, an inspiration that if indeed we do only have one life, let it be lived as a Hitched Chick.

Acknowledgments

Heartfelt thanks must first go to all the Hitched Chicks who gave up their time to bare their souls and talk to me about their marriages. Subjected to lengthy, intimate inquisitions for no reward other than a few drinks (and a bowl of fries and mayo if they were lucky), they responded with humor, consideration and candor. Each and every one provided an immeasurable contribution to *The Hitched Chick's Guide* and (I wish to acknowledge again) my perspective on marriage, including my own. Some were already precious friends ("Suzannah, Ellis, Lucy, Anabelle, Stella, Patti, Gabrielle"), many became friends and I remain in touch with too many to mention out of genuine affection and interest in the progression of their lives.

As warm and approachable as I like to think I am, I couldn't have met many of these amazing women if so many single friends had not offered up their entire greeting card lists of married colleagues, acquaintances and family members. Kate, in particular, you were a major star and I hope you find *The Hitched Chick's Guide* invaluable as you embark on your own marriage this year.

Special thanks to my agent, Susan Raihofer, whose enthusiasm and support for me and this book never once waivered. Her guidance anchored me when, at times, I was about to pop, and her cheerleading calls and e-mails energized me through those long summer days and nights of non-stop writing. Susan, I wish I could have taken you up on your invitations for cocktails more often, but I'm determined to make up for it now!

There aren't many editors who approach their work with as much vigor and dedication as my St. Martin's editor, Alicia Brooks, whose generosity and sweetness camouflages her all-out ballsiness. Alicia, your insights and attention to detail have been invaluable. I hope you'll now be able to go home to your gorgeous husband at a civilized hour.

My great appreciation and affection, too, goes to Elizabeth Beier, whose advice and phone calls were always an inspiration.

My thanks to the wide variety of experts—from financial whiz Ginita Wall to sexy Melissa Brockgreiten, Youth Intelligence's Jane Buckingham and the brilliant Dr. John Gottman—who helped and inspired me. Plus Helen Gurley Brown, mentor and an all-around role model, whose revolutionary *Sex & the Single Girl* has pride of place on my bookshelf.

Finally, enormous thanks to my parents, especially my mother, who is always my number one fan. Mom, you've never mentioned it, but I know your telephone bills are *huuuge*—reading mammoth chunks of this book to you over the phone from New York to Newcastle was an expensive pastime, but your feedback is always positively considered and greatly appreciated. To my daughters, Rosie and Daisy, whose little love notes slipped under my study door and big hearts I cherish more than anything in the world. And to my husband, Martin: You always said marrying me would be a roller-coaster ride, but our relatively short journey together—with its breathtaking highs and heartaching dips—has already enriched my life beyond measure. Thank you for listening, transcribing, reading and discussing into the wee small hours. Without you, this book wouldn't have been possible, since without you, I'm sure I never would have had the desire or courage to get hitched.

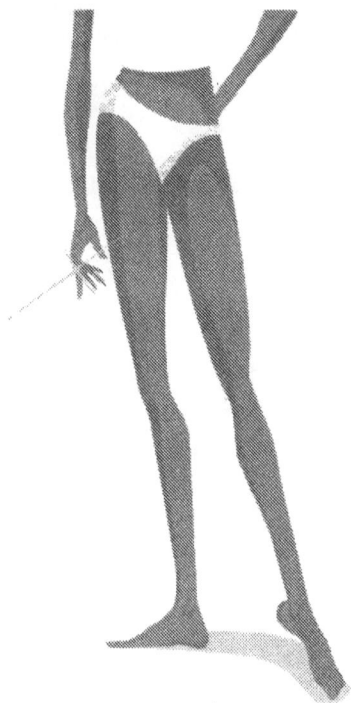

Mandi Norwood was born in Manchester, England. She has spent the past two decades working on women's magazines, both in the U.K., where she was editor in chief of *Company* magazine and *Cosmopolitan*, and the U.S., as editor in chief of *Mademoiselle*. She currently lives in New York with her husband, Martin, and two young daughters, Rosie and Daisy and is now the editor in chief of *Shop Etc.*